SITE PLANNING

Environment, Process, and Development

R. Gene Brooks

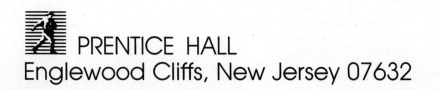
PRENTICE HALL
Englewood Cliffs, New Jersey 07632

Library of Congress Cataloging-in-Publication Data

BROOKS, R. GENE, *(date)*
   Site planning.

   Includes index.
   1. Building sites—Planning.   I. Title.
NA2540.5.B76 1988   720   87-1302
ISBN   0-13-811258-4

Editorial/production supervision and
   interior design: **Kathryn Pavelec**
Manufacturing buyer: **Lorraine Fumoso**

 © 1988 by **Prentice Hall**
A Division of Simon & Schuster
Englewood Cliffs, New Jersey 07632

Printed in the United States of America

10 9 8 7 6 5 4 3

ISBN   0-13-811258-4

PRENTICE-HALL INTERNATIONAL (UK) LIMITED, *London*
PRENTICE-HALL OF AUSTRALIA PTY. LIMITED, *Sydney*
PRENTICE-HALL CANADA INC., *Toronto*
PRENTICE-HALL HISPANOAMERICANA, S.A., *Mexico*
PRENTICE-HALL OF INDIA PRIVATE LIMITED, *New Delhi*
PRENTICE-HALL OF JAPAN, INC., *Tokyo*
SIMON & SCHUSTER ASIA PTE. LTD., *Singapore*
EDITORA PRENTICE-HALL DO BRASIL, LTDA., *Rio de Janeiro*

Contents

part II An Environmental Inventory and Assessment

part III The Site in Change

part IV   Streetscape and Site
           Improvements

18 Land Use Controls *260*

19 The Site Planning Process *283*

appendix A Stations Providing Local Climatological Data *310*

appendix B Sun Pegs for Various Latitudes *313*

Index *317*

Preface

The intent of this work is to coalesce under one cover the principles, issues, and inter-relationships that are considered in the site planning process. Since application is the acid test of most theory, this text leans to the side of practice. Aside from brief chapters on history, ethics, and environment, the majority of the book examines the basic components, issues, and methods that make up site planning and development.

The assumptions here are that:

1. There are a cluster of common issues that must be addressed and resolved in the development of any site plan.
2. The specifics of reality are far more complex than is academic doctrine.
3. In the final analysis the critical question in the design of any site relates to its *reason*. Long after the scholarly discussions of design juries are only a vague memory, the questions posed by review boards, clients, legislative authorities, and citizens will be: ''Why?'' ''What was the rationale for that decision?'' ''What were the alternatives to this proposal?'' Some of the questions will be polite and a smile will follow any but the most nonsensical answer. There will also be circumstances in which every word, sentence, and punctuation of the answer will be scrutinized for flaws in a defendant's competency.

Reason or rationale are often found in the two elemental bases of design: form and function. The argument as to which of these two principles should enjoy the dominant position is ongoing. There is a segment of the design professions that supports the position that the creative processes are diluted when functional or technical issues are anything more than benign agents in a problem. Advocates of this philosophy suggest that the creative mind works at its highest degree of potential when the constraints of the problems are minimal. This view holds that form must be the principal consideration since function left to its own devices rarely creates a design of any aesthetic achievement, and more often than not results in solutions devoid of spirit. The opposing opinion suggests that functional reasoning must be the primary consideration; otherwise, anything of any size can be any place. The functionalist view holds that beauty, in form, is a very subjective consideration, and points to the passing of numerous design styles as evidence of its capricious nature.

Most practioners, regardless of their philosphical persuasion, are of the opinion that there are few benign agents in the problem-solving process. This more holistic alternative holds that the more we know about a problem, the more responsible our solution will be. This does not impugn the value of form, but what every professional knows is that his or her creative judgment has become more precise with experience and research.

Although we know and recognize that the site is a common design problem with a set of common community-related issues, there is some question as to whether the site planning process is always activated with common sense. Common sense is that collection of resources that each person knows will emerge, when all else fails, to act as a mental safety net. "Use your common sense" is the teacher's last-gasp demand that students reach down into their minds, underneath all the material piled on by peers, the media, and society, and activate that collection of gray matter that would rescue you from a fate worse than death: permanent and everlasting stupidity! What is often forgotten is that the first hope is not for stellar innovation but for good judgment. Other good things follow.

Given the mix of philosophical differences and professional biases today toward land, design, and structure, the concept of site planning enlists an array of responses. The pervasive dilemma is that many approach the process of site planning as though their work is isolated, independent, and immune to the impacts of nature, legislation, and economics. While each of these will influence the disposition of any man-made change to the site, the challenge is to develop a plan of aesthetic achievement that reflects the natural attributes of the site in concert with the law and fiscal responsibility.

Prior to applying any theory to site planning, it is critical to understand that like other design issues, site planning is a process of interrelated investigations. Our common sense tells us that questionable soils, impossible slopes, and drainage swales are all conditions that need to be approached with some degree of caution. Since the extent or range of a site's problems are dependent on research and analysis, these are the obvious first steps in the procss. Problems emerge most often when intuitive decisions, keyed to form, are based on optimistic conclusions from partial data. Almost every professional has had at least secondhand knowledge of a situation in which a "brief analysis" would suffice until the financing became firm; then things really took a turn for the worse. Although the illusions created by the magician are something that we can see, our common sense tells us that we cannot believe everything we see. If that is a quality on which one builds good judgment, it would follow that the character or quality of any site is never so transparent that it can be evaluated simply by what we see.

An understanding of the influence of climate on a site is another aspect of site planning that requires the use of common sense. Similar to the site's physiography, these issues are critical enough that one neither assumes nor guesses as to the seasonal paths of the sun. If a garden court's success is dependent on direct sunlight, would not the documentation of that illumination be an essential part of the early research? If we recognize that the east and west sides of a building will receive the highest heat load in the summer, would not orienting the building to minimize the heavier heat loads have been more cost-effective than the sun screens and additional air-conditioning requirement for the east–west alternative? If we understand that the sun can provide supplemental heat and light to a room, would not it have been more responsive to have oriented the building in such a way as to exploit this energy that nature gives so freely? Is common sense of such little currency that it has no value without eclectic theory?

It must be added, that, in reality, site planning problems are seldom black or white. The contour lines may run perpendicular to the preferred orientation of a structure; or the zoning envelope forces the building into a broad swale which bisects the property;

or the flattest area of the site is shadowed from the winter sun by a multistory structure. Since almost every problem has conflicting objectives, the process dictates the development of criteria on which alternative action might be based; otherwise, anything is possible. The site planner must have accrued sufficient acumen to recognize when a subjective decision creates a condition that violates common sense. In a professional context this is called judgment.

The National Architectural Accreditation Board (NAAB) has four general categories on which they review the design component of architectural programs for accreditaion. They are *analysis, synthesis, communication,* and *judgment.*[1] Judgment is without question the key property, as it integrates both technical and artistic components in its process. Other educational institutions have similar criteria which require that some aspects of the educational process address this critical element. Almost regardless of the issue or test, judgment is the critical ingredient, as it provides the direction to the other three skills. What it is easy to forget is that judgment rests on a foundation of common sense.

The relative success of any solution must be judged in part on its response to people. Interpretation of the designer's intent has long been a focus of debate, with little evidence provided by postoccupancy evaluation. If data were not already limited, research by Albert Ames, Earl Kelly, and Handley Cantril document the elusive nature of common perceptions.[2] Put briefly, perceptions of the physical environment are influenced by language, meaning, and past experience. Although reality exists in the form of tangible objects, reality filtered through the central system also exists somewhere behind our eyes.

In other words, perceptions are reality. Although the intent of the work may be one thing, its meaning, like language, can be colored or diffused for many reasons. This is particularly challenging for the designer who seeks to create something that rises above the purely functional requirements of a problem. For those engaged in that arduous struggle, most resist anything which compromises an aesthetic achievement. But what of solutions that focus first on the resolution of technical problems, yet are a delight to the eye? A Formula 1 Grand Prix car or a 12-meter America's Cup competitor of almost any vintage are good examples of solutions based primarily on the laws of physics, but sacrifice nothing for aesthetics. How is it that some purely technical solution can sometimes result in something so aesthetically pleasing? A similar question could be framed regarding the aesthetic quality of the implements and artifacts developed by primitive cultures, whose survival was the final judge of every technical achievement. The quality common to the achievements of both intellectual and unskilled cultures is what Vitruvius referred to as beauty.

The vague and elusive qualities of beauty are such that a useful definition does not exist. The canard that "beauty is in the eye of the beholder" tells us nothing other than to emphasize the very subjective nature of the term. In *Design: Purpose, Form and Meaning*, John Pyle advances the concept that the "communication of meaning [is] the real concern that lies hidden behind [aesthetics]."[3] The implication is that an "object's" aesthetic quality must be measured by the intent communicated through its form. Although functional success does not ensure an aesthetic achievement, functional failure is generally indicative of an ill-conceived design. In the search for the "ever new," the sage advice of Mies van der Rohe that "it is much better to be good than to be original" has a certain ring of truth.

Sooner or later your judgment will be put to the test. That is the nature of the design profession as all seek to demonstrate their understanding and creativity. Those

---

[1]National Architectural Accrediting Board, *NAAB Criteria and Procedures* (Washington, D.C.: NAAB, December 1984), p. 14.

[2]Neil Postman and Charles Weingartner, *Teaching as a Subversive Activity* (New York: Dell Publishing Co., Inc., 1969), pp. 89–91.

[3]John F. Pyle, *Design: Purpose, Form and Meaning* (New York: W. W. Norton & Company, Inc., 1979), p. 101.

who enjoy a flourishing practice know that relative success is based on their command of fundamentals, which permit them to reach beyond those basics. They will also testify that failure to recognize and resolve basic problems can jeopardize both project and practice. "First things first" applies to you as well as to your physician. Just as a physician's judgment must be based on fact, reason, and fundamentals, no small part of yours should do likewise.

I believe this book is different from the numerous other publications listed in your library's card catalog to the degree that it seeks to examine the three forces at work on every site in their most basic terms:

1. The natural site conditions; the significance of the site's natural context and critical resources
2. The process and methods of altering the site to accommodate man-made components
3. The legal controls that delineate the extent to which the site can be changed, and their collective interrelationships in site planning.

Each of these three topics must be understood in a comprehensive way, as they both support and encumber each other in a dynamic process. Not only are they operationally inseparable, but a working knowledge of their finer parts is critical to diagnosis and design. Ignoring any one of these constituents invites criticism and solutions of dubious results. Although the book is light on theory, there is a broad overview of the background and history behind the changes in philosophies and values that have affected site planning. Although it is valuable to understand "how to do it," it is equally important to have some insight into "why" something is done. The intent of this larger perspective was to provide the reader with a grasp of the past as the basis upon which to reckon with change.

The bias maintained throughout the book is that change is, for most sites, a requirement. But accepting change and improvements does not imply that radical change is the best under any circumstances. The site planner's role is a continuing process of balance and reconciliation. It begins with an intellect that can recognize those qualities of a site that make it unique and continues as a process that integrates change in a way that respects those attributes, thereby enriching the architecture and the lives of its occupants.

R. GENE BROOKS

Acknowledgments

As with most books of this scope, there are contributions, beyond the author's, that it is important to recognize. I have been the fortunate benefactor of the aid of numerous people without whom the quality of the book would be far less. It is for those personal gifts of time, energy, and tolerance that I am very grateful.

First, a word on the contributing authors. Dr. Ernest Buckley is a registered professional engineer and the Dean of the College of Engineering at South Dakota State University. Dr. Buckley has had a long and distinguished career as a practicing professional, teacher, and author. What I want to recognize here is that Dr. Buckley's participation, like Truett's and Michael's, goes well beyond that of his text.

George Truett James is an Associate Professor of Architecture at The University of Texas at Arlington where he has been teaching in the areas of design, building energy use, environmental controls, and computer systems. Truett's M.ARCH degree provided the background for his research, study, and outstanding publications on thermal loads and building energy analysis utilizing microcomputers.

Michael Ostdick is a registered landscape architect practicing in Santa Barbara, California. Michael's pursuit of his MLA degree resulted in awards from the School of Architecture and Environmental Design at The University of Texas at Arlington as well as the American Society of Landscape Architecture. As my GTA, Michael saw with me the potential for a text that could bridge the gap between the popular notions of site planning and the realities of practice. What follows will hopefully help others to understand the interdisciplinary perspective of the authors towards site planning.

Special thanks to Richard Ferrier, John McDermott, and Andrzej Pinno for their good grace as they alternately served as counsel. Their willingness to endure hours with me in the doorway of their offices to unravel an idea was a geniune test of their friendship. I am indebted to them for their honest criticism and ability to see the forest when I found myself ankle deep in leaves.

My abiding thanks to the secretarial staff of the School of Architecture and Environmental Design at The University of Texas at Arlington, in particular, Barbara Abbott, Linda Tilley, Gelynn Majure, and Danny Earnest, who patiently kept it all together through change after change. I am forever in their debt. For their continued encouragement and support, I also owe a special thanks to Sandra Chipley, Tom Galbreath, Philip Neeley, and Richard Odlozil.

As always, I am grateful to my wife, Betty, for her understanding over these past many months. Her support and forbearance made even rejection letters and rewrites tolerable. Every new author should have a spouse with the ability to find a positive side to impending catastrophe. For mine, I am forever grateful. And finally, I wish to dedicate this book to my boys, Mark and Dan. While their patience was not entirely elastic, they eventually accepted their mother's caution, ''Don't bother Dad, he's working on the book'' as a tolerable reason for my seclusion.

chapter 1
Historical References

A CONTEXT OF RELIGION AND AUTHORITY

History is a principal resource in developing an understanding of any design discipline, as it permits an analysis of a particular set of events relative to their context and subsequent implications. History is the enviable 20–20 hindsight. Aside from the opportunity to separate the myth from the reality, history provides the opportunity to identify primary models and scrutinize their applicability to current conditions. One of the problems with an examination of the early history of site planning is that it was a natural extension of architecture and city planning. These two disciplines have been the principal sources of literature and practice, which provided their common theory, form, and order.

For many, city planning is an active component in the review of site planning. Alberti's suggestion that a house was a small city oversimplified the complex nature of cities and their real applicability to site planning and architecture. While studying the evolution of towns and villages is an engaging endeavor, the commonalities between a city's form and site-specific planning problems can have marginal corelationships. Although the plan for a city may have been the subject of some deliberation relative to its shape and physical development, a site in that city may or may not have been influenced by the same or similar criteria. The best example of this point is that although there were plans for ideal cities (Fig. 1-1), for good reasons we do not see plans of ''ideal'' sites. Although site planning has relied on town planning for theory and formal models, scrutiny of the real implications of that process, and analogies, can become obviously thin. What might be relevant in the relationship between town and site planning may not be the form as much as the prevailing social or ethical philosophy. The perception of physical plans also creates some problems in translating the city to the site. The form of a city is a reflection of the social, political, cultural, and economic forces at work in that society over an extended period. The quaint medieval streetscape we visit and enjoy today may have been a steaming sewer in the fourteenth century. Our inclination is to interpret the success or failure of history through our own values of good, bad, order,

1

Figure 1-1 Plan of ideal cities.

chaos, and so on. Transferring forms and physical models of the past to the twentieth century is one of the prevailing reasons for the sea of differences between the visions of planners and the reality of today. If the visual and environmental results of the twentieth-century city are dubious (for which there is some supporting evidence), they may be based, at least in part, on a superficial understanding of history.

The scale and authorities controlling site planning in history are also worth noting. The large land ownerships controlled by king, pharaoh, or maharaja did not lend themselves to the scale of site planning in the sense that we use it today. Properties were often administered by noblemen and leased to smaller tenants, who built structures, raised livestock, and/or farmed. Since each tenant was a part of a larger organizational structure, in urban European history there appears to have been less emphasis on individual land ownership and building and more on the plan or development of a community. Most of the models taken from architectural history are of major monuments created for monarchs or religious institutions, wherein an expression of a culture could be articulated. The significance of the smaller site planning problem (vernacular architecture) has been considered less profound, as it relied on conventions and ethics as opposed to formal intellectual ideas. What may be learned from site planning in history is an appreciation for the relationships that the ancients structured between man, earth, deity, and the physical implications of those alliances to site and settlement. Although the relationships vary, decisions were nonetheless based on conventions that focused to define place, to separate the sacred from the secular, and in the process, to survive.

To the ancients, existence and well-being had a direct functional relationship with the environment. All the elements that provided them with food, clothing, and shelter were directly attributed to the recognition of earth as deity. To the American Indian, "Father Sky and Mother Earth" were a union that gave meaning to life beyond the scope of the daily essentials. As such, the reverence held for the relationship between man and earth was one of survival, ethics, and religion. Rapoport's interpretation of Deffontaines in *Geographie et Religions* is: "The founder [of the site] chooses the location not from geographical conditions but by seeking to conform to the decisions of the Gods."[1]

Numerous cultures believed the decisions associated with the location of a building, or the placement of a structure or community, to be a process that obligated one to consult the gods before a stone was turned or a field plowed. Since the earth was one of the few "known" quantities, it is easy to understand the importance attributed to nature and the cosmos. Finding the place for a community settlement, house, or field was no casual decision, particularly for the religious person. If human beings were to establish any sense of order in a world of chaos, the place must be fixed, or to quote Mircea

---

[1] Amos Rapoport, *House, Form and Culture* (Englewood Cliffs, N.J.: Prentice-Hall, Inc., 1969), p. 75.

Figure 1-2 Mont St. Michael.

Eliade: "If the world is to be lived in, it must be founded."[2] Some definition between that place which was sacred and that which was secular was of prime importance. Sometimes, "signs" or visions provided one level of decision making, and when those did not occur, a reasoning process was employed.

NATURE, PLACE, AND FORM

Among the myths and rites associated with the definition of sacred places, the physical qualities of nature were an ever-present resource. Springs, trees, and particularly hills and mountains were often identified as sacred precincts. Stones and rocks have also held a special reverence with people throughout time. The most holy shrine of Islam at Mecca contains a stone that is believed to have fallen from heaven. Although Americans feel the compelling urge to carve faces in mountains, the ancients considered rock outcroppings to mark places "where the essence of the earth could still be perceived."[3] These were considered to be holy places in which dwelled the earth's spirit and were often visited to "obtain states of heightened vision."[4] Many religions have references in their liturgy to holy mountains or hills. In an effort to integrate theology with the daily activities of the practitioner, numerous mountain/hill forms became sites for convents, monasteries, mosques, and churches (Fig. 1-2). Dominant earth forms obviously provided excellent visual metaphors which could easily be integrated into those of the prevailing religion.

As an example, the Hebrews consider Palestine to be holy high ground, as it was not submerged by the great flood described in the Old Testament.[5] The Islamic faith believes the *Ka'aba* to be the highest place on earth, as "the pole star bears witness that it faces the center of Heaven."[6] The ancient Greeks sought to identify sacred precincts

---

[2]Mircea Eliade, *The Sacred and the Profane* (New York: Harcourt Brace Jovanovich, Inc., 1957), p. 2.
[3]Nigel Pennick, *The Art and Science of Geomancy* (London: Thames and Hudson Ltd., 1979), p. 22.
[4]Ibid.
[5]Mircea Eliade, *The Myth of the Eternal Return*, Bollingen Series XLVI (New York: Pantheon Books, Inc., 1954), p. 10.
[6]Ibid., p. 15.

Figure 1-3   Ziggurat.

by pronouncing Mt. Olympus to be the home of the Greek gods and Delphi to be the center (navel) of the earth. The center of the world was also a feature to which many cultures attached religious significance. In the twelfth century, the alignment of the sun on Jerusalem on the summer solstice was such that it prompted declarations that the city was the center of the earth. Although the perception of the center of the earth might vary from one religion to the next, the concept that embraced the heavens was common to many. The rationale relative to the summer solstice was also the criterion used by the Chinese in locating the center of the world and the capital of the perfect Chinese sovereign.

Although there was doubt among many ancient cultures relative to an earth-born deity, the physical power and visual spectacle of the heavens were sufficient to create an abundant number of myths associated with the sky. The heavens became the home of gods for many cultures, as its infinite quality created concepts of eternity and omnipresence. Although human beings enlisted various conventions to locate the center of the world, the corollary to that was often an ''axis mundi,'' or vertical axis, through the center connecting the earth to the heavens. That concept became manifest in the construction of man-made mountains (*ziggurats*) or temples whose design attempted either to connect the secular to the sacred or to imitate the cosmos in its design (Fig. 1-3).

In the temple of Queen Hetshepsut near Deirel Bahari, a mountain has been utilized as a surrogate for the pyramid. This decision not only embodied the notions associated with the sacred quality of hills, but successfully shadowed attempts to place the temple in time (Fig. 1-4).

The physically prominent was only a segment of the significance of nature to the ancients. To the religious, nature was never something that transpired by virtue of its own processes. ''Nature is never natural; it is always fraught with a religious value.''[7] Nature was a daily reminder of an inexplicable power that left only evidence of its meaning. The vegetation cults were not based on the appearance of spring as an annual birth as much as on the ''prophetic sign of the mystery.''[8] Although the secular view of trees may have been no more than an expression of continual birth and death, to many ancients the tree was the symbol of cosmos whose fruit could impart infinite wisdom, power, and eternal life. Trees were simple expressions of the same perceptual phenomenon: a mystery of inexhaustible life and energy. Trees were attributed particular importance in antiquity, for they were links between heaven and earth and believed to be the residence of specific spirits. Europeans had identified numerous religious and ethical meanings with trees. In Germany, it was believed that elves and spirits lived under oaks,

---

[7]Eliade, *The Sacred and the Profane*, p. 116.
[8]Ibid., p. 151.

Figure 1-4 Temple of Queen Hetsheput.

elders, and firs. Care was taken to avoid damaging or uprooting these particular species in case one should, in the process, disturb their mythological tenants.[9] In German law, trees were the meeting places of the secret vigilant Vehnic Courts.[10] Scandinavian tribesmen believed that trees housed the spirits of deceased family members. The "old religion" did not die with Christianity. As a part of their land-clearing process, Finns and Swedes in the New World would recite incantations to the tree spirits prior to burning the fallen timber.[11]

An ancient Irish law stipulated that the destruction of any one of the seven holy trees (apple, alder, birch, hazel, holly, oak, and willow) was punishable by the fine of a cow, an extremely valuable property at that time.[12] The attitude of reverence for trees was not limited to ancient Europeans but continues today. Nigel Pennick reports in *The Art and Science of Geomancy* that construction work on a Singapore site was halted by the local workers' refusal to cut a holy tree, until labor from outside the Malaysian community was hired to remove it.[13]

CONVENTIONS AND INVENTIONS

Since survival was based on the delicate balance between the whims of nature and individual needs, primitive cultures invented various strategies to explain the world, creation, and cosmos. Aside from the nature-related forms discussed earlier, some cultures sought to develop principles that would serve to guide a change in the earth's form. The effort to provide some structure to the unknown, earth or cosmos, was the essence of countless settlements, all of which sought answers to a series of questions. The first was: "Where is the right place? How do we locate the appropriate site for a settlement that maintains the balance among earth, sky, and deity?" The second might have been:

[9]John R. Stilgoe, *Common Landscape of America, 1580–1845* (New Haven, Conn.: Yale University Press, 1982), p. 8.
[10]Pennick, p. 19.
[11]Stilgoe, pp. 7 and 176.
[12]Pennick, p. 20.
[13]Ibid.

Figure 1-5 Stonehenge.

"Where is the holy ground? Where are those sacred zones that it is important to recognize? What are the limits of the settlement, or what is its form?" Although the first two questions might be reversed, the question of form and direction was always one that required the use of various rituals.

The art of *geomancy* provided guidance and direction for site planning of the great pyramids of the Gizeh in Egypt, Stonehenge in Britain, and the Forbidden City of Peking. "In geomancy, the world was conceived as a continuum in which all acts, natural and supernatural, conscious and unconscious, were linked . . . one with the next."[14] In respecting that concept, one exercised great caution in any act which sought to modify that symbiotic relationship.

Probably the most notable example of the ancient geomancy is Stonehenge at Salisbury. The significance of this site was not fully understood until the publication in 1965 of *Stonehenge Decoded* (Fig. 1-5). Contrary to earlier theories, research indicated that the structure was not a temple but a calendar which documented and forecast changes in the seasons as well as the lunar eclipse phenomenon.[15] Imagine the range and scale of unknown quantities in the thirteenth century B.C. and the impact of a structure that could predict the alignment and arrangement of the sun and moon. The structure provided a partial insight into the tenuous sequence of planting, cultivation, and harvest, upon which survival depended. The significance of Stonehenge to a community surrounded by an environment that was the source of both life and death was obviously profound. The impact of early geomancy is probably more obvious when we consider its contribution to our collective knowledge in terms of something as simple as direction. Although the concept of direction is attributed to man's individual orientation—front, back, left, and right—the division is also reflected in the geometry of the globe: two poles and east–west. The division of direction into corresponding colors was considered and adopted by cultures throughout the world and is illustrated in Table 1-1.

As to the shape of the settlement, the Roman model was a circle. Using the cardinal (four) points, the circle was then quartered.[16] The form of Roman cities reflected the criteria of Vitruvius, who theorized that the shape of the city was created from the crossing of two roads, dividing the world as a compass, and surrounding the region of that intersection with walls.[17] A similar quartered system was also employed by ancient cultures in Bali and Asia, which followed a ritual of separating settlements into four sections that collectively resembled a square. The construction of the Sioux's sacred lodge also reflects the cardinal points, with four doors, four windows, and four colors.[18]

The concept of direction and orientation provided a basic mechanism for the development of various geometric typologies (squares, circles, crosses, pentagons). These

---

[14]Ibid., p. 8.
[15]Ibid., pp. 31–35.
[16]Christian Norberg-Schultz, *Existence, Space and Architecture* (New York: Praeger Publishers, 1971), p. 23.
[17]Ibid., p. 22.
[18]Eliade, *The Sacred and the Profane*, pp. 45 and 46.

TABLE 1-1 Division of Direction and Color

		DIRECTION			
CULTURE	Center	East	North	West	South
Aztec		Red	White	Black	Blue
Chinese	Yellow	Blue	Black	White	Red
Irish		Red	Black	Green	White
Hindu		White	Brown	Yellow	Red
Maya/Hopi	Blue-green	Red	White	Black	Yellow
Tibetan	White	Blue	Green	Red	Yellow

Source: Nigel Pennick, *The Art and Science of Geomancy* (London: Thames and Hudson Ltd., 1979), p. 96.

techniques and methods were employed in the development of specific sites as well as ideal cities. All were based on the belief that man was inextricably linked to the planet. As Tao Te Ching summarized: "The world is a holy vessel . . . let him that would tamper with it, beware."[19] Although each culture nurtured a philosophy that was unique to a region or a continent, the common quality was one that integrated the physical, natural environment with the supernatural, religious one; and it was man's obligation to maintain a balance between them.

The Chinese geomancy, Feng Shui, provides a number of excellent examples in which mountains correspond with planets. In Feng Shui there are functional analogies concerning the ancient landscape that provide guidance toward any change in the relationship between man and earth. An established set of complex rules governs the practice of Feng Shui. One particular theory was that evil spirits traveled only in a straight line and could not turn corners.[20] Buildings were sited and designed with the specific purpose of providing an indirect access that would "trap" or shield a home from intrusion by an evil spirit. Although a person unaware of this principle might interpret the plan to be a classic "linking" or "transition zone," the reality of the rationale is quite different.

The geomancer believed that each site was vested with natural aura or forces. The "place" could be fixed when the forces were enclosed for a purpose rather than allowed to seep away into the external continuum. An eastern Indian society employed an astronomer to fix the forces in the preparation of a building site. The astronomer identified the location for the building cornerstone, which was believed to be the location of the snake's head supporting the world. A sharpened stake was driven in the earth to "fix" the symbolic snake of chaos, and the cornerstone was set on the stake. The ritual was repeated at each construction site to create symbolic form from the amorphous.[21]

Although to some cultures "fixing" the place was a site-specific convention, to the Romans, there was a relationship between sites and people. *Genius loci,* or the "spirit of place," was a Roman concept in which every person had his or her own guardian spirit, genius, or guiding force that was trying to shape his or her character. The concept of *genius loci* goes back to the *diamon* of the Greeks and reflects ancient man's perception of life and destiny. "In particular he recognized that it is of great existential importance to come to terms with the genius of the locality in which his life takes place."[22] *Genius loci,* like geomancy, emerged to give meaning to a relationship between places and people. Since at any one time, many people may inhabit a site, *genius loci* must be multivalent. Although *genius loci* relies on the physical quality of a site and reflects a distinct character, that character is laced with "complexities and contradictions."[23]

Most people understand that our individual worlds are neither common nor per-

---

[19]Pennick, p. 162.

[20]Ibid., p. 66.

[21]Eliade, *The Sacred and the Profane*, p. 54.

[22]Christian Norberg-Schultz, *Genius Loci* (New York: Rizzoli International Publication, Inc., 1980), p. 18.

[23]Norberg-Schulz, *Existence, Space and Architecture*, p. 69.

a   b

c   d

Figure 1-6 Four basic models of site planning.

ceived with common values from a background of common experiences. To complicate
an already questionable perceptual problem, there is another view which suggests that
the substance of urban life emerges from the interaction of people, not from the physical
place. It is within this multifaceted context of place occupied by people of various cultural backgrounds that site planning functions.

   If, as Christian Norberg-Schultz maintains, ''man's existence is dependent upon
the establishment of meaningful and coherent environmental image of existential
space,''[24] then the methods by which ''meaningful and coherent'' emerge become critical to the process. Over time, many early conventions conceived to assist in the process
of giving meaning to sites and settlements fell into disrepute. Successes were either
extremely limited or perceptually biased, as few rituals endured that can be applied to
any site. Although myths and rites dissolved in the light of knowledge, what we can
glean from the centuries-long process of change is the evolution of four basic forms used
to fix a place or form space.

   1. The image and form of the object building are capable of fixing a place (Fig. 1-6a).
   2. A collection of independent structures, which although unattached, create a co-
      herent image of place (Fig. 1-6b).

[24]Norberg-Schultz, p. 114.

Figure 1-7 Villa Rotunda.

3. The form of a building can be such that a place may be fixed by the enclosure of its facades (Fig. 1-6c).

4. Although the kinetic implications of the word "path" are somewhat contradictory, paths are nonetheless capable of forming coherent, meaningful images[25] (Fig. 1-6d).

These four concepts and their numerous variations make up the basic man-made models. All are common in the built environment. There are, on occasion, similar qualities in the natural environment. Each of us has been in places where the view, treeline, landform, or water's edge was in its own way a coherent identifiable place without the introduction of man-made invention. The one concept that has only recently become more clear is the relationship between man and the natural environment. Fewer resources and an expanding population are easily overshadowed by a technology that has taken man into a realm once considered to be the home of gods. This larger perspective has made society more conscious that the balance between earth and man is as acute as ever.

The challenge of creating place thus has two interlocking parts: to form space that permits a plurality of interpretations, but to do it in such a way as to recognize the existing "place" and integrate the identity of man with the identity of earth.

PLAN, ORDER, AND SITE

The development of ancient conventions and rites framed the parameters of site planning for numerous cultures as each sought to bring order to a world of chaos. Although methods to fix or define a place varied, the most common form of man-made invention was the building. History is rich with examples of this site planning model. Some are more successful than others at creating an image of place, as opposed to an object, as concepts of structure easily dominate context and landscape (Fig. 1-7).

Another site planning model was mastered by the Egyptians, who were expert at the development of paths acting as "place" (Fig. 1-8). An extensive number of their monuments used the path (sequential images) in conjunction with buildings to magnify the funerary ritual. Large-scale land ownership, stratified social orders, and well-articulated religious principles provided a context and structure through which various cultures functioned to create place.

Hellenic Greece, like other societies, sought to create some man-made order in the

[25]Ibid., pp. 39–53.

Figure 1-8 Plan of pyramid complex of Sahura.

Figure 1-9 The Acropolis.

field of nature (the cosmos). The prevailing theory was that "the ordering of space on earth would mirror the order of the universe."[26] In pursuit of that order, the Greeks evolved two additional basic site planning models: a place defined by a collection of buildings and a place defined by an enclosure of structures.

The Acropolis is an outstanding example of place given identity by an arrangement of unattached buildings. The site and composition of structures convey a clear image of the precinct separate from the individual achievements of classical architecture. The Greeks, as did others, ascribed a value to high, physically prominent areas (Fig. 1-9). It naturally followed that the sacred site for the city of Athens would be located on a visibly prominent hill with the mortal complement of the community at the base elevation. The physical quality of historic Athens and its districts relies heavily on the Ionic order's preoccupation with the finite. This predisposition to develop plans of fixed, forever-controlled shapes influenced decisions associated with both town and site planning.

---

[26]C. A. Doxiadis, *Architectural Space in Ancient Greece* (Cambridge, Mass.: The MIT Press, 1972), p. 20.

Figure 1-10 The Acropolis; plan 530 to 450 B.C.

Since the Acropolis was initially a fortress, its site planning incorporated vestiges of that earlier role, which may partially account for its barren quality. An "end state plan," as such, did not apparently exist until some time between 447 and 437 B.C.[27] Temples were built, disassembled, and moved over a period of years to accommodate new structures and additions and to identify the correct relationship between structure and site. Figure 1-10 illustrates the changes in the Acropolis in the period between 530 and 450 B.C.[28]

Whereas the Acropolis was sacred, an agora was completely secular, and plans often reflected the differences. The agora at Corinth is an example of a site plan that develops an identity from the enclosure of building facades (Fig. 1-11). Whereas the Acropolis was conceived as a group of individual building *volumes* designed and positioned to create a specific spatial quality, the Corinth agora consisted of a series of structures designed to control the quality of exterior space with *facades*. The agora at Miletus (Fig. 1-12) is a reminder that although different models were employed in different regions, each was a deliberate, conscientious effort to create an exterior spatial identity.

Although there is a marked difference in the concept of the buildings' arrangement, there is a similarity in the treatment of the ground plane and vegetation. The sites for various agoras and their planning almost totally exclude vegetation, or integrate natural

[27]Ibid., pp. 36–38.
[28]Ibid., p. 29.

1 Northwest Shops
2 Captives Facade
3 Basilica
4 Peirene
5 Peribolos of Appolo
6 Julian Basilica
7 Upper Terrace
8 South Stoa
9 South Basilica
10 Northwest Shops

Figure 1-11   The Agora at Corinth.

landforms. Although the Greeks' attitude toward the role of vegetation in the context of building is not clear, the absence or inclusion of living plants as a part of the site did not occur by chance.

Numerous public spaces throughout Hellenic Greece were developed without a network of geometric systems (radial, orthogonal, hexagonal, etc.), but C. A. Doxiadis maintains that many utilized an organizational structure based on geometry and the visual quality of space. His research supports the notion that the siting of structures in numerous locations throughout Greece was based on a system of "polar coordinates." This concept builds on the premise that with man as the observer, each object (building) should be located on a site relative to man's view.[29] *Architectural Space in Ancient Greece* contains extensive documentation of 15 sites that were developed on the basis of a strict set of Euclidean principles. Doxiadis's hypothesis is that numerous structures in major public spaces were oriented relative to a fixed view from a propylon in accordance with a predetermined set of geometric angles.

The Altis at Olympia (Fig. 1-13) incorporated aspects of place defined by building facades, a collection of structures, an object building, and a path. When multiple concepts are used to reinforce the role of others, the potential for creating an enduring image

[29]Ibid., pp. 4 and 5.

Figure 1-12 The Agora at Miletus.

Figure 1-13 The Altis at Olympia.

is increased substantially. It should be noted that the Roman Forum of Trajan and the Imperial Forum are excellent examples of building facades used to give form and image to a place (Fig. 1-14). Whereas the Forum of Trajan evolved as an assembly of monuments and temples around a common open zone, the Imperial Forum was designed to enclose and define space with a building form. Both contain easily identifiable spaces which are visibly coherent and rich in variety.

1   Forum of Trajan
2   Forum of Augustus
3   Forum of Nerva
4   Forum of Vespasian
5   Forum of Romanum
6   Forum of Cæsar
7   Basilica Aemilia
8   Basilica of Constantine
9   Basilica Julia
10 Temple of Venus and Rome
11 via Sacra

Figure 1-14 The Roman Forums.

Although neither the Acropolis nor many agoras were developed with an orthogonal grid, the concept had been in use in urban societies of the Mediterranean and the Middle East from the third millennium. The fact that the grid had been the organizational structure for Greek cities with high topographical relief implies that the decision to employ the system had little to do with a site's natural quality but relied more on some grand-design decision. The city of Priene was developed with an orthogonal grid on topography so steep that many streets took the form of stairs. Others have attested to the Greeks' concern for topography in site planning, and their preoccupation with creating physical order in a natural context is clear. This is consistent with the decisions of various cultures throughout history which relied on the geometry of the grid to create order in an unstructured environment.

The proliferation of the grid street system has been attributed to the Greek planner Hippodamus. His work is visible in numerous Greek colonial towns, which have qualities similar to that of his home, Miletus (Fig. 1-15). Although the orthogonal system was not a new concept, it was continually under refinement. Dinocrates, the town planner for Alexander the Great, universalized the grid pattern plan as he sought to give a common physical order and/or form to the conqueror's world. But in spite of the proliferation of the orthogonal plan popularized under the reign of Alexander, the form survived the test of time only in those societies that saw a value in the geometry beyond its functional capabilities.

By the second century before Christ, war and corruption had seriously affected Greece's former Golden Age and it was little more than another Roman province. Unlike Greece, Imperial Rome was never a democracy and the previous Greek attitudes toward the finite were never embraced by the Romans. The philosophy of the Roman Empire may best be expressed as "colonial expansionist," with Rome at the center of the universe. The grid was immensely successful, as it was simple to establish and easy to expand. It was easy to manipulate the size of the township, and the regularity of the grid facilitated control and access. Numerous Roman colonial cities established throughout

Figure 1-15 Plan of Miletus.

Italy and Europe were based on the orthogonal grid. Long after the collapse of the political empire, various cities, including Paris, London, Vienna, and Cologne, flourished on the sites of former Roman cities and included remnants of the original grid plans.[30]

ORDER IN THE WILDERNESS

The grid became a common organizational system throughout Europe and was particularly useful in the expansion of colonial settlements. Although the grid had variations that reflected the nuances of each culture, the model successfully accomplished two objectives: It provided a clear organizational structure, as it had in the past, for the development of settlements, and it facilitated the subdivision of land.

For tenant farmers in Europe, where land was a scarce resource, cooperation and community were physical and economic necessities. The word "community" was most accurately defined in the concept of *landschaft*. According to John Stilgoe, this word, which is German in origin, traditionally implied a cluster of dwellings, fields, meadows, and homes for about 300 people. This was a collective enterprise that objectified a self-sufficient agricultural community of tradition, purpose, order, and strength.[31] More than the notion of land as an area or property, *landschaft* was thought of as a space defined and ordered by man. Similar to other concepts, *landschaft* implied a common bond or obligation between men and the land. When resources were limited, cooperation and community were paramount concerns to individuals. *Landschaft* was apparently a concept applied primarily to agricultural communities, as the building-dominated townships related little to either land or community.

Seventeenth-century European society was extremely stratified into classes, families, and social orders. There was some comfort in the traditions of the European class system, as everyone knew his or her "place" in society. But for the energetic, ambitious individual who sought a higher station in life through risk and work, the new world was an opportunity to change that predetermined place. Any immigrant, of whatever craft or profession, who sought a new life and identity knew the potential in colonial settlement.

---

[30]Leonardo Benevolo, *History of the City* (Cambridge, Mass.: The MIT Press, 1980), p. 221.
[31]Stilgoe, pp. 11–13.

Although the European hierarchy focused on the community first and the individual second, the American model reversed that relationship and codified the concept in the Bill of Rights. The significance of the relationship between property and status was not a phenomenon of colonialism in Europe. Historical precedents favoring those who own property date to the Roman Senate, which was "restricted by the *Lex Claudia* of B.C. 218 to Land owners."[32] The ownership of property in the new world meant social, economic, and political change, all of which were eagerly sought by indentured servants and free men alike.

Settlement of the New World occurred at a time of technological innovation and change in agricultural methods. This change shifted the role of the farm from that of a self-supporting family enterprise to that of a market-oriented establishment.[33] In addition to the change in economic conditions, there was a change in the "value" of community. Many settlers had misgivings about any collective controls that resembled Old World methods. Although colonial governments had policies for land assignments that supported the structure of village or township, few took shape.

In the New World, land was plentiful. The ethical and socioeconomic structure that was the foundation of the *landschaft* in Europe was not visible in America. But in spite of the disappearance of common pastures and collective maintenance, the concept of *landschaft* did not disappear overnight. Until the middle of the eighteenth century, recollections of its physical quality were the scale by which settlements in New England were measured. As attention shifted from community to individual concerns, the social fabric and its physical component were also undergoing change. Since the larger, market-oriented farms did not lend themselves to the spatial organization of the *landschaft*, the need for a surrogate structure emerged in the form of neighborhoods.[34]

Whereas rural communities struggled with social, economic, and physical transitions, urban townships were somewhat more secure, with their own identity. The prevailing text on city planning was "The Ordering of Towns," published in 1683.[35] Among the various recommendations of this broadly read manuscript was the postulate that an ideal town should be 6 miles square. Although there may have been disagreement on the site of a town, various shapes, particularly the orthogonal form, were generally accepted and followed. The grid plan enjoyed widespread use in colonial America. The organizational structure was well known and implied that the community had established a preconceived plan and order for its growth. The system was obviously an intellectual concept and as powerful a statement of man and order as could be made in an environment of nature and disorder. Unlike the ancients, who relied on conventions or myths to separate secular from sacred or provide an order for a site or settlement, the colonists were intellectually well prepared. With a few notable exceptions (Annapolis, Boston, and Washington), the grid was the prevailing planning strategy. Visiting Europeans often commented on the extensive use of the grid in American cities. An Englishman, Francis Baily, noted on his arrival in America:

> That perfect regularity in which [Philadelphia] is built, is not to be approved by some; but it is what I most admire; indeed it accords so much with the ideas of the Americans in general that it is a practice which is almost universally adopted in laying out their new towns and improving their old.[36]

The grid as a matrix provided numerous variations relative to the siting of municipal buildings and public parks, and in view of its widespread success, it became the

---

[32]William Alexander McClung, "The Mediating Structure of the Small Town," *Journal of Architectural Education*, Spring 1985, p. 4.

[33]Stilgoe, pp. 80–81.

[34]Ibid., p. 82.

[35]Ibid., p. 99.

[36]John W. Reps, *Cities of the American West: A History of Frontier Urban Planning* (Princeton, N.J.: Princeton University Press, 1979), p. 3.

conceptual model of the unexplored territories, although in his journal, Francis Baily would later recant on his enthusiasm for the grid:

> I have taken on occasion to express my approbation of the American mode of laying out their new towns . . . but I think that often times it is sacrifice of beauty to prejudice, particularly when they persevere in making all their streets cross each other at right angles without regard to the situation of the ground.[37]

The fact is that throughout history the grid was the plan form used by various civilizations when the objectives were to establish colonial townships or to control empires. The orthogonal plan was simple, easy to comprehend, embraced a rational (intellectual) quality, and expedited the survey and allocation of land parcels. Although the grid was a widely accepted form for many urban areas, expanding the concept to include territories larger than most European nations had some dubious implications. But the Continental Congress of the 1780s found that the frontier was as insecure as the nation's treasury. In an effort to resolve both problems, Congress began to consider liquidating its extensive land holdings west of the Appalachians. The idea was to generate income from the sale of the land while encouraging settlement and stabilization of the western frontier.

It was one task to develop a set of policies for the political structure of a democratic society but quite another to formulate strategies for the physical development of that society in an uncharted land. Accepting the fact that formulation of the Declaration of Independence and Constitution was no small achievement, the articulation of a mechanism for the actual settlement of the frontier was also a major challenge.

The strategy that was ultimately adopted by Congress was based, in part, on two developments. The first was a collection of surveying constants promulgated by an English inventor/surveyor, Edmund Gunter. Gunter developed a surveying "chain" of 100 links with a total length of 66 ft. The chain's value was in the multiple uses of its lengths. Eighty lengths of Gunter's chain on either side of a square enclosed a square mile, which had an area of exactly 640 acres (Fig. 1-16). The second development was the publication "The Ordering of Towns," mentioned earlier. These two marginally related events provided the regimen for the 1785 law to survey the territories west of the Appalachians.[38]

In spite of Jefferson's presence as chairman of the committee responsible for the development of a survey strategy, the Congress did not totally embrace the concepts developed by his committee. It did, however, seize on two important recommendations. One was the development of a survey that would be comprehensive and lock the uncharted territories into an orthogonal grid. Second, the orientation of the grid was to be based on lines of longitude and latitude. The legislation mandated townships 6 miles square, with subdivisions of 36 parcels of 640 acres throughout the territories. This was in complete accord with Jefferson, who visualized a democratic society as a nation of free men on individual farms with a minimal number of cities.

The implementation of a grid that was locked into a north–south longitude (meridian) was, however, doomed to failure. Congress did not have the presence of mind necessary to understand that there would be substantial errors in a format which required that a survey be based on true north–south alignments that converged at the poles. In spite of vocal criticism of the methodology, Congress in its "wisdom" prevailed. Although that august body would spend the next three congressional sessions creating legislation to correct the flaws inherent in the original act, the conceptual power of the grid was very pervasive. Although urban in origin, the indelible field of the grid was transformed into fence, plowed field, and road. Although the philosophical base of the idea

---

[37]Ibid., p. 13.
[38]Stilgoe, p. 100.

Figure 1-16 Depicting area measure of Gunter's chain.

had nothing to do with the environment, there is nothing that compares with the impact of the orthogonal grid on the American landscape.

RECONCILING VISION WITH REALITY

The fact that the grid worked only part of the time did not appear to matter. Like other dogma, we used it where it met little resistance and modified it to accommodate difficult conditions. Even though the construction of roads was relegated to alignments that were on the grid and not on the diagonals, people struggled through. It was almost as though we did not control the system. The myth of the solution endured despite its incredible flaws.

The power of an image or idea can sometimes take on a larger-than-life or mythical state and dupe otherwise rational people into trading a perfectly good cow for a handful of magic beans. History is resplendent with examples wherein the more preposterous the proposal, the broader the appeal.

Revolutions are often blinded by the light of change to the implications of their solutions, and the modern movement of the 1920s was no exception. The issues that gave rise to the revolution in art, architecture, and city planning in the second decade of this century had various roots. The "City Beautiful" movement, which began in the 1890s, had provided the initial impetus for a credible change in city planning in the United States. This had been followed closely by the "Garden Cities" movement conceived by an Englishman, Ebeneezer Howard. Howard, like other social reformers of the era, believed the city to be the antithesis of everything humane and worked to develop alternative strategies to resolve various English social problems. Howard's solution was a series of low-density, satellite new towns in the rural hinterlands of London (Fig. 1-17). Lewis Mumford, Sir Patrick Geddes, and Clarence Stein were all anti-city, and all actively supported the development of these new communities in Europe and the United States, with varying degrees of success.

The acceptance of the Garden Cities concept by architects, landscape architects,

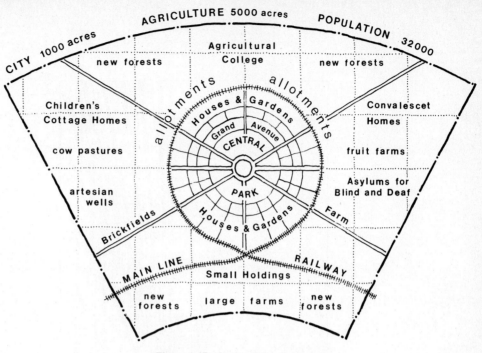

Figure 1-17 Garden Cities Concept plan.

and city planners on both sides of the Atlantic provided an intellectual setting for Le Corbusier's "Radiant City." Unlike the low-density settlements of Howard and Stein, Le Corbusier's vision was of a city of high-rise towers set in a tablet-like park. Le Corbusier explained:

> Suppose we are entering the city by way of the Great Park. Our fast car takes the special elevated motor track between the majestic skyscrapers: as we approach nearer, there is seen the repetition against the sky of the twenty-four skyscrapers; to our left and right on the outskirts of each particular area are the administrative buildings, and enclosing the space are the museums and university buildings. The whole city is a Park [Fig. 1-18].[39]

Although the plan of the Radiant City was physical, it was also an attempt to structure a social utopia based on what he called "maximum individual liberty." Although Le Corbusier accepted the concept of Garden Cities, he maintained that "the solution was to be found in the *vertical* Garden City."[40]

The city as a physical and social problem was first on the agenda of the Congress Internationaux d'Architecture Moderne (CIAM). Le Corbusier had been instrumental in organizing this prestigious group of architects and city planners, who in 1931 pledged their skills to solving urban problems. Le Corbusier had spent years giving shape to his invention. Although part of it was due to the success of the Garden City, part must also be attributed to the physical magnitude and simplicity of the proposal. The visual and aesthetic clarity of the site planning of Greece were to become visible qualities of his large-scale design proposals. He attributed importance to the role of the "shaper of the city," which came to be an implicit part of his work in South America and Algiers. Le Corbusier held the opinion that the architect would give shape, order, and stature to the

---

[39]Jane Jacobs, *The Death and Life of Great American Cities* (New York: Vintage Books, 1961), p. 21.
[40]Ibid., p. 22.

Figure 1-18 Radiant City.

landscape with architectural achievement. In these projects Le Corbusier approached the plan as though "the ground is clear, even if it is occupied."[41] This conceptual bias was consistent with earlier comments in which he expressed the need of clear and level ground to receive a building; the "aesthetic of a carpet." This absence of any natural qualities provided an unencumbered canvas for art. To the revolutionary, the meaning of culture, land, environment, and society mattered little. To Le Corbusier the city was similar to what A. Choisy saw at the Acropolis: "a site which fire had cleared."[42]

Redevelopment proposals for older European cities were constantly thwarted when the planner was obligated to address the problems of small individual property owners. Unlike the Acropolis, the city was a patchwork of small land parcels which created a serious impediment to large-scale planning proposals. With funding from various French industrialists, Le Corbusier worked to resolve the problems of urban Paris. When the need to resolve the problems associated with individual properties distorted the plan, Le Corbusier simply suggested dissolving the concept of individual properties. In defense of his 1930 plan for that city, he concluded: "The unification of the land, a true revolution in the sacred concept of property . . . we must demonstrate that there can be no modern city planning without the unification of the land."[43]

The concept of the Radiant City, the Voisin plan for Paris, and Le Plan de Paris enamored architects and city planners alike. Although supporters of the Garden Cities movement were appalled at the densities suggested by de Corbusier, the simplicity with which the visionary resolved the problems of low-income housing, traffic, and office, commercial, and retail space was greeted with genuine enthusiasm. He brought order to the chaos of the city.

On the other hand, Jane Jacobs, author of *The Death and Life of Great American Cities*, suggests that there is nothing undesirable in something that appears to be visually chaotic.[44] There is nothing fundamentally wrong with a city because it cannot be interpreted by a simple key. She contends that the nature of the city is complexity, that the structure of the city is a mixture of uses, and that understanding the city as a total organism requires understanding its smaller parts first.

What we see and understand better now is that in the rush to rebuild and resolve new social challenges, the modern movement discounted everything that gave meaning to the culture and natural aesthetics of landscape. Working from the premise that the industrial revolution could provide the technology to resolve the housing problems of the world, variations in property, community, context, topography, vegetation, and geomorphology restricted the development of solutions appropriate for mass production and consumption. Since the machine was the solution, the problem had to be scaled to accommodate the limitations of the machine. This limited view of problems and solutions is not unusual, as revolutions in general are often skewed by polemics and segmented views of reality.

The postwar audience of two continents sifted through the precepts and proposals of the visionaries, then extracted and applied the physical components where the need seemed to fit. Although the social rationale for the movement was critical to developing a supporting constituency in sufficient numbers to make the products credible, some simply accepted and applied the form and image products.

The redevelopment policies and programs of the postwar U.S. government were not incongruous with the physical concepts promulgated by the international school of the modern movement. Housing and slum clearance programs were features of the 1949

---

[41]Francois de Pierrefeu and Le Corbusier, *La Maison des hommes* (Paris: n.p. 1942), p. 73. Cited from "The Terrain of Architecture," *36 Lotus International*, 1982.

[42]A. Choisy, *Histoire de l'architecture*, Tome 1, p. 238. Cited from "The Terrain of Architecture," *36 Lotus International*, 1982.

[43]Le Corbusier, "Rapport sur le parcellement du sol des villes," *L'Architecture vivante*, Spring–Summer 1931, pp. 21–22. Cited from "The Terrain of Architecture," *36 Lotus International*, 1982.

[44]Jacobs, pp. 223–226.

Housing Act, which promised "a decent and safe living environment for every American family." The theory was to turn the wartime U.S. industrial and technological force into a peacetime power that would transform cities and suburbs into utopian communities. The will of the people, expressed through its Congress, created a cornucopia of development programs that focused on housing and urban renewal. Subdivisions, inner-city neighborhoods, and sites were developed by legions of entrepreneurs who leveled hills and filled valleys to make way for millions of acres of imageless housing. The grid provided the guidelines for the front- and side-yard setbacks. Each house repeated the same interval, prescribed by the geometry of the streets. All the site planning, as such, was done in the context of the design of the streets and the establishment of the subdivision regulations and zoning ordinances.

It was not that Americans lacked the technology to approach the problem with more sensitivity; it was almost as though we did not have the time. It was easier to plan and redevelop the cities with the "carpet aesthetic" and the structure of the grid. The grid provided the order, the revolution, the new architecture, and the planning. There were few who challenged the despoilment of the landscape. It was simply viewed as an unfortunate, albeit acceptable cost of "progress." And, of course, the myth endures.

The indelible nature of the grid and the simplistic ideas of early twentieth-century modernists left a legacy of sites and communities devoid of social life and natural landscape. Although the intent of all was a built environment of "better" quality, "better" is a subjective value judgment. Some contend that "better" is not necessarily neat and orderly. On occasions, "better" might have qualities of disorder or a wider variety, where the site and structure become a backdrop for the daily activities of people. One of the many common oversights associated with site planning is accepting the way in which people will, or will not, use a site, regardless of the site planner's intent. Where the visionary is oblivious to the "warts and all" of society, the experienced site planner understands and accepts the varieties of preferences expressed by people, culture, and history on a site. Jane Jacobs's message to planners was: "A city cannot be a work of art."[45] The search for visual order has very definite limits. Nature has an order of its own. Plant communities, soils, topography, and microclimate are all part of an interrelated system. Although these components may appear to be without visual order, it does not mean that there is an absence of order. Making the site plan a work of art means understanding the limits of those things that should not be changed and having the creativity to bring those components together into a unified whole. Although art is of value, and important in making something of life and reality, it is not a substitute for either.

---

[45]Ibid., p. 372.

chapter 2

Environmental Ethics: Commandment or Condition?

INTRODUCTION

The fact that a site must accommodate change is, in most instances, an acceptable condition. How that change will take place and under what circumstances is in large part influenced by the philosophical attitudes of society. Since the values of society find a way of materializing themselves into laws and ordinances, or the lack thereof, the impact of a society's value system cannot be casually dismissed. Although the foundation of a culture's values may have various roots, probably one of the most profound is religion. The guidelines for acceptable behavior in society are often corollary with those believed to be important theocracy. Remember Prohibition?

Recall from Chapter 1 the influences of early religions on changes to the natural landscape. The dominant religious perspectives in America today, however, are generally moderate in their view relative to the environment. Accepting the fact that various members of the clergy may take a vocal position concerning a specific issue of environmental quality, a collective religious consensus on the environment appears to be some time away.

Although religions exert potent and enduring pressure on the ethics of society, they realistically share that influence with the social, economic, and political character of a culture. It appears that when all four forces can be brought together into a single movement, a society's ethics are more articulate and visible. Such was the case in the colonial era in this country.

THE JUDEO-CHRISTIAN ETHIC IN THE NEW WORLD

Land ownership in Europe was rigorously controlled by the aristocracy. The prevalent arrangement was one in which the common people leased land and, as tenants, worked to produce an income that was shared with the landlord. People's lives were tied to the land socially, economically, and culturally. The parcel of property they were permitted to till was often allocated year after year to the same family, yet no one that worked a "strip," as it was called, fenced that property, as there was a common strength in the collection of farms. The order of the cultivated fields in the wilderness provided an image of collective strength and reinforced the social compact among individuals, community, and nobleman.[1]

A permanent house or structure was an equally valuable commodity. Although the cotter or laborer had a crude shelter, it was temporary and was considered a dwelling, not a house. A house was different not only in its more permanent quality, but also because it was one of the components in what the English considered a "stead." John Stilgoe writes in *Common Landscape of America* that the "stead" held a meaning which integrated the building and the land, recalled today in our concepts of homestead and farmstead.[2] So important were land, homestead, and their meaning in the community that punishment of a serious crime such as heresy would result in the destruction of one's home and the plowing of the yard. The stead provided and ensured a family of status and position in the community for which there was no substitute.

Immigration to the New World provided an opportunity for land ownership that was, for most people, unattainable in Europe. However, many found the cost of their land to be terribly severe. Of the few true wildernesses remaining in Europe at the end of the fifteenth century, none compared to those of North America. The New World was almost incomprehensible. The dimensions of the land, savages, and climate comprised a very hostile set of conditions. The fact that the survival rate of the Jamestown colony was only 20% provides grim documentation of the impending hostility of the New World.

To the settlers the dream of economic independence in America far outweighed the cost in hardships. To the mass of European and Asian immigrants to follow, land and property meant the right to vote and, as such, gave one a role in controlling his destiny. The relationship between land ownership and voting privilege was a part of the ideology of the architects of the new republic. Compared to the political structure of the colonies, a democratic government did not exist in most European countries in the seventeenth century. Despite later reforms, which permitted voting rights by those other than the propertied class, the concept of equating the ownership of land with the right to vote died hard. As recently as the early twentieth century, when women's suffrage was a topic of national debate, the city of New York permitted women to vote only when they owned property and only when taxes were an issue.

If the fruits of economic and social gain were not enough incentive, the permissive attitudes of colonial governments associated with religion were very desirable. Pocahontas's spouse, Captain John Smith, suggested to his followers that settlement of the New World was a holy war. One only had to recall God's commandment to Adam and Eve, in Genesis 1:28:

> And God blessed them, and God said unto them, be fruitful and multiply and replenish the earth and subdue it and have dominion over the fish of the sea and over the fowl of the air, and over every living thing that moveth upon the earth.[3]

Captain Smith, and many who followed, visualized their efforts to be in complete accord with those of Jehovah. They maintained an anthropocentric view which held that *man* was the central aim of creation and, as such, enjoyed the right of dominion over the earth. The pervasive philosophy was one of dominance over all things, with the caveat that the results would be for the glory of God. This anthropocentric view was Judeo-Christian in origin and obviously had little respect or tolerance for other religious perspectives. It was sympathetic to the political and economic goals of New World settlement and, as such, provided religious reinforcement for other motives.

---

[1] John R. Stilgoe, *Common Landscape of America, 1580–1845* (New Haven, Conn.: Yale University Press, 1982), p. 13.
[2] Ibid., p. 14.
[3] *Holy Bible*, King James Version (New York: Abradale Press, 1969), p. 2.

The interpretation of Genesis 1:28 has been a topic of debate by religious scholars for some time. In Hebrew, the key word in the text is *khibshuah*, which translates as "fill the earth and subdue it." Other references in the Old Testament using the word are very harsh, as it is based on the root "to trample, tread underfoot, to force humble, ravish."[4] The Greek translation is not as caustic, and where it is used elsewhere in the Old Testament expresses simple domination.

Josephus, a Jewish historian writing around the first century A.D., stated that God commanded human beings "to take care of the plants."[5] An ancient commentary on this passage of the Old Testament claims the following: "If he merits it, he is to have dominion, if not he descends to the lower level with other animals."[6] Josephus's text implies that the dominion over creation depends on the responsibility that human beings display in exercising that dominion.

In this light, the concept of covenant between man and God maintains man as the agent of the creator. As Robert Gordis, a modern Jewish scholar, has put it: "The Hebrew and Jewish interpreters would prohibit exploitation." Judaism goes much further and insists that man has the obligation not only to conserve, but also to enhance, because man is the "co-partner of God in the creation."[7]

The interpretation of the same scripture by St. Thomas Aquinas rendered a similar picture. The largely ignored work of the thirteenth-century Italian priest and scholar suggests a more pluralistic attitude. Thomas Aquinas, an outstanding theologian of the Catholic Church, believed that the Biblical text implied that man's obligation to the earth was as a steward, with God at the center of the universe. This stewardship role implied further that man was a link in the chain of the environment, and as the most "intelligent," the role of dominion was more that of "keeper" with an obligation of preservation. Whether Thomas Aquinas was influenced by Josephus is open to speculation, but the similarity of their conclusions suggests that the literal interpretation of "dominion" had disputed theological support.

John R. Stilgoe is of the opinion that "Christianity destroyed the ancient oneness of man and nature."[8] To early Christians, the wilderness was pagan and the place of idolaters. Even the word "wilderness" has as its roots "the nest of the wild [beast]" and was considered to be beyond the realm of man's control.[9] Christianity, as a religion, was objectified in settled land, not woods. The farmhouse in a setting of tilled soil and flourishing pasture was all a part of man's abstract concept of order, harmony, and peace.

The attitudes of dominance and concepts of ownership were unknown to many of the Indians of America, to whom the earth and environment were an extension of the family unit. The land was not owned; it belonged to everyone. This was reinforced by the religious belief that deceased family members were reincarnated as parts of the landscape—"my brother the tree, my father the pond." The absence of a land ownership concept by many Indian tribes was another stroke of luck for the colonists.

Armed with the commandment of God in a land of incredibly abundant natural resources, they embarked on an enterprise to subdue an entire continent and, in the process, bring Christianity and civilization to its inhabitants. To support the exploitation process, the few regulations that did exist in the New World became fewer as one moved toward the frontier. This collection of circumstances propelled the frontier farther to the West, but more important, it crystallized the national land ethic: growth. Growth ma-

---

[4]A. B. Davidson, *Analytical Hebrew and Chaldee Lexicon of the Old Testament* (MacDill A.F.B. Fla.: MacDonald Publishing Company), p. 369.

[5]Josephus, quoted in *Antiquities*, Vol. I (Grand Rapids, Mich.: Baker Book House, 1974), pp. 1–3.

[6]Midrash, *Genesis Rabbah*, Vol. VIII (New York: Bloch Publishing Company, Inc.), p. 12.

[7]W. Gunther Plaut and Bernard J. Bamberger, *The Torah; A Modern Commentary* (New York: Union of American Hebrew Congregations, 1981), p. 25.

[8]Stilgoe, p. 8.

[9]*Oxford English Dictionary*, Vol. 11, pp. 3778–3779; Kersey, *A New English Dictionary*, under "Wilderness"; Hoskins, *The Making of the English Landscape*, pp. 95–103; Tuan, *Landscapes of Fear*, pp. 73–86.

terialized the essence of America as a land in which an ambitious person could find economic independence, with minimal governmental interference, through the development of the land and its resources. This perception of the Americas, which began with the landing of Sir Walter Raleigh in 1584, is visible today in the massive urban/rural migration fueled by regional economic change.

MANIFEST DESTINY

The extremely mobile nineteenth-century population found new frontiers regardless of whether they followed the timber industry from Illinois to Oregon, the cattle drives from Texas to Kansas, or gold and silver from Colorado to California. This mobility encouraged an exploitive view of the environment and galvanized the concept of land as a commodity. The successful entrepreneurs who converted natural resources into economic fortunes became models for others to follow. In light of the immense hardships encountered by the colonists, the ability to successfully convert an adversary environment into one of financial gain only improved the balance sheet. In the process of forging a democracy with a willingness to accept all comers, progress became a creed.

The birth of the nation spawned an expansionist philosophy that enjoined the imagination and aspirations of millions. Economic progress and the industrial revolution meant jobs and increased wealth for the entire population. The growth achievements and opportunities of the young nation could be measured by the multitudes of emigrants who left families and homelands to begin again. The risk of starting over in America was small considering the tales of success, wealth, status, and progress carried by those who survived the hardships.

The vision of progress was the engine of the future. But visions, like myths, not only ignore and shed the flaws of reality but survive to create utopian images. Currier and Ives engravings of colonial America portray a bucolic setting extrapolating the picturesque from the genuine and, in the minds of many, is still that of ''New England'' today. We forget that the working conditions of the urban poor at the turn of the century were essentially voluntary slavery. Separating myth from reality poses a problem for a society, as it involves the examination of larger-than-life personalities or events in real, accountable terms. What exacerbates the problem is that it requires scrutiny of society's own values in the process.

- What was Thomas Jefferson, author of the Declaration of Independence, doing with a house and yard full of slaves?
- How many black free men actually received the one mule and 40 acres promised by the federal government at the close of the Civil War? (It has been estimated that the acreage involved would have approached that of the size of the state of Montana.)

Others have observed that we keep two sets of books: one myth, one reality. This is a much more convenient arrangement, as it permits a society to present one set of ideals while living with another. Such was the situation when seventeenth-century references to the settlement of the New World as a ''Holy War'' were reincarnated in the policy of ''Manifest Destiny.'' In an editorial supporting the annexation of Texas in 1845, journalist and diplomat John Louis O'Sullivan suggested the tenet that ''territorial expansion of the nation is not only inevitable but divinely ordained.''[10] In his detailed account of the American Indian's struggle with the U.S. government, *Bury My Heart at Wounded Knee*, Dee Brown suggests that Manifest Destiny ''lifted land hunger to a lofty plane.'' To the Indian, the policy implied that the white man was the ''dominant race

---

[10]*United States Magazine and Democratic Review*, July–August 1845.

and, therefore, responsible for the Indians—along with their lands, forests, and mineral wealth.''[11]

Rationalization of the numerous American Indian treaty infractions was extensive and almost always based on the view that land and its inherent resources were commodities. Furthermore, without federal intervention and control, the expertise to manage the resources adequately would not be available. The policies and development philosophies of our political leaders of the early nineteenth century were heavily influenced by the British economist Adam Smith (1723–1790). Smith's publication *An Inquiry into the Nature and Causes of the Wealth of Nations* was an extensive examination of the distribution of industry and commerce in Europe. Smith's thesis was that a minimum of governmental interference promoted the best use (production) and distribution of capital. This concept of noninterference, or laissez-faire, was based on Smith's theory that each person, permitted to act in his or her own best interest, would create a condition that was in the best interest of all. Obviously, any meddling by government with free competition in the market would create negative effects.[12]

Even if we accept the concept that land is a commodity and essential to the long-term welfare of the nation as a whole, why do we not care for the resource better than we do? Knowing that land resources are finite, should we seriously allow the extraction of resources or the deposit of waste to occur without review, control, or comment by local, state, or federal government?

The "land as commodity" philosophy maintains that whatever resource imbalance might exist can be corrected by the fundamental entrepreneurial spirit that built this country. The opposing opinion maintains that the land is a resource, not a commodity. This philosophical position suggests that land is not necessarily "owned" by anyone, as the land lives on while ownerships change over time. These two opposing positions are not always as polarized as presented here, but the basis for disagreement is operationally close.

The "resource" philosophy suggests that the solution to various environmental problems requires an examination of the limited resources of the planet and the interdependencies of one resource on another. This conservation ethic holds the view that we have squandered our resources for decades and it is time for another accounting. The political bias of the conservation ethic is diametrically opposed to that of Adam Smith and suggests that the laissez-faire market is essentially responsible for the massive water and air quality degradation which has resulted from industrial practices that have treated the environment as a public toilet. To add insult to injury, the public has had to establish a cabinet position at the national level to manage and monitor the problem. One observer quipped that air quality standards have been in the hands of the American private sector for years, and the benefits of their criteria have provided us with the latest addition to the dictionary—"acid rain."

A QUESTION OF VALUES

This conflict between land as a resource and land as a commodity has been a topic of extensive debate and consternation. The model of this confrontation between the land and ethical standards is probably best illustrated in Garrett Hardin's treatise "The Tragedy of the Commons." Hardins rejoiner to Adam Smith's theory was based on an accepted practice in fourteenth century England that permitted neighboring property owners the right to graze in the "wastes" or moors belonging to a manoral lord. These common property rights were often multiple in any one field, as both cultivation and

---

[11]Dee Brown, *Bury My Heart at Wounded Knee* (New York: Holt, Rinehart and Winston, 1970), p. 8.
[12]*Funk and Wagnalls Encyclopedia*, Vol. 21 (New York: Funk & Wagnalls, Inc., 1976), p. 422.

THE EVOLUTION OF ETHICS

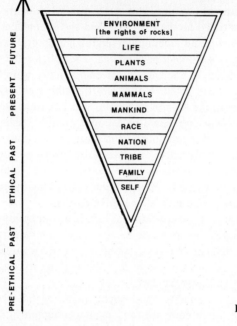

Figure 2-1   Diagram of ethical relationship.

grazing might occur simultaneously. This was a difficult situation at best as the quality of the commons was dependent upon a *quid-pro-quo* relationship between those who shared the rights to these fields. When population densities were low and the natural processes imposed certain limits on the number of livestock, the common pasture was easily capable of supporting the demands of both man and beast. Time and circumstances had worked to create and maintain a balance between the commons and livestock as a resource. Although each herdsman recognized the importance of the commons as a resource to all, each also decided that his own best interest would be better served by adding one animal to the commons. The rationale was that the economic value of one animal was well worth the ''fractional'' impact on the quality of the commons. Considering the fact that the costs would have been paid for by a marginal degradation to the commons and the rest of the community, every herdsman elected to increase his herd by one. The results: an overgrazed commons and poor herds. Livestock that could survive in a healthy environment at limited levels failed to produce in comparable quantity or quality. The net effect of uses that attempted to extend the holding capacity of the land beyond its realistic potential was the generation of serious long-term economic and environmental losses. This absence of a ''quid-pro-quo'' relationship with each person, as well as the land, produced predictable results.

Observations on this relationship that exists among man, environment, and an ethical standard have been made by many. In an essay by Roderick Nash on Aldo Leopold, Nash developed a model of the ethical relationships, illustrated in Fig. 2-1.[13] The model suggests that the first quid-pro-quo relationship existed when man adopted the attitude that someone else's life was more important than his or her own. When ''survival of the fittest'' was no longer the creed on which man chose to exist, a change in our ethics became plausible. Over time, this change has generally expanded from the individual to include family, tribe, and nation. Although some have adopted an attitude that some mammals (other than human beings) have ''rights,'' extending the concept to include plants and rocks creates serious debate.

---

[13]Roderick Nash, ''Do Rocks Have Rights?'' *Center Magazine*, November–December 1977, p. 6.

There have been proposals put forth which support the argument that the environment does have rights. Christopher Stones' *Should Trees Have Standing?* discusses the principles behind legal "standing," which he suggests exists when we establish national forests and parks. The Grand Canyon is a collection of rocks and is, furthermore, considered a national treasure. The decision as to the extent of those rights is based on values, priorities, and our ethics at the time.

The "man dominant" position implied in Genesis has had a definitive effect on the philosophy behind our government and legal system. That philosophy had been practiced in the United States for over 200 years without caveat or question—until recently. It may be time for a reevaluation of the canons which support that philosophy in view of the range and scale of environmental problems that confront the United States today. Even if the more moderate attitude of man-steward is wrong, how much worse could the impending results be?

The primary concepts associated with developing an understanding of man's relationship with the environment can best be summarized in the four basic laws of ecology formulated by the renowned environmentalist Barry Commoner.[14]

The first law is: "Everything is connected to everything else." The development and preparation of life itself is dependent on interrelated processes. Commoner's second law is: "Everything must go somewhere." This is really the basic law of physics—matter is indestructible. There is no "waste" in ecology or nature; nothing is discarded. Principal among the reasons for the environmental crisis today is that we have extracted extraordinary amounts of natural resources, converted them into other forms, and discharged the residuals without realizing that everything must go somewhere.

The third law is: "Nature knows best." This axiom is sometimes difficult for us to accept, for in many instances we look to technology to solve our problems. Even the concept of recycling is concomitant with the natural processes. One of the characteristics of living systems is that for every organic substance produced by a living organism, there exists somewhere in nature an enzyme capable of breaking down that substance. The essence of this is that no organic substance is synthesized without provision for its degradation. The fourth law is: "There is no such thing as a free lunch." In ecology, just as in economics, this law warns that every gain is won at some cost. The tenets of the three previous laws are incorporated in this precept. Because the global ecosystem is a connected whole in which nothing is gained or lost without an imperative for improvement, anything that is extracted by human effort must be replaced. Payment cannot be avoided; it can only be delayed.

---

[14]Barry Commoner, *The Closing Circle* (New York: Alfred A. Knopf, Inc., 1971), pp. 33–45.

chapter 3

The American Value System in Change

THE NATIONAL ENVIRONMENTAL PROTECTION ACT

With an understanding of why the "man dominant" ethic was so pervasive, it is easy to understand why it was unchallenged for so many years. Although growth and change fueled the most envied economy in the world, both qualities were unsuspecting harbingers of costs that would be paid by other generations.

The 1960s were a time of traumatic social unrest in the United States. Technological changes in communications provided the media with the capability for a verbal and visual daily accounting of the nation's activities and leadership. While the economy enjoyed a flourishing peacetime growth, it was also a time of introspection. People began an active wholesale inquiry into the methods, ethics, and values of government and industry. The sentiment of Congress was that something was wrong with the conduct of various governmental policies and agencies which convoluted the trust of natural resources and fiscal management of the people.

Although the sentiment of a need to change was one thing, the language of the Supreme Court in a 1954 ruling provided the basis on which the public's health, safety, and welfare would later be considered:

> The concept of the public welfare is broad and inclusive. The values it represents are spiritual as well as physical, aesthetic as well as monetary. It is within the power of the legislature to determine that the community should be beautiful as well as healthy, spacious as well as clean, well-balanced as well as carefully patrolled.[1]

The Court's 1954 ruling in *Berman* v. *Parker* was a landmark decision relative to environmental quality, as it stated in lucid terms that there were issues beyond the monetary that were valid qualities of every community. Congress reinforced the Court's concern by adopting legislation based on the premise that the environment has an intrin-

---

[1]Berman v. Parker, 348 U.S. 26,33 (1954).

sic value to society. The National Environmental Protection Act of 1969 (NEPA) was to have a profound effect on the way the federal government and American industry would do business.

Although it is not imperative that every site planner understand the intricacies of the legislation, a working knowledge of the law's intent, the procedure, and its impact on state environmental and land use controls is worthwhile. Following the national legislation, the number of state and local ordinances designed to supplement NEPA and/or to correct oversights have been extensive. The proliferation of additional legislation reflects the fact that the concept of environmental quality is no longer an abstract idea; rather, it is an issue that individuals and government can legitimately control.

NEPA: POLICY STATEMENT AND PROCESS

The National Environmental Protection Act of 1969 (Public Law 91-190) is probably one of the most controversial and significant laws in recent history to sort its way through the legislative process. For the first time the Congress promulgated legislation which mandated an active federal role in the maintenance and control of the environmental quality of this nation. The purpose of the legislation is to

> encourage productive and enjoyable harmony between man and his environment; to promote efforts which will prevent or eliminate damage to the environment and biosphere and stimulate the health and welfare of man; to enrich the understanding of the ecological systems and the natural resources important to the Nation.[2]

The text of the legislation is separated into two primary sections. The first, Title I, is a statement of national environmental policy: Sections 101(b) and (c) are as follows:

> (b) To carry out the policy set forth in this Act, it is the continuing responsibility of the Federal Government to use all practicable means consistent with other essential considerations of national policy, to improve and coordinate Federal plans, functions, programs and resources to end that the Nation may:
>
> (1) fulfill the responsibilities of each generation as trustee of the environment for the succeeding generations;
> (2) assure for all Americans healthful, safe, productive and aesthetically and culturally pleasing surroundings;
> (3) attain the widest range of beneficial uses of the environment without degradation, risk to health or safety or other undesirable and unintended consequences;
> (4) preserve important historic, cultural, and natural aspects of our national heritage, and maintain, whenever possible, an environment which will support diversity and variety of individual choice;
> (5) achieve a balance between population and resources use which will permit high standards of living and a wide sharing of life's amenities; and
> (6) enhance the quality of renewable resources and approach the maximum attainable recycling of the depletable resources.
>
> (c) The Congress recognizes that each person should enjoy a healthful environment and that each person has a responsibility to contribute to the preservation and enhancement of the environment.[3]

The thrust of the legislation was to engage every federal agency in a balanced decision-making process that considered the total public interest. This carried with it the obligation of each federal agency to critique, through an Environmental Impact Statement, its projects and to provide other agencies or private parties with that evaluation.

---

[2]*Federal Register*, Vol. 38, No. 147, Part II; Council on Environmental Quality, *Preparation of Environmental Impact Statements*, Title 40, Chap. V, Sec. 1500.1.

[3]The National Environmental Policy Act of 1969, Public Law 91-190, 91st Congress, Session 1075, January 1, 1970.

The hope was that this would ensure a more coordinated collective effort on programs and projects throughout federal, state, and local entities. Prior to NEPA, interagency conflicts were the standard bill of fare. The Federal Highway Administration was supporting the construction of highways in national parks and the Corps of Engineers was financing projects that would eliminate millions of acres of farm and park land.[4] Congress saw the need for an agency or entity that would coordinate interagency operations as they affected the environment.

NEPA incorporated provisions similar to those of the earlier National Full Employment Act of 1940.[5] Both laws recommended the establishment of a national policy for the environment and a Council of Environmental Quality (CEQ). The role of the CEQ was to act in an advisory capacity to the President. NEPA departed from its predecessors by prescribing an "action forcing mechanism" which required participation by all federal agencies.[6] The fact that it was mandatory prior to any action was without precedent. Observations relative to the scope and implications of NEPA have been that it was the "single most important change in land use regulation [in the United States] since zoning."[7]

We know now that the effect of this legislation on the environmental design professions has been significant beyond the scope of the law itself. First, the legislation welded into prominence the concept that the physical environment was something of value to be considered in terms other than economic. Second, not only has the issue of environmental quality become something of value from a national perspective, but it also has filtered down to townhall meetings and grade-school classrooms throughout the United States. The growth of an awareness and consciousness of the environment as something that requires stewardship has been nothing short of remarkable.

Third, regardless of any other accomplishments, the legislation delineated a process that bound each federal agency into a role of inventory, analysis, and an examination of alternatives. The process has proven to be valuable to the federal establishment in the scrutiny of feasible options, but it has also become a model for state and some local environmental legislative clones. The review process and citizen participation in the law had a major impact on those federal agencies that had an inclination for translating a community's best interest into agency projects.

Federal action has been interpreted to mean that there are either one or both—federal control or financial participation—in a project or program. Major federal action generally implies that the action is of significant proportion and importance such that it will require a substantial amount of time, financial resources, and planning if implemented.[8] Another good guideline for interpreting a "major" action is that it is any action which creates an environmental impact that could become controversial. The crucial point here is that it is better to address potential negatives early, to avoid reference of "omission" or bias later.

As with any good problem-solving methodology, the Environmental Impact Statement begins with research. The first step is an environmental inventory and generally requires a comprehensive survey of a site's existing ecology. The inventory would include documentation of a site's physical, cultural, and biological character. In addition to those qualities normally mapped for a site planning problem (see Chapter 4), to comply with EPA's standards the inventory should also include a quantitative water and air analysis, herpetofanno and wildlife (mammals and aquatic) evaluation, and identification

---

[4]Richard N. L. Andrews, "Impact Statements and Impact Assessment," Vol. III, *Management and Control of Growth* (Washington, D.C.: Urban Land Institute, 1975), p. 150.

[5]Robert Gladstone and Robert Witherspoon, "EIS's and Development: Origins/Evolution/Impact," Vol. III, *Management and Control of Growth* (Washington, D.C.: Urban Land Institute, 1975), p. 141.

[6]L. W. Canter, *Environmental Impact Assessment* (New York: McGraw-Hill Book Company, 1977), p. 14.

[7]Gladstone and Witherspoon, p. 142.

[8]*Preparation of the Environmental Impact Statement*, published by the Federal Highway Administration, National Highway Institute, and V.T.N. Consolidated, Inc., p. 8.

of any rare or endangered species.[9] Since inventory is the basis on which an impact will be evaluated, the quality and scope of this research is obviously critical to the entire process. Any omissions or oversights in this initial phase would seriously undermine an impact statement's credibility and value. The law's comprehensive nature and process almost demand an interdisciplinary approach.[10] For an Environmental Impact Statement (EIS) to respond adequately to the scope of issues, the contributions of a biologist, a landscape architect, an engineer, a city planner, and an architect may all be necessary.

Initially, the NEPA applied to all federal agencies; those responsible for a proposal were also responsible for preparation of the NEPA statement. Subsequent changes through the courts and Congress have exempted NEPA in limited circumstances and amended the legislation to permit the Secretary of Housing and Urban Development (HUD) to vest the NEPA responsibility with local governments requesting federal community development block grants.[11] Although there are some exceptions to the law, NEPA requires that any proposal receiving federal financial assistance for "major federal actions significantly affecting the quality of the human environment" be accompanied by an EIS.[12] Obviously, questions concerning the definition of "major" have led to an extended number of arguments. Although some environmental constituents, such as water and air quality, can be measured and quantified against a given set of quantitative parameters, measuring the aesthetic value of a scenic vista or historical monument eludes even the most innovative analysis. Some federal agencies have developed their own guidelines in an effort to provide consistent distinctions between major and minor federal actions. It must also be noted that the term is "federal action" and, as such, includes any change in federal policies. For example, the courts required the Interstate Commerce Commission to prepare an EIS on their proposal to abandon a group of railway lines.[13]

THE ENVIRONMENTAL ASSESSMENT AND IMPACT STATEMENTS

The assessment segment of the process obligates the investigator to "evaluate the consequences of a proposed action" on each of the elements described in the inventory segment. Just as this stage implies, "it is necessary to (1) predict any change in each environmental constituent, (2) identify the scope of any change on each environmental descriptor, (3) determine the implications or significance of the anticipated change on each element."[14]

The value of this stage of the EIS is in the anticipated assessment of change and, obviously, implies a forecast of the future. Although there are legitimate techniques for predicting the results of certain actions on some elements, such as water quality, there are some problems associated with predicting the impact of a change in air quality relative to a wildlife habitat. Efforts to further evaluate the short- and long-term effects on elements that were difficult to quantify initially has been an obvious criticism of the EIS process.[15] The biases of those involved in the preparation of the document are also no small factor, as interpretations, which are unavoidable, have and will create a context for disagreement. Just as it was important in the inventory stage for interdisciplinary involvement, it continues to be so in this phase as well.

---

[9]Canter, p. 2.

[10]Ibid.

[11]42 U.S.C., 5304 (h).

[12]42 U.S.C., 4332 (2) (c).

[13]City of New York v. United States, 337 F. Supp. 150, 3 ERC 1570 (E.D.N.Y. 1972); Aberdeen and Rockfish R.R. v. SCRAP, 442 E.S. 289, 7 ERC, 2009 (1975).

[14]Canter, p. 2.

[15]Ibid.

Following the environmental assessment and the determination that an EIS is necessary, part (c) of Section 102 defines the considerations that are obligatory in the preparation of the EIS. The first point to be addressed is "the environmental impact of the proposed action."[16] A coupling amendment to the original guidelines now requires a statement that describes the proposed action.[17]

Although many consider the nature of an environmental impact statement to be one that is essentially negative in its considerations, it is entirely plausible that a project may contain several very positive impacts. Popular notions are first, that the EIS is a herald of problems associated with a proposal; second, that the EIS will focus only on the adverse and will be confirmed by the accompanying technical and descriptive documentation. The basic intent of NEPA is an "environmental full disclosure law" and, as such, implies that both positive and negative effects will be documented and considered in the evaluation of a proposal.[18]

The second component required under Section 102 is the identification of "any adverse environmental effects which cannot be avoided should the proposal be implemented."[19] This is the critical "problem statement" of the process and is pivotal to the development of a comprehensive and objective statement. Failure to honor either of these issues lays the groundwork for future criticism.

The third question focuses on the range of feasible alternatives, considered as solutions, to achieve the initial problem objective, or, as the legislation states, "alternatives to the proposed action." The inability of various agencies to take this section seriously has created numerous lawsuits. Problems are created by the pervasive attitude of some agencies that prepare an EIS to support a preconceived alternative. One of the most enlightening evaluations is the way in which agencies consider the "no project" or "do nothing" alternative. Since this alternative requires careful scrutiny of both positive and negative impacts under "no action," it provides a good basis for the evaluation of other alternatives.

The fourth stipulation under part (c) requires the agency to identify "the relationship productivity."[20] The motive behind the inclusion of this language is that each generation should be cognizant of its obligation as steward or trustee of the environment. The question is: What options or resources are being reduced or eliminated from future use by an action today? This question is a companion to the next requirement—to identify "any irreversible and irretrievable commitments of resources which would be involved in the proposed action should it be implemented."[21] The response demands that the agency not only consider the desires of today relative to the needs of tomorrow, but compels an accounting of the long-term, permanent environmental costs.

A sixth component requires the agency to discuss the objections or issues expressed by reviewers. Two additional sections were added to the CEQ guidelines in August 1973. Both are intended to expand the potential of the EIS as a planning and decision-making document. One requires a response relative to the proposed action's impact on federal, state, or local land use policies. The second amendment also requires a discussion of other federal policies or programs that might mitigate any adverse consequences of the proposed action. These additions to the original law not only require that the EIS be more specific in addressing local land use controls and policies but permit the EIS to consider the contribution of other federal agencies in alleviating any potential negative effects.

---

[16]42 U.S.C. 4332 (2) (c).

[17]Ibid.

[18]Elaine Moss, ed., National Resources Defense Council, *Land Use Controls in the United States* (New York: The Dial Press/James Wade, 1977), p. 36.

[19]42 U.S.C. 4332 (2) (c).

[20]Ibid.

[21]Ibid.

INTENT AND OMISSIONS

Probably, the most significant criticism of NEPA focuses on the process itself. The radical character of the legislation and the composition of the law's language over a brief period of time created natural compromises. The ambiguity and "implied" analytical requirements of the final law have been universally criticized by supporters, protagonists, legal scholars, and judges.[22] Although NEPA created a process for and awareness of federal participation and review, the law was silent on two crucial points. First, the CEQ was provided with no statutory authority to approve or disapprove projects. Second, the problem was compounded further by the fact that many individual agencies are also without the specific legal power to mandate compliance.[23] The final decisions often rest with the federal agency proposing the project and/or state agencies participating in the review.

But what would appear to be a "Catch-22" loop in the law has been remedied by the process and by human nature. In spite of the law's silence on final action, as a practical matter, citizen organizations took their role in the process very seriously and have "been and will continue to be largely responsible for finally assuring compliance with NEPA."[24] Interestingly enough, the EIS (Section 102) was not a component of the original legislation proposed in 1969.[25] The action-forcing provisions of the law were added following public testimony on the Senate Bill 1075 and are attributed to Lyton Caldwell. Those recommendations were developed as a mechanism to require federal agencies to address environmental issues with a comprehensive, objective process. This was dramatically different from the normal agency bias, and the "conflicting mission" issue was at the seat of Caldwell's criticism.[26] Although the inclusion of the EIS became an addendum to Senate Bill 1075, the obvious lack of the additional rigor that structures guidelines for decisions and mandatory compliance has never found its way into law.

In spite of intentions, the "actions" forced by NEPA have taken on two entirely different characteristics. First, the Environmental Impact Statement has taken on a "life of its own." Ostensibly, the preparation of the EAS, and EIS if necessary, was to have provided a base of data, documentation, and forecasts on which a judgment could be made. Only the most naive believed that only those projects that had no negative environmental impact would be built. The point of the process was to identify the extent of the recognized and potential losses, the implications of the loss, and the preparation of that information in a way that could be reviewed and understood by both the public and private sectors. The problems associated with the documentation of the data and the prognosis of various alternatives become a paper "swamp." The complexity and verbosity of assessment and impact statements become analogous to an intellectual purgatory. Developers and federal agencies submitted assessment and impact statements in multivolume form in which the proponent sought to overwhelm adversaries with technical jargon, data, and forecasts. Instead of the EIS emerging as a document of enlightenment, it became a wall, and war, of words.

Second, although the intent of the EIS was to function as a mechanism for an integrated planning process, it has been utilized by both public and private sectors as a method to justify a decision made significantly earlier in the process. The tragedy here is the misconception of many agencies as to who the original "client" is. This is not an uncommon attitude of some bureaucracies; the missions of a bureau often take on an

---

[22]Gladstone and Witherspoon, p. 142.

[23]Canter, p. 4.

[24]Mary E. Brooks, *Housing Equity and Environmental Protection* (Washington, D.C.: American Institute of Planners, 1976), p. 22.

[25]Canter, p. 4.

[26]Andrews, p. 151.

importance above and beyond those whom the agency serves. As a result, one of the primary objectives of the law is still unfulfilled.

When it became obvious that NEPA and its process were to become part of the way we would do business, those who believed that progress was incarnate in bricks and mortar predicted that strict adherence to the law's goals would result in an economic debacle. The genuine intent in the law's efforts to improve the planning process by an open evaluation of proposed actions was blurred in the rhetoric which shackled the future of the construction industry with the burden of the new law. The criticism was not completely unjustified; as M. E. Brooks comments in *Housing Equity and Environmental Protection*: "Increased exposure through public notice, possible public hearings and greater opportunities for citizens' suits increases the likelihood of a challenge on environmental grounds. . . . The actual impact of these delays is often so costly as to render a project no longer economically feasible."[27]

The popular misconceptions by both professionals and laypersons concerning NEPA begin with the difference between the Assessment and the Impact Statement. It is critical to recognize that the process has two stages, the first of which is the assessment. As mentioned earlier, this stage begins with an inventory and continues on to its more important function: prediction. The principal failing of most assessments is that they are more inventory and less prediction. If the site planner remains mindful of NEPA's purpose to anticipate environmental impacts and identify those alternatives which can best mitigate those impacts, the importance of the predictive function will probably not become subordinated to bookkeeping.

Predictions should also remain separate from the evaluation process. Predictions are estimates, or forecasts, by professionals of empirical data within a fixed time period. An evaluation of impacts can be made by professionals or laypersons and is a matter of judgment. Although predictions must be made with professional rigor, evaluation of the impacts may be a matter of "social preferences" and thus could be made by anyone.[28] The Impact Statement is pursued only if the consequences of the Assessment Statement warrant a more extensive analysis. Every case does not require the more definitive second stage, because the magnitude of the direct or indirect effects simply may not justify additional evaluation and analysis.

Criticisms of NEPA imply that the process is somehow never ending, as the scope of research and analytical analysis is ambiguous. That observation is not without some validity, as state and local legislation are often better. Oversights concerning the more definitive aspects of environmental research are commonly more specific at the state and local government levels, as they can be more responsive to regional circumstances. Richard Andrews suggests that in lieu of the methodology currently employed, the scope of the inventory data gathering could be reduced dramatically by restricting the inventory function to those "resource functions that are intertwined with the proposed action."[29] Following that first item the research would focus on "selective baseline studies of parameter values that define those systems."[30] This finer level of detail would provide the basis for the development of forecasting methodologies which examine a resource system's "sensitivity" to various alternative changes.

Although NEPA has some serious faults, it is hard to imagine anyone concerned with the quality of life suggesting that we regress to the process prior to NEPA. Although the legislation and its administration may be less than perfect, the principal function of the EAS/EIS as a planning and decision-making process remains valid. The proliferation of toxic chemicals has brought us to the realization that environmental quality cannot be left to the "good will of good men." Although NEPA may not leave the EPA minding the store, it enjoys the clear legal authority to review the entries and check the books.

---

[27]Brooks, pp. 33–34.
[28]Andrews, p. 153.
[29]Ibid. p. 154.
[30]Ibid.

An Environmental Inventory and Assessment

chapter 4

Mapping:
The Method of Inventory

INTRODUCTION

Each of us at one time or another has become exasperated with the response we got from a verbal description and has exclaimed: "Do I need to draw you a picture?" or, as a rhetorical question in an explanation, asked "Do you get the picture?" The implication is that "you may not understand what I have said, so I will resort to a more remedial form of communication: pictures." We have heard that "a picture is worth a thousand words" and "a model is worth a thousand pictures." Both expressions reinforce the fact that pictures provide us with a method of communication that permits us to understand conditions that words cannot describe. This is not to say that words are less important than pictures, but drawings do permit us to delineate some things that are better portrayed in drawings or maps.

It would be outrageous for us to think of design without drawings. It is equally absurd for us to design without analysis, to analyze without documentation, or to attempt documentation without drawings. Without documentation of a site's character, the assessment of a site is relegated to memory and perceptual bias.

Many professions understand the importance of good documentation and the translation of something into visual evidence for clarity or comparison. The physician uses x-rays, an electrocardiogram (EKG), brain waves, and CAT scans, all of which help provide a better "picture" of an individual's physiographic character than can be obtained otherwise. The social scientist uses pie charts and graphs. The importance of the translation of information from numerical or statistical status is not only for the purpose of clarity, but also to provide us with the ability to compare and examine visually the relative significance of each constituent.

If each of us recognizes the value of inventory, documentation, and analysis, why is it not employed more rigorously? The explanation may vary from case to case, but the theme is common. Someone—architect, engineer, landscape architect, or client—is applying predetermined solutions to a site without regard for the site's environmental character or context. It is likely that "solutions" of similar origin in an operating room would provide grounds for a malpractice suit.

Since no site exists within a static, pristine set of conditions, it is common for an activity or circumstance off-site to affect or limit the long-term use and development of a site. The physician's inquiry as to a family's health history has the same intent. Man-made or natural, conditions and qualities need to be mapped before a complete picture of a site's assets and liabilities can be clearly evaluated.

Mapping often provides us with the basis for some clear decisions, or at least, some intelligent questions: "If these are the circumstances, why do I have this property?" This brings into the process a most important person: the owner and your client. Your documentation, analysis, and recommendations for a site create the first level of understanding upon which the client will participate in the site planning process. Your credibility will be based on the accuracy and objectivity of the research and your perception as to:

1. The conditions of a site's environmental quality and context.
2. The opportunity for change as it relates to your client's program.

THE METHOD OF INVENTORY

Since the quality of each site will vary, the scope of the inventory needs to be sufficiently inclusive as to consider all reasonable variables. The role, value, and contribution of a site's various natural systems are in part based on their species, condition, maturity, stability, and diversity. Although a higher level of detail in the site inventory provides for a more ecological response, the following are qualities common to most sites that require documentation.

Topography: Topography is a collection of contour lines, a two-dimensional graphic representing a three-dimensional character. The documentation of a site begins with topography as contour lines describe the form and shape of the site's floor (Fig. 4-1). Reading and understanding topography are important, as any change in contour or slope will either reduce or increase water runoff patterns, increase or reduce erosion and/or sedimentation, and potentially influence a site's entire stability.

Collectively, contour lines describe another characteristic: slope. Slopes portray the relative incline of a site and are documented in percentages. A slope is expressed as a percentage of vertical rise or fall over a horizontal distance of 100 ft. For example, if the topographical change is 20 ft across 100 ft of horizontal distance, the area has a 20% slope. Site-specific slope analysis is often broken into smaller percentages: for example, 0 to 4%, 4 to 8%, 8 to 16%, 16 to 20%, and above 20%. Slope analysis is by far one of the best techniques for documenting and quantifying a site's physical topographical character. The resulting picture provides an instant understanding of steep slopes as well as more accommodating grades. Figure 4-2 is an example of a slope analysis of a 4.6-acre site. See Chapter 9 for a detailed description of slope analysis.

Soils: We look but rarely see soils. Most of the time we see only examples of our misuse and misunderstanding of their capabilities. Soils can be considered for their engineering qualities: depth, permeability, shrink/swell characteristics, chemicals, slope, stability, or resource potential. Although the identification of soil types is good information, when coupled with slopes, a definitively more complete picture of a site's tolerances becomes visible. Soils and topography are essential indices used in evaluating the most appropriate and inappropriate locations for structures. The shape of the site (topography) is the basis for drainage analysis. Soils and slopes collectively identify those areas that are unstable, susceptible to erosion, or conversely, suitable for a building site and tolerance to regrading.

Figure 4-1 Topography.

Figure 4-2   Slope analysis 4.6-acre site.

Subsurface Geology: Subsurface geology and geomorphology provide the site planner with a historical perspective of the site's natural evolution. Of all the documentation relative to a site's ability to support buildings or structure, none is more crucial than subsurface geology. Although bedrock provides an excellent base for foundations, rock outcroppings are a sure sign of rock near the surface and a sure warning of potential problems in subsurface excavation (Fig. 4-3).

Rock exists in numerous categories, and what needs to be identified is the depth of rock strata, the depth to bedrock, and the rock's density and permeability. The existence of rock on a site can mean extensive construction costs. Its removal can change a site's stability, settlement potential, and dispersal of groundwater and have an impact on local wells, wetlands, bogs, and swamps. See Chapter 5 for a more detailed review of geology, soils, and their common characteristics.

Hydrology: Water in one form or another is a part of every site. The surface water is easy to identify and can often become an amenity for a site. Water affects a site as:

1. Precipitation that becomes runoff
2. Groundwater or as standing surface water in a pond
3. A water course traversing the site

Since water can change its "contribution" to a site from amenity to a serious problem, the experienced site planner recognizes the potential for both and develops plans to

Figure 4-3 Rock outcropping.

accommodate that change. Chapter 7 provides a comprehensive overview of hydrology and surface water as they influence site development.

Marsh and Wetlands: Probably one of the most misunderstood roles and functions of water for many years was the marsh. For years, developers, architects, engineers, and planning commissions expended an enormous amount of energy filling marshes and swamps. What many failed to understand is that the marsh is a most sensitive environment and absolutely crucial to some fish in the food-chain cycle. Various states have passed legislation that prohibits the filling of wetlands. Probably one of the best examples of wetland protection was expressed in the 1972 decision by the Wisconsin Supreme Court in *Just* v. *Marinette County.* In sustaining the county's prohibition against wetland filling, the court stated:

> An owner of land has no absolute and unlimited right to change the essential natural character of his land so as to use it for a purpose for which it was unsuited in its natural state and which injuries the rights of others. . . . The changing of wetlands and swamps to the damage of the general public by upsetting the natural environment and the natural relationship is not a reasonable use of that land which is protected from police power regulation. . . . [N]othing this court has said or held in prior cases indicate [sic] that destroying the natural character of a swamp or a wetland so as to make that location available for human habitation is a reasonable use of that land when the new use, although of a more economical value to the owner, causes a harm to the general public.[1]

Aside from their contribution to the environment, swamps and marshes are inherently poor building sites, as they have high shrink/swell levels, collapsing soils, and by their nature, drain poorly. There are two other areas that one must approach with caution:

1. Development in areas with a high water table
2. Development in areas that have been the location of filling or dumps

Almost any project developed in areas of a high water table invites a myriad of problems

---

[1]201 N.W. 2d at 768.

that only begin with the structure. The question that one should ask in the development of any site with a high water table is: "Is this an intelligent place for this project?"

Sites of prior filling or dumps are always rather obscure and sinister. Unless there is a caveat in the land purchase contract that permits the buyer to void the contract if any unusual subsurface conditions arise, in the language of the vernacular, "what you see is what you get." There is nothing quite as demoralizing as core samples that yield bits of plastic milk cartons and domestic tin. The implications are, hopefully, obvious. The additional costs associated with a foundation on a landfill can turn an inexpensive property and profitable development into a financial debacle. It is not that foundations cannot be designed for the minimal bearing capacities of a landfill, but unless the cost of the property was very low, the foundation costs can be prohibitive.

Vegetation: Plant cover is the most sensitive index of soil and weather conditions. For example, willow, hemlock, and red maples mark areas that are poorly drained; oak and hickory associations grow on warm, dry land; and spruce and fir grow in cold, moist places. Each locality has a matrix of soil, water, and temperature characteristics for trees and ground cover.

Each site has a range of levels of plant life that needs to be considered, from the dominant canopy down through the trees of the understory, shrubs, and prostrate ground covers. Trees need to be located and identified by type, height, density, and character (canopy or understory) and noted as to their age or condition. There is often a range of grasses, shrubs, and vines that exist on a site prior to our "arrival" which enjoy a healthy relationship with the wildlife and major vegetation. A change in the site's conditions will probably change the quality of ground cover as well. In the process of site analysis, make note of the uniqueness of the wild flowers, grasses, and vines. If lost, many take from two to three years to germinate, even if successfully transplanted. Some may never again be successful. See Chapter 6 for further explanation relative to evaluating existing vegetation and its role in site planning.

Wildlife: The habitat of small birds and animals is directly affected by any major modification of the environment. The variety of species and their migration patterns will be influenced by any change in the site's natural condition. Sensitivity to the various wildlife habitats and their contribution and dependency on the environment is an important quality of every good site plan.

Microclimate: In an examination of any site, consider its latitude, slope, and exposure to the sun on a seasonal basis. Sites sheltered by hills or bluffs may have dramatically different microclimates than those in similar areas with different orientations. The exposure of a building to the sun is one of the most significant issues to be considered in site planning. This impact cannot be underemphasized and is a very powerful and critical part of site analysis. The sun is a source of energy that should be exploited, and understanding its influence and potential contribution is very important.

Air movement is influenced substantially by slope and vegetation. If unspoiled by tree cover, wind speeds at the crest of a hill may be 20 percent greater than on flat topography. This higher wind speed at the crest generally means that the wind is quieter on the leeward side of a hill as opposed to the windward side. Although the hill crest tends to shelter the leeward side from the more intense winds, it also implies that snow drifts are deeper off the crest and down the hill (Fig. 4-4).

Cold air floods are a nocturnal phenomenon on open slopes. A layer of air near the ground is cooled by the ground beneath it, which loses heat by radiation outward to the sky. This film of cold air flows downhill as a shallow sheet, gathering as a stream in an open valley or forming in a pool when blocked by a "dam" of topography, tree cover, or buildings.

Precipitation: Development changes the impact of precipitation on almost every site. The addition of impervious surfaces frequently increases runoff, alters water tables, and

Figure 4-4 Wind/snow at crest of hill.

has been a principal contributor to increased erosion and aquifer pollution. For these reasons the seasonal patterns, intensities, and major storm periods (snow and rain) need to be considered. The National Weather Service is an excellent source of data associated with precipitation and wind patterns for various regions. This documentation should be integrated into the site planner's analysis (Fig. 4-5). An extensive review of the rationale and methods appropriate to document and interpret microclimate is presented in Chapter 8.

DOCUMENTATION

The most common method of collating and documenting site research is with a series of maps or overlays. The first, or base map usually reflects the information identified in parts I and II of the site planning checklist (p. 54–55). The base map is normally limited to those elements that lend themselves to graphic presentation. Although zoning might be part of a textual report, boundary lines and constraints should be part of the documentation. The base map will become the common controlling map for all research. A common method of documentation is to separate specific activities, or site constituents, into their smallest parts. This process is most effective when each environmental constituent (soils, slopes, vegetation, etc.) is translated to maps of the same scale as the base (Fig. 4-6). The value of the method is that it permits the site planner to examine one environmental element, such as surface water, or the collection of numerous elements. This system of overlays can be applied both to a site of 1 acre and to a regional planning problem of thousands of acres.

Proper and accurate documentation begins with avoiding secondary and dated sources. Local, state, and federal governmental agencies are all excellent sources of primary information. It is imperative that the site planner become familiar with the agencies both as a source of information and to become cognizant of their requirements. Since local governments are almost always involved in development, a working understanding of their ordinances, codes, and processes is essential. Such agencies might include the following:

City
    Planning and zoning commissions
    Parks and recreation departments
    Building inspection
    Public works and utilities
    School districts
    Traffic and transportation

Figure 4-5 Climate graph.

SOIL TYPES

7	Arrents
31 32	Ferris-Helden Clay Series
34	Frio Slity Clay
41 42	Helden Clay Series
43 44	Houston Black Clay Series
53	Lewisville Clay Loam

Figure 4-6 Individual inventory maps.

SLOPE ANALYSIS

- 0-5%
- 5-10%
- 10-15%
- 15% & Above

Figure 4-6 (*cont.*)

VEGETATION

Overstory 30' & Above
Understory Less Than 20'
Shrubs 18"-8'
Aquatic Plants
Ground Covers Less Than 18"
Cultivated Crops

Figure 4-6   *(cont.)*

HYDROLOGY

⬓ U.S. Geological Survey of Flood Plain

▤ Severe Erosion Area

◀ Major Drainage Swale

← Minor Drainage Swale

▪▪▪ Ridgeline

⋯⋯ Estimated Flood Line

Figure 4-6 *(cont.)*

SITE RECONNAISSANCE

* Primary High Point
* Secondary High Point
* Wet Area
* Severe Erosion Area
* Area Unique in Character Due to Topography or Vegetation

Figure 4-6 (*cont.*)

County
County commissioners or judges
Flood control districts or river commission
Parks and recreation department
Health departments
Highway department

State
Highway departments
Water rights commission
Coastal zone management agency
Health department
Department of natural resources or parks and recreation

Federal
Department of Agriculture
    Soil Conservation Service
    Forestry Service
Department of the Army
    Board of Engineers for Rivers and Harbors
    Coastal Research Center
    Corps of Engineers
    Mississippi River Commission
Department of Commerce
    National Oceanic and Atmospheric Administration
    National Ocean Survey
Environmental Protection Agency
Housing and Urban Development
Department of the Interior
    Bureau of Land Management
    National Park Service
    U.S. Geological Survey

Of these agencies, there are three federal agencies that collect data on a national scale that can be utilized at the local level. The first is the Soil Conservation Service (SCS). The mission of this agency focuses on three areas: soil and water conservation, natural resource surveys, and community resource protection and development. SCS has a variety of staff nationwide, including engineers, soil scientists, agronomists, biologists, economists, foresters, geologists, archaeologists, landscape architects, cartographers, and environmental specialists.

For the site planner, the soils surveys are extremely valuable, as they provide the base data on which land suitability analysis can be made. The research relative to physical properties and chemical characteristics of soils is usually mapped and published on a county-wide basis (Fig. 4-7). The information in the SCS survey can easily be translated and mapped to identify the characteristics of the soils relative to a particular site and its ability to support development. Because of the large land areas and interval of testing, the survey maps should be used as a guide; they are not site specific. As a result, small pockets of soils different from those mapped may be found on a site. Nonetheless, the quality of the dominant soil type should be recognized and considered in the site planning process. No knowledgeable site planner ignores the importance of understanding the quality of a site's floor: soils.

The second is the United States Geological Survey (USGS). The USGS quad sheet at 1 in. = 1000 ft (1:12,000) is probably the most widely used resource available from USGS. These "topo" maps identify urbanized areas, tree cover, surface water, existing

Figure 4-7 Soil Conservation Service map.

roads, railroads, power lines, buildings, contour lines, and bench marks (Figs. 4-8 and 4-9). This is a primary resource for many where more detailed information is unavailable. Although the topo quad sheet is the staple of USGS, the agency has extended their research to include other earth science data. One such area is flood hazard mapping.

Because of the federal government's involvement in flood insurance programs, USGS inaugurated a program of floodplain identification. Maps delineating the location of those areas that have a 1% chance of flooding (a 100-year flood) are part of USGS's water resource mapping. The initial mapping focused on those areas where flooding and development problems existed. The next phase is to identify those areas where future

MILE

WYOMING

QUADRANGLE LOCATION

ROAD CLASSIFICATION

Primary highway,   Light-duty road, hard or
hard surface   improved surface

Secondary highway,
hard surface   Unimproved road

⬡ Interstate Route   ⬭ U.S. Route   ◯ State Route

RAWLINS PEAK, WYO.
SE/4 RAWLINS PEAK 15' QUADRANGLE
N4145—W10715/7.5

1983

DMA 4567 IV SE—SERIES V874

Figure 4-8   USGS map.

INTERIOR—GEOLOGICAL SURVEY, RESTON, VIRGINIA— 1985

ROAD LEGEND

Improved Road ....
Unimproved Road ....
Trail ....

)Interstate Route   )U.S. Route   )State Route

BLUE MESA WEST, WYOMING

PROVISIONAL EDITION 1985

43108-H4-TF-024

1 MILE

WYOMING

QUADRANGLE LOCATION

1	2	3
4		5
6	7	8

1 Gillies Draw
2 Dutch Nick Flat SW
3 Dutch Nick Flat
4 Red Ridge
5 Blue Mesa East
6 Hamilton Dome
7 Gloin Reservoir
8 Little Sand Draw

ADJOINING 7.5' QUADRANGLE NAMES

Figure 4-9 USGS map.

development and flooding could create hazards. Although not available for every urban area, maps have been completed for a limited number of communities and are available from the Department of Housing and Urban Development.

USGS has also mapped land use cover, geological hazards, and surface water. The geological hazards studies focus on earthquake and volcano eruption and provide information on fault systems and active seismic zones. Surface water studies have concentrated on stream discharge and quality analysis and are part of the National Stream Quality Accounting Network (NASQAN) monitoring program. Groundwater is another series of environmental studies under the purview of USGS. Although limited, these studies assess present groundwater supply and identify emerging hydrological problems associated with their continued use.

USGS provides an extensive range of services, from complete cartographic separates to remote sensing. Although the scale of the data is often large, in some cases it may be the only source of information.

Site Planning Checklist

I. Legal
   A. Plat or boundary line survey
      1. Easements
      2. Right-of-way lines
      3. Acreage
      4. Oil and gas transmission lines
   B. Restrictive covenants or deed restrictions
   C. Existing land uses and buildings
   D. Zoning (existing and proposed)
      1. Permitted uses or special exceptions
      2. Density
      3. Setbacks/height limits
      4. Coverage
II. Planning Data
   A. Adjacent land uses
   B. Utilities
      1. Water
      2. Sewer (storm and sanitary)
      3. Gas
      4. Electric
   C. Roads, alignment, and rights-of-way (existing and proposed)
      1. Major thoroughfares and freeways
      2. Primary arterials
      3. Secondary collectors
      4. Tertiary streets
      5. Service drives
   D. Public parks and open space
III. Environmental
   A. Topography: minimal 2-ft interval
      1. Slope analysis
   B. Drainage
      1. Off-site considerations
         a. Watershed: above and below site
         b. Existing development in watershed
         c. Proposed development in watershed
         d. Potential impacts
      2. On-site drainage characteristics
         a. Drainage patterns
         b. Swales
         c. Existing inlets, culverts, or drains
         d. Areas of erosion or siltation

C. Hydrology
    1. Surface water
        a. Existing and intermittent water courses
        b. Floodplains
    2. Subsurface: water table and aquifer
D. Vegetation
    1. Tree cover: types and species
    2. Understory
    3. Ground cover
E. Geology and soils
    1. Surface soil characteristics noting high shrink/swell soils or high water table
    2. Subsurface geology: noting bedrock and depth to frostline
F. Climate
    1. Precipitation: annual rainfall and seasonal variations
    2. Solar analysis
    3. Wind: direction and velocities

The development of the data outlined above is critical to intelligent site planning, and it will also be invaluable in the event of site-related litigation.

An Environmental Inventory and Assessment

chapter 5

Geology and Soils

by Michael E. Ostdick

INTRODUCTION

Geology is the study of the earth. The fundamental principle that underlies most of geology is that the present processes occurring on the earth have occurred throughout geologic time. Subsurface geology and geomorphology provide the site planner with a historical perspective of what has happened to a site as well as what potential problems may be encountered.

There are three basic types of rocks, which are classified according to their origin: igneous, metamorphic, and sedimentary. Igneous rocks are produced from solidifying melt or magma. Metamorphic rocks are rocks that have been changed by high temperature and pressure within the earth's crust. Sedimentary rocks are weathering products of preexisting rocks that are deposited near the earth's surface by wind, water, ice, and biological activity.

SUBSURFACE GEOLOGY

The type of rocks in underlying formations gives a good indication of their ability to accept the load of a building. Different rock types have varying bearing capacities for safe loads on earth foundation beds that need to be investigated when considering extensive building loads (Table 5-1). Equally as important a consideration in known earthquake regions is that buildings on bedrock will be damaged less than those built on less consolidated, easily deformed material such as natural or artificial fills.

The layer below which rocks and soils are saturated with water is called the water table (Fig. 5-1). This level changes with the seasons. In general, it is a reflection of the surface topography but is more subdued, that is, has less relief than the surface topography. The action of groundwater is controlled by the physical properties of the rocks. The most common reservoir rock—rock porous enough to hold and filter water—is sandstone.

TABLE 5-1 Safe Loads on Earth Foundation Beds

Material	Load (lb/ft^2)
Hard rock	80,000
Medium rock	30,000
Hardpan	20,000
Soft rock	16,000
Gravel	12,000
Sand, firm and coarse	8,000
Clay, hard and dry	8,000
Sand, fine and dry	6,000
Ordinary firm clay	4,000
Sand and clay, mixed or in layers	4,000
Sand, wet	4,000
Clay, soft	2,000
Alluvial soil	1,000

Source: J. D. Carpenter, ed., *Handbook of Landscape Architectural Construction* (Washington, D.C.: Landscape Architecture Foundation, 1973), p. 239.

Figure 5-1 Soil classification chart. (Courtesy of U.S. Department of Agriculture.)

Groundwater is a very valuable economic commodity and is recovered from wells for domestic, industrial, and agricultural use. In areas where groundwater is used extensively, care must be taken that, on the average, no more water is withdrawn in a year than is replaced by natural processes. This can be determined by monitoring precipitation and the water table's fluxuation. The conservation of groundwater is very important because groundwater moves very slowly and many years may be required to replace water hastily removed.

SURFACE GEOLOGY AND NATURAL PROPERTIES

Rocks on the crust of the earth are subject to weathering due to climatic changes. Rainfall and freeze/thaw cycles contribute to the fragmentation of the rock mass. These fragments, together with plant and animal remains, promote soil formation and evolution. Erosion due to rain and snowmelt ultimately creates the three-dimensional forms of swales, valleys, summits, and ridges common in the landscape.

Soils are composed of mineral and organic matter, air, and water. The mineral matter varies in size and texture from fine grains to large rocks. The organic matter, which occurs mainly in the topsoil, accounts for about 1 to 6% of the soil content. It is the topsoil that is critical to all plant life; if completely removed, the newly exposed layer of soil must begin the long process of decay and decomposition to establish a new layer of topsoil.

Every soil type has a distinctive texture. The size and mineral grain content depend on the mineralogical composition, climate, period of weathering, and the method of transportation. Coarse-grained textures include boulders, gravel, and sand, while fine-grained textures include fine silts and clays. How these mineralogical components are arranged within the soil mass is referred to as soil structure. Soil structure is a critical consideration when designing drainage systems, dams, and embankments.

Soils are classified as being either organic or inorganic, and by grain size. Following are the four classifications for soil by grain size:

1. *Gravel*—particles over 2 mm in diameter.
2. *Sand*—0.05 to 2 mm. The finest grains are just visible to the eye; gritty to the touch.
3. *Silt*—0.002 to 0.05 mm. The grains are invisible but can be felt; smooth to the touch.
4. *Clay*—under 0.002 mm. Smooth and floury or in stiff lumps when dry, plastic and sticky when wet.

STRUCTURAL AND DRAINAGE CHARACTERISTICS

The site planner must be aware of the structural limitations and potentials of a specific soil in order to make the appropriate design and construction decisions. This preview of the engineering characteristics will provide an introduction to the terminology commonly used in a discussion of soils.

Soil elasticity refers to a soil's ability to return to its original shape after temporary deformation as a result of loading. Closely related to elasticity is soil plasticity. This is the trait of soil to be deformed under loading and to maintain the deformed shape without cracking or crumbling. Elasticity and plasticity play a significant role in the structural design of building foundations, wall footings, and the preparation of the subgrade or the subbase of paved surfaces.

Shearing strength is the result of friction between the soil particles. The cohesion of these particles, and consequently the shearing strength, vary depending on the soil's water content as well as numerous other factors. Soil stability is directly dependent on the shearing strength of the soil. This characteristic is critical to the soil's ability to support footings and to maintain steep banks and slopes.

The portion of volume change or deformation due to compression through the expulsion of pore water is referred to as soil compressibility. Compressibility is directly related to soil structure and past stress. Compaction is the ratio of volume decrease to air expulsion. For on-grade structures, it is recommended that fill areas for foundations and areas to be paved be compacted to 95% maximum density (ASTM standard). Failure to do so may cause settling, and consequently, foundation slippage and/or fracturing.

Shrinkage and swell result from the buildup and release of capillary tensile stress in pore water and vary with the moisture demand of clay materials. Soils with severe shrink/swell potential should be avoided where possible, but may be overcome by conscientious planning and responsive design. Some clays are so expansive that elevation changes of 12 to 18 in. are commonplace.

The "angle of repose" is the degree of incline beyond which soil must be reviewed when considering the construction of landforms with new fill. The limiting angles for soils range from 18% for very wet clay and silt to 45% for hard rotten rock (Table 5-2).

Capillarity is the action by which water rises in a channel in any direction above the horizontal plane of the supply of free water. The degree and rate of capillarity is determined by the number and size of channels. Slow in dry soils, more rapid in silt soils, and variable in gravels and coarse sand, capillarity is an important consideration for subgrade pavement design and site construction procedures.

Permeability is the soil's capacity to transport water. It depends on the size and number of continuous soil pores. Permeability varies with the void ratio, grain size, distribution, structure, and degree of compaction. Coarse-grained soils are generally more permeable than are fine-grained soils.

Liquid limit is the minimum moisture content at which the soil will flow under its own weight.

PERFORMANCE STANDARDS

The life-support capacity of soil is based on pH level, organic content, friability, drainage, temperature, and leaching in relationship to the requirements of a particular plant material.

Structural suitability of soils is dependent on soil strength, location, and type. Soil

TABLE 5-2 Angle of Repose

Material	Angle of Repose	Slope Ratio
Sand, clean	33°41'	1.5:1
Sand and clay	36°53'	1.33:1
Clay, dry	29°44'	1.75:1
Clay, damp, plastic	18°24'	3.0:1
Gravel, clean	36°53'	1.33:1
Gravel, sand, and clay	36°53'	1.33:1
Soil (average)	33°41'	9.5:1
Soft rotten rock	36°53'	1.33:1
Hard rotten rock	45°	1:1
Cinders	45°	1:1

Source: J. D. Carpenter, ed., *Handbook of Landscape Architectural Construction* (Washington, D.C.: Landscape Architecture Foundation, 1973), p. 227.

classification systems group soils that will perform in a similar manner when densities, moisture content, water table, climate, and slope are similar. For specific information as to soil performance criteria, refer to the ASHTO Classification System and the Unified Soil Classification Systems for proposed use in relation to its structural properties, past performance, and required tests.

Surface and subsurface drainage systems are affected by the structural characteristics of a given soil, moisture content, and location of the water table. The aforementioned considerations should be reviewed when designing subsurface facilities.

An Environmental Inventory and Assessment

chapter 6
Vegetation

by Michael E. Ostdick

LANDSCAPE CHARACTER

Regardless of the size of the landscape being viewed, it has an intrinsic character. This character is composed of the basic components of nature: land and rock forms, vegetative patterns, water, and structures. An understanding of these elements is basic to the design of a responsive and creative new landscape.

An examination of the landscape character of the eastern United States reveals that one of its most valuable natural resources is the scenic quality of its rural landscape. The attractiveness can be perceived from a variety of features, with the integral scenic element being vegetative cover and patterns created by that vegetation as a visual resource. In contrast, cropland and grassland are the dominating vegetation of the interior regions of the United States, while the Appalachian region is dominated by mixed hardwoods in the north and pine–hardwood forests in the south. Mixtures of deciduous and coniferous species create considerable contrast, as does the broad variety of shrubs and grasses. Each region possesses well-defined characteristics in terms of terrain and vegetation as well as visual character.

A plant finds its niche based on a number of variables, ranging from soil, orientation, amount of light, and rainfall to the influence of man and animals. A group of closely growing plants has a natural simplicity. When a landscape has achieved the full climax state of high forest, the dominant trees may be few in number and limited to one species compared with the shrubs and ground-cover layers. They are visually as well as ecologically dominant; thus the qualities of unity and simplicity again relate to this different type of natural landscape. The key issues here are the quality of unity and the degree of simplicity. Contrast in these natural landscapes is usually short-lived, as the bold instances of color vary with the seasons.

There are two ways in which ecology serves as a basis for planting design. When an actual on-site analysis is not possible, it is within the realm of reason to make a conjectural analysis of a site's natural vegetation and to develop a planting plan on that basis. In another approach, the plants are selected in accordance with the soil/climate

Figure 6-1

aspect, appearance, and other relevant environmental determinants. This method is used with the knowledge that if competition from other plants is removed, success is likely. This second approach does not necessarily base plant selection on plant adaptation or aesthetics.

The plants in an ecologically based design should be selected in a way that they will contribute to a biotic community rather than a plant community. In turn, each biotic community should be able to reside congenially in the habitat. In order to have a basis for this type of approach, one must understand the principles of cover and food bondage. Cover bondage refers to the link between the dominant plant and the habitat. The dominant plant modifies the habitat, forming microclimates and zones of plant communities.

Food bondage is a three-way link between the flora and fauna and the habitat. One must remember that although wildlife is highly mobile, the animals are restricted by the flora of the habitat. The habitat relies on the flora and fauna to replenish the nutrients of the soil. The goal of any proposed planting design is to develop an ecosystem that provides balance and stability. Care must be taken so that the habitat is not radically changed by the encroachment of man.

EVALUATING EXISTING VEGETATION

The documentation of the existing vegetative cover is an integral step in the site planning process. Plant materials can be categorized into three general divisions: canopy trees, the understory, and ground covers. Canopy trees are defined as those trees that define or limit the overhead plane (Fig. 6-2). The understory is a combination of small trees, large shrubs, and climbing vines which develop under the canopy trees and can form a physical barrier much like a wall. Ground covers are grasses, prostrate vines, and wildflowers which define the base plane.

Criteria should be developed for the evaluation of the existing vegetation. The following are some basic standards for evaluation:

1. Aesthetic value. Consideration should be given to form, texture, foliage color, flowering habits, autumn foliage, bark and crown characteristics, and type of fruit.
2. Disease resistance. Consideration should be given to maintenance costs and the methods for treating the disease.

Figure 6-2

3. Life span of the trees. An obvious aspect of vegetation criteria is its normal expected life.
4. Wind firmness. Shallow-rooted trees will blow over easily if they have been growing in a close stand.
5. Wildlife value. Plants with nuts and berries provide animals and birds with food during the fall and winter.
6. Comfort index. Tree cover can reduce summer temperature by as much as 10 degrees.
7. Sudden exposure to direct sunlight and the ability to withstand radiated heat from proposed building and pavement are both necessary considerations.
8. The space needed for future growth and the relationship to electric and telephone lines, driveways, walkways, and water and sewer lines must be documented to avoid damage to vegetation and facilities.

Ultimately, the site planner must recognize two or three basic rules of trees that have grown in the woods.

1. They have shallow roots and should be conserved in a clump.
2. Even mature trees will not survive a violent change in their habitat.
3. A change in the groundwater or microclimate will likely be fatal.
4. The area around most trees should never be filled, as it disturbs the access of air, water, and minerals.

Root systems must have water, sunlight, and food. Wells or retaining walls can be used to hold back dramatic grade changes. When trees are removed from a site, the surface temperature will increase, and erosion often increases unless steps are taken to prevent it. The loss of major trees results in an impact on wildlife and subsurface stability, as well as general aesthetic degradation. Every effort should be made to retain as many as is possible while adopting strict design standards to reduce the amount of ultimate loss due to grading and paving.

THE ROLE OF PLANT MATERIALS

The role of plant materials in site planning and development should not be overlooked or considered a remedial task for the ''gardener.'' The design components available to architects for the design of interior space are pertinent to the design of exterior spaces. The physical materials by which these design concepts are implemented are quite different. The major materials of a building are static elements, whereas the materials (i.e., plants) of the landscape are constantly changing due to growth and seasons. The base plane or floor becomes grasses or ground cover, the walls become hedges or masses of shrubs, the ceiling becomes the canopy of a tree or a vine on a trellis. Outdoor rooms can be created through a combination of architectural elements. Each element can exist by itself but is enhanced by sensitive blending with others.

Plants play primary functional roles in the following:

1. Wind control
2. Erosion control
3. Energy conservation
4. Wildlife habitat

WIND CONTROL

There are three principles that can be employed to control the wind: obstruction, filtration, and deflection. Obstruction can be achieved with plant materials by selecting species whose foliage and branching habit are dense. If year-round protection/obstruction is desired, evergreens are a must. Plantings should be spaced such that the mature plants will interwine/mesh with each other and form a dense obstruction. Where space allows, staggering the plants will help prevent leaks or breaches in the plantings. The specific selection of a plant for this use should take into account soil, climate, and so on. Those plants that are marginally suited for the microclimate of the site should not be considered. Hardy, vigorous plants are a preference rather than plants of questionable hardiness and unreliable growth.

Filtration can be achieved by such simple techniques as selective pruning. For example, a site is bordered by a grove of deciduous trees that surrounds an existing lake. It is highly desirable to take advantage of the cool breezes off the lake, yet the trees at the water's edge give a nice sense of space and scale to the property. By selectively pruning and thinning out the lower limbs of the trees, the desired effect is achieved. When selecting trees that will allow air to pass through their structure, consider more upright trees with sparse branching rather than those with hanging limbs and dense branching.

Deflection is redirecting the wind in the hope of either taking advantage of its effect or trying to mitigate its impact. The use of planting masses can guide or direct wind flow to or from an area. See Chapter 8 for more detail on site and climate.

EROSION CONTROL

Plants can play a major role in reducing erosion. Shrubs and grasses that have dense, spreading root systems can bind the soil and prevent unstable slopes from eroding. As discussed in Chapter 13, there are several products on the market, such as jute mats and plastic webbing, that are designed to be used on slopes that are to be planted. The keys to the selection of plants for this use are soil, climate, soil pH, amount of water available, and plant adaptability. The regional offices of the Soil Conservation Service are a good source of information regarding suitable plants for erosion control.

ENERGY CONSERVATION

The impact of plant materials on energy conservation should not be underestimated. Chapter 8 provides an extensive review of the various methods in which plants influence a microclimate and contribute to energy-efficient site planning.

WILDLIFE HABITAT

Although the process of development reduces the area of the natural habitat for animals, careful and sensitive site planning can limit major incursions. The preservation of existing habitats and their supplementation through the careful selection of plants should be a consideration of the site planner. Plants not only provide food but also protection and materials for nest building. County agricultural extensions and local environmental clubs are commonly good informational resources regarding wildlife and plants. In addition to the vegetation's value as food and protection for wildlife, the site planner should assess the potential for integrating existing habits with the new use, the character of the new microclimate, ongoing water requirements, and the relative health of the vegetation and its maintenance over time.

THE PLANTING PLAN

Developing a planting plan should not be an attempt to reproduce nature. Plants serve a natural and necessary function in the ecological cycle and are thus subject to the hardships and cycles of nature. As such, planting plans should not include rigid principles, the success of which are dependent on the perfection of plants or their maintenance. The development of plants through time and seasonal changes can be an aesthetic contribution to every site. Plants can also be used in the following ways:

- In combination with a building or building complexes for the extension of architectural lines or as a foil to screen or enhance the quality of architecture
- As a silhouette against the sky or reflection in water or as skyline trees
- To define space or a sheltered area, or function as a buffer between activities, or create a sense of openness
- To enhance a view, block a view, frame a view, or even be a view
- As an educational resource.

The following are some of the principles that should be considered in the development of a planting plan:

1. The plan should reflect a predominance of one type of plant or a similar texture, color, or form within any grouping.
2. Exercise some restraint relative to the number of different plants used in the plan.
3. Select those plants that have a common soil, climate, and water requirements.
4. Since maintenance of formal (clipped) hedges is a time-consuming operation, consider growth habit and mature size in the selection of plants.
5. In an informal plan, plants should be located so as not to rely on the quality of any particular tree.

The plant selection process should be based on at least one of the following criteria:

1. A plant's ability to live and flourish in a specific environment
2. Knowledge as to the existing trees on a site or their healthy growth on adjacent sites
3. Plants that require low maintenance and/or low water requirements
4. Plants for a specific purpose, such as shade, contrast, color, or size

NATIVE PLANTS AND DROUGHT-TOLERANT PLANTS

Native plants are plants that are indigenous to a site or region. Over the years certain species have adapted to the climatic conditions of the region and become a significant part of the site's inherent character. The species identified on any given site can be used as an indicator of how well proposed plantings may do and indicate what modifications to existing conditions may be necessary.

The significance of using native plants should not be underestimated. Native plants are more naturally drought tolerant, as they are more acclimated to the seasonal variations in the microclimate of their environment. This attribute means that their water requirement is often less than that for other ornamental species. In the west and southwestern United States, where water is scarce, drought-tolerant native plants constitute the majority of a designer's plant resources. But regardless of a plant's drought-tolerance capability, there are few plants that can survive without water when first being established, and native plants are no exception. The difference between native plants and ornamental plants is that after the native plants are established, they can be left on their own, without irrigation. Ornamentals, on the other hand, may not last a week, let alone a month or two, without supplemental irrigation.

Sources for information on native plants and drought-tolerant plants include the regional offices of the Soil Conservation Service and the County Agricultural Agents. These agencies typically have pamphlets available on these topics and have experimental stations that can be visited to see what the plants look like under water-restricted conditions.

An Environmental Inventory and Assessment

chapter 7
Hydrology

THE HYDROLOGICAL CYCLE

The influence of water on a site is multifaceted. The most obvious is in the form of surface water as it vacillates from amenity to adversary. Understanding how and under what circumstances that change takes place is part of the site planner's obligation. The influence and impact of surface water, for instance, are not always dependent on the capriciousness of nature. The physical intervention of man has created impacts in some circumstances which, if matched by natural phenomena, would have been considered catastrophic.

Compared to the movement of surface water across a site, subsurface hydrology is very obscure. Historically, the site planner's concerns relative to subsurface hydrology were limited to the impact of groundwater on development. More recently, however, the importance of water as a resource and the maintenance of its quality have come to be recognized by all levels of government. But despite general agreement relative to the scope of the problem, water quality, quantity, and equitable distribution continue to elude comprehensive solution in many regions. As with other site components, many local governments play substantive roles in the review of development and water-related issues and thus their function in the process cannot be overemphasized.

Theory and study of the movement of water dates to Anaxogoras of Clazomene (500 to 428 B.C.).[1] His observations of the hydrological process were remarkably accurate considering that they were based on empirical evidence. However, later scholars, such as Plato and Aristotle, disagreed with Anaxogoras's theory. It was not until 1674 that a French research scientist's quantitative analysis of water volumes in the Seine River basin confirmed the concept of precipitation's change into groundwater recharge and runoff, transpiration, and evaporation to form again in the atmosphere as precipi-

---

[1]Harry W. Gehm and Jacob L. Bregman, eds., *Handbook of Water Resources and Pollution Control* (New York: Van Nostrand Reinhold Company, Inc., 1976), p. 16.

Figure 7-1   (Photo by Kenneth Roemer.)

tation.[2] Subsequent research continued to expand and confirm the hydrological phenomenon, which, driven by solar radiation, continually recycles the resource (Fig. 7-2).

   If solar energy drives the process, surface water must be considered the fuel for
the process. Because of the size and extensive heat storage capacity of the oceans, the
critical link in the process is the relationship between the atmosphere and the seas. The

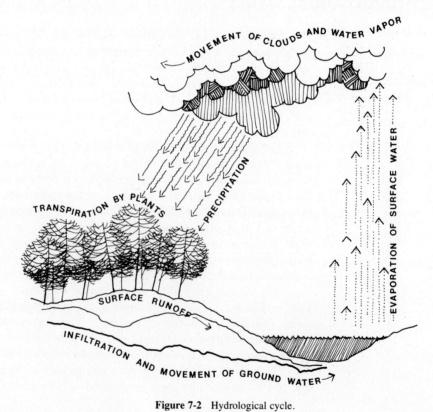

Figure 7-2   Hydrological cycle.

[2]Pierre Perrault, *De l'origine fontaines* (Paris: Pierre le Petit, 1674).

oceans function as an immense reservoir, which, through evaporation, transfers moisture to the atmosphere, where it is distilled and distributed throughout the globe.

Precipitation is the key conversion of the process that sustains the cycle. Its effect on the site depends on topography, soils, land use, and vegetation. While the topography determines the path and flow of water, the soils attest to a site's ability to absorb precipitation. Land use is a variable that provides the site planner with an insight into an area's runoff potential. Everything in the way of vegetation, from prostrate ground cover and grasses to mature overstory, affects precipitation as it falls to the site.

Rainfall is dispersed by vegetation through transpiration and interception, although there is some problem with differentiating between the two. The leaves of plants intercept water in its free fall to the soil, permitting evaporation from the vegetation. Healthy plants also withdraw water from the soil and transpire moisture through their leaves in the photosynthesis process. Although the relative amounts of water transferred through transpiration and interception are small, both contribute to the entire hydrological process.

Table 7-1 identifies the principal storage and fluxes in the hydrological cycle, which are divided into two general classifications: surface and subsurface water. Examined more closely, precipitation falling on the site is dispersed in various ways. The water may either be absorbed into the soil and become part of the groundwater supply or recharge established aquifers. This absorption process is referred to as infiltration and is the natural downward movement of water through the surface soil. When the zone of aeration (Fig. 7-3), is sufficiently saturated, deep percolation occurs. But until the supply of the water exceeds the holding capacity of the soil, groundwater recharge does not occur. It also follows that if the subsoil in the zone of aeration is poorly permeable, groundwater recharge will occur at a very slow rate regardless of the amount of water in the zone. When this condition occurs and the water moves laterally as well as down, the process is known as groundwater underflow.[3]

TABLE 7-1 Principal Parameters of the Hydrological Cycle

STORAGES	FLUXES[a]
Atmospheric water	Evaporation
Oceans and seas	From bare and vegetated land
Lakes and reservoirs	From oceans and other water bodies
River channels	From snow and ice
Swamps	Horizontal vapor flux
Biological water	Precipitation
Moisture in soil and unsaturated zone	Runoff
Groundwater	Infiltration; deep percolation
Frozen water	Recharge, underflow, and discharge
Icecaps	
Glaciers	Rates of movement
Pack ice	
Ice shelves	
Permafrost	

[a] *Other fluxes affect the hydrological cycle, such as ocean currents and heat fluxes. Although not included in the discussion that follows, they would not be overlooked in water balance studies. Heat fluxes, for example, affect evaporation, but we deal here only with evaporation, once it has been determined or estimated; similarly for other factors.*

Source: Harry W. Gehm and Jacob L. Bregman, eds., *Handbook of Water Resources and Pollution Control* (New York: Van Nostrand Reinhold Company, Inc., 1976), p. 17.

---

[3]Gehm and Bregman, pp. 8–10.

soil water zone

zone of aeroation

pellicular and
gravitational water

intermediate
zone

capillay water

capillary zone

water table

ground water

zone of
saturation

bedrock

Figure 7-3 Section through surface illustrating groundwater.

RESOURCE DISTRIBUTION AND CONFLICTS

An introduction to subsurface water would be incomplete without an explanation of
aquifers. The two general types, confined and unconfined, reflect the geological context
of the soils above and below the aquifer. A popular notion is that an aquifer is an
underground river; it is more often analogous to a water-saturated container of sand.
Although there are unique geological conditions in which impervious soils occur both
above and below the more porous aquifer, "confining" its recharge potential to a limited
zone, the "unconfined" aquifer stores water in the pore spaces of rock, sand, and gravel.[4]

The capacity for most unconfined aquifers to absorb additional groundwater is
limited and many are overflowing. This is evidenced by water that continues to flow in
creeks and streams during dry periods. This movement of water from springs and aquifers into tributaries, rivers, and bays by diffused percolation is known as groundwater
outflow. Whereas in some cases the supply is modest, in contrast, the Snake River in
southern Idaho is fed by a group of springs at the collective rate of 6000 ft^3 per second.[5]

The large Ogalala formation is an example of a confined aquifer that has a modest
annual recharge. The Texas high plains segment of the aquifer receives little or nothing
from adjacent resources and exists primarily on an endowment from a time when there
simply was more rain.

Lakes, rivers, and swamps are also contributors to the total surface water area.
Depending on the size of the body of water, local climate and hence the hydrological

---

[4]Ibid., p. 37.

[5]Ibid., p. 10.

processes can be influenced by lakes. The Great Lakes of the midwestern United States are an example of the effect of the amount of surface water on the climate of an extremely large region. The Great Lakes are the result of unique geological formations; other lakes may simply be wide places in a river. Where the number of circumstances in which lakes were formed by a natural change in the river's edge are limited, the construction of dams (reservoirs) which exploit natural river basins are numerous. Once constructed, reservoirs function in essentially the same way as natural lakes. The thousands of smaller natural lakes are either topographical depressions supplied by groundwater outflow or exist above the water table and provide groundwater recharge through deep percolation.

Swamps, bogs, and wetlands were for years considered nuisances and misunderstood as to their role in a region's ecology. Swamps and wetlands are areas where the water table is essentially level with the land. This physical relationship permits the water to flow unabated from the water table into a topographically shallow elevation that contains the groundwater. Although the lake is usually an easily visible amenity with numerous contributions to make to a site, the swamp was historically something to fill and prepare for development. Since the late 1960s, however, the role of swamp in the food-chain cycle has become common knowledge. Ordinances and legislation controlling the filling of wetlands have been adopted by numerous state and local governments. See page 44 for the salient portion of the Wisconsin Supreme Court's opinion concerning wetlands in that state. The site planner needs to be aware of the environmental implications, as well as the portending disasters of development in swamps, bogs, or marshes.

The special qualities of the river's edge are valuable in the same way that bays, lakes, and the sea contribute to the city. The poetic Chinese reference to the river as "threads of sea" acknowledges the kinship between the two. The deeper truth to the Oriental observation is that the river dominates edges beyond its normal flow. Just as the sea responds to climatic changes and affects the land at its edge, so does the river. Although these edge conditions are often the most highly valued for their views and special relationships with the river, they can also be the first to be damaged in the event that the river breaches its normal banks. These areas are probably some of the most critical to, the site planner, who knows that the difference between the river's edge and the river's domain can be critical to life and property.

Because of the importance of water in sustaining man, conflicts associated with its use have existed since there were two who claimed absolute rights to a single resource. The origin of the word "rival" has reference to those who shared the water of a river or irrigation channel. As a result of those conflicts, laws associated with either the quality, quantity, or distribution date to proclamations of Gaius Caesar in 45 B.C. Recognition of the relationship between water and public health came much earlier. Mesopotamian cities following the Mosaic law and Zoroastrian religion had developed sanitary sewer systems by the middle of the third millennium.[6] Contrary, however, to the very early awareness of the import of water quality, later societies were not so adept. As late as the mid-nineteenth century, poor sanitation standards were widespread in English cities and responsible for cholera and typhoid epidemics in London. American cities were no better, as Chicago used Lake Michigan for water supply and sewerage disposal concurrently at the turn of the century.[7]

The law was the process through which conflicts were resolved between civilized people. In the United States, water rights and the legal doctrine were inherited from the English. England's riparian law reflected the environmental context of that water-rich country, which placed little value on the ownership of water. Water was commonly shared by all and each person owning property adjoining a water source was entitled to use the water. However, each was also obligated to return the water to its course without change in its quality or reduction in its quantity to every downstream riparian property

[6]Charles E. Warren, *Biology and Water Pollution Control* (Philadelphia: W. B. Sanders Company, 1971), pp. 3–4.
[7]Ibid., p. 5.

Figure 7-4   Colorado River diagram.

owner. This was a fairly civilized quid-pro-quo relationship, as it held everyone's right to use the water to be equal. This concept was easily assimilated into early American law. The eastern seaboard of America was similar to that of England insofar as its water resources were concerned. There was little rationale for changing the concept of water law until the settlement of the arid west, and more particularly, with the discovery of gold. Since the popular mining techniques of the time required the utilization of streams, a reevaluation of the long-established ripararian doctrine became necessary. As gold was being mined on public land, custom was that the first to appropriate the water (for whatever use) enjoyed rights superior to those of people downstream. This change in practice resulted in a radical change in the concept of water rights in the west. The antithesis of riparian doctrine emerged as the "doctrine of prior appropriation." This concept, which maintains that the quantity and quality of water can be changed by anyone who appropriates the resource first, is practiced in the 17 states of the Lower 48 west of the Mississippi. Figure 7-4 illustrates the application of the prior appropriation doctrine to the Colorado River in its 1400-mile flow from Wyoming through Mexico to the Gulf of California.[8]

    Problems associated with water will always focus on quantity (allocation) and quality (pollution control). The arid plainsman dreams of the construction of canals to import water from a better-endowed neighboring state to "make the desert bloom."

---

[8]Thomas Y. Canby, "Our Most Precious Resource: Water," *National Geographic*, August 1980, p. 176.

While hope springs eternal, the financial assistance to support such projects does not, as skeptical voters mount sturdy opposition to dubious water projects in various western states. The reality of the situation is that economic pressures dictate continued use of agricultural techniques that require high water use in the face of reduced water reserves, putting the future of affected farming communities in jeopardy.

If depletion of major aquifers were not enough, continued extraction of groundwater beyond its limits for recharge contributes to yet another water-related malady: subsidence. In most cases the process of pumping oil, gas, and/or water creates little, if any, perceivable reaction on the earth's surface. In some conditions, however, extensive removal of those resources has created collapsed areas in the surface geology. As an example, limited areas of the San Joaquin Valley of California have experienced over 30 ft of surface subsidence since 1925. To aggravate the problem, development (i.e., impervious surfaces), eliminates effective groundwater recharge as the resource is being extracted. Although water is not the sole constituent which when removed induces subsidence, it is the only one of the three (gas, oil, and water) capable of recharge through natural processes.

Although it is not within the purview of the site planner to solve problems associated with water resource management, it is important to understand the by-products of a society that has both abused and neglected one of its most life-sustaining elements. What is important is to understand the concern and rationale for stricter on-site detention policies, storm water management guidelines, and water conservation controls. Each municipality, like individuals, adopts those regulations that reflect its environmental context, local values, and economic health. The problem in the past has been a lack of perspective associated with a value system which failed to recognize that mankind shares a common, critical, and limited provision.

SURFACE WATER: STREAMS, CREEKS, AND RIVERS

From the beginning of recorded time, one of the most desirable areas of human settlement has been near rivers, lakes, and seashores. The cradle of civilization at the delta of the Tigris and Euphrates valley tells us something of the attraction to the water's edge. The early rationale was easy to understand. The soil of the rivers' bottomland was fertile, rich, and a valuable resource that, with nature's own natural processes, replenished itself. The ebb and flow of the Nile has sustained one of the oldest civilizations on earth beyond the level of its contribution in the food-chain cycle. Similarly, the Yangtze in China and Ganges in India have significance beyond the scope of agricultural resource to their respective countries.

The attraction to the water's edge is natural, since the sea and tributaries provide man with food as well as a transportation system. The commerce and exchange of ideas and cultures supported by the sea acted as a powerful industry that shaped the establishment and growth characteristics of every coastal nation in the world. The rise and fall of tides have long been well understood and the location of buildings or structures at the water's edge has respected those inevitable changes. In most cases, people have recognized the incredible force in hurricanes and typhoons. Settlements on the water reflect a range of issues, all of which focus on identifying that location which provides the best protection from violent storms and a topographical configuration that supports the unhampered access of deep-draft vessels. Man had historically accepted the intransigence of nature and knew that decisions which spurned well-established natural patterns jeopardized their safety and well-being.

The industrial revolution provided man with the ability to construct machines that could defy (at least momentarily) the forces of nature. Our perceived abilities to control nature appeared to be limited only by our ability to conjure and build the appropriate device. In terms of water and flood control, these devices have taken the form of dams,

Figure 7-5   Dam.

reservoirs, channel realignment, levees, and seawalls (Figs. 7-5, 7-6, and 7-7). In many communities popular political strategies often support the design of a system that treats symptoms of the problem instead of the problem at its source. Floods, floodplains, and urbanization are interrelated factors that typify the problem–symptom relationship. Floods are not a modern phenomenon and are a problem only when they create property damage or become a threat to human health. Our methods for dealing with the threat of flood often focus on structural techniques, which is natural considering the fact that man-made urbanization contributes to the problem so significantly. Although structural methods have helped curb the destructive power of floods and flooding, they do not solve the problem entirely. The problem is that structures present the illusion of man conquering the forces of nature through technology and lead many to believe that there is a technical solution to every problem.

Figure 7-6   Channel realignment.

Figure 7-7 Sea wall.

SURFACE WATER AS A PROCESS

To understand the problem comprehensively involves a recapitulation of the hydrological process, runoff, the drainage basin, and the floodplain. Precipitation falling in a watershed or drainage basin does two things: It is either absorbed into the soil in the process of infiltration, or it moves across the surface of the land, always seeking a lower elevation. This second process is referred to as runoff and occurs when the amount of water applied to a surface occurs at a rate or volume beyond the ground's ability to absorb it. Another condition exists where the surface is completely impervious and will not accept any water. Impervious surfaces are not just man-made (i.e., buildings, parking lots, roads, etc.) but may also occur in nature.

It is the runoff from each site in the watershed that contributes to the first order of streams. These are the "fingertip tributaries,"[9] the smallest landforms in the system. They have no other contributors, but when merged create a second order of stream. Second-order streams merge to form thirds, and third orders join to create a fourth. The bottom of the drainage basin or floodplain is created by the fourth-order stream[10] (Fig. 7-8), which is formed by long periods of erosion, deposition of nondissolved sediment, and subsurface geology. Although the runoff is incapable of being absorbed, if it traverses any soil, it will transport weathered sediments in three ways:

1. The particles that are carried in chemical solution are called the dissolved load.
2. Small particles such as silt and clay are kept in suspension by turbulent water flows. These particles are called the suspended-sediment load.
3. "Larger particles of sand and gravel or rock fragments roll, slide, or bounce along the bed of a stream. As the velocity of the stream is reduced, the larger particles of non-dissolved sediment drop to the bottom."[11] "This sediment is called alluvium. The surface of the alluvium, from the edge of the fourth order stream to the base of the valley walls, is called the flood-plain of the river."[12]

---

[9]Arthur L. Bloom, *The Surface of the Earth* (Englewood Cliffs, N.J.: Prentice-Hall, Inc., 1969), p. 55.

[10]Thomas Dunne and Luna B. Leopold, *Water in Environmental Planning* (San Francisco: W. H. Freeman and Company, Publishers, 1978), p. 498.

[11]Bloom, p. 59.

[12]Ibid., p. 52.

Orders

1 ···········
2 ⌒⌒⌒
3 ⌒·⌒·⌒·
4 〜〜〜

Figure 7-8   Four orders of streams.

The principal impact of this transportation of particles is erosion. The basic process of stream erosion is the scouring action of the sand and gravel along with the moving water. That process produces three distinctly different types of erosion. The first is an action of "downcutting," which results in lowering the depth of the stream channel. The second and most noticeable is an action called "headward" erosion. This occurs when the velocity and amount of water are such that the water is forced "upslope." Slope retreat is the third major effect of erosion. This sideways erosion causes the valley walls to recede from the channel.[13] All of these result in increased deposition of sediment in the streambed, thus raising the bed and the level of floodwaters.

Erosion not only destroys valuable land, it pollutes rivers, streams, and lakes. A major source of water pollution in many communities is sediment. Sediment in the form of suspended solids in waterways creates special problems to water quality. Increased turbidity reduces the amount of sunlight a stream receives, thus "inhibiting the growth of aquatic plants and habitat. Sediment also settles to the bottom of the stream to form oxygen-demanding sludge."[14] This organic debris increases the amount of decomposing bacteria, resulting in an algae-choked, biologically depleted stream.

The pollution and sedimentation problems created by urbanization are often more visible than the companion thermal and chemical pollution. Thermal pollution results from a loss of natural vegetation and ground cover to roads, parking lots, and buildings. Although the process must be accepted as that which goes with urban development, it does raise the temperature of the runoff. The same can be said of the chemical pollution that occurs as precipitation washes petroleum and other chemical residues from parking lots, roads, sanitary landfills, and industrial activities into surface drainage systems and groundwater supply.

Water quality and quantity are related to both land and water management. Poor land and water management leads to the removal of vegetation, loss of soils through erosion, destruction of wetlands, and an increase in impervious surfaces. Alterations of stream flow can also impair the natural method of purifying runoff. Local land use and development regulations must be adopted if a community is to maintain a stable surface

---

[13]W. K. Hamblin and J. D. Howard, *Exercises in Physical Geology*, 5th ed. (Minneapolis, Minn.: Burgess Publishing Company, 1980), p. 72.

[14]U.S. Dept. of Agriculture, Soil Conservation Service, *America's Soil and Water: Conditions and Trends* (Washington, D.C.: SCS, December 1980), p. 30.

and groundwater supply while mitigating the damage due to flooding and groundwater pollution.

FLOODS: DESCRIPTION AND REGULATION

Developing appropriate regulations to control water problems is no simple task. Rivers and streams traverse various municipal and state boundaries which rarely reflect the geographic limits of watersheds. Counties and townships are often hampered with minimal data, diminishing economic resources, and marginal intraregional cooperation in their effort to develop a program and policies that reflect local environmental and development conditions.

Although the problems of flooding are primarily local in nature, in 1966, the U.S. Geological Survey and the U.S. Congress sponsored reports that recommended changes in flood control policy. Among other recommendations, the congressional report, "A Unified National Program for Managing Flood Losses," directed federal agencies to implement a national program for flood insurance.[15] The Water Resources Council worked for four years on a report ultimately released in 1972 which supported federal assistance to state and local governments that sought to adopt flood control and flood-plain management enabling legislation and zoning ordinances.

The development of the new regulations was sponsored, in part, by the interest of communities in the flood insurance programs. According to a December 1980 report by the Soil Conservation Service, 21,000 communities are subject to floods.[16] For many communities without some strategy to control existing flooding conditions, continued development and associated runoff only exacerbate the problem. As mentioned earlier, the most prevalent community strategy to control flooding is structural and would include the following:

1. *Dams and reservoirs.* These are designed to hold or retard the flow of water in a watershed and release the water at a flow rate that will minimize downstream damage.
2. *Levees.* These are designed to confine flood water to a channel.
3. *Channel improvements.* These usually involve methods to increase a channel's capacity or to improve its ability to discharge water.[17]

The second strategy of flood control is regulation, which can be separated into two subdivisions: site and nonsite. Site-specific regulations control the land use within the stream corridor and in the buffer zones immediately adjacent to the corridor. In addition to protecting life, minimizing public expenditures, and preventing and/or reducing flood damage to property, land use control strategies strive to define and allocate land to its most appropriate use.[18] Some of the instruments of regulatory approach are subdivision regulations, floodplain zoning, local building codes, and parks and open-space acquisition programs. Other municipal policies that might restrict the extension of public facilities (water, sewer, roads, etc.) would obviously retard the future development of flood-prone areas. Generally, the most effective regulatory strategy couples land use controls and public policy.

Nonsite regulations complement the site-specific regulations and focus on land use or development regulation in the entire watershed. It must be emphasized that neither site-specific nor nonsite regulation alone is usually a sufficient approach. Nonsite regu-

---

[15]U.S. Congress, House, Unified National Program for Managing Flood Losses, 89th Congress, August 10, 1966, House Document 465.

[16]U.S. Department of Agriculture, Soil Conservation Service, p. 28.

[17]Jon A. Kusler and Thomas M. Lee, "Regulations for Flood Plains," American Society of Planning Officials, Report No. 277, February 1972, p. 6.

[18]Ibid., p. 7.

lations reflect the more holistic perspective of flood control mechanisms and are devised to reduce the impact of future growth within the watershed in flood-prone areas. Conceptually, the nonsite regulations seek to lessen the negative environmental impacts with runoff control ordinances and/or erosion and sedimentation control ordinances.

Faced with shrinking budgets and rising demands for services, many municipalities can no longer find the financial resources or public support for additional storm sewers. Numerous local governments have preferred to adopt mechanisms that limit the amount of runoff from any specific development to the hydraulic capacity of the existing, in-place system. There are variations on these policies which may, for example, require on-site retention of a specific storm with a companion release rate. Although the criteria may vary from one watershed to another within a community, normally the objectives are the same. In some communities the developer may be given the flexibility to use a variety of methods, provided that the impact on the existing systems does not exceed prescribed limits. In many cases, this on-site storm water detention not only prevents additional runoff from flooding downstream areas, but is frequently more economical than standard storm sewer construction. It also forces the site planner and client to evaluate the existing environment carefully as part of the planning process.

EROSION AND SEDIMENTATION CONTROL

Unlike runoff control ordinances, erosion and sediment control ordinaces are concerned principally with regulating the process of construction as it influences runoff and its quality. Most ordinances of this character center on two objectives: acceptable site-clearing methods and on-site detention during construction. Many communities have adopted policies that require developers to submit erosion and sedimentation control plans prior to receiving building permits. The rationale is easy to accept when communities are periodically faced with expending hundreds of thousands of dollars to remove sediment from their rivers and reservoirs. Many, in fact, have found the financial burden of removing the silt so expensive that they simply acquire new properties and build new reservoirs.[19]

The following are typical examples of erosion abatement methods:

1. Build sediment basins or traps to keep soil on the site. Stabilize cut-and-fill slopes with temporary diversions, beams, bench terraces, or dikes to intercept and divert storm runoff.
2. Leave vegetation on the site as long as possible. Plant temporary turf or ground cover promptly after grading.
3. Use jute matting or a similar stabilizer on slopes to protect seed or plants.
4. Preserve trees and shrubs on one side of the stream to provide shade and maintain wildlife habitat.
5. Reduce runoff velocity with grade stabilization structures, grassed waterways, or energy dissipators.

Although site-specific policies are critical to address the problem at its source, it is equally important for communities to understand the importance of adopting land-use control regulations for properties in flood-prone zones. Without both programs in place, communities are often reminded that half-hearted efforts are rewarded with equal results.

FLOODPLAINS

In spite of the public's growing awareness of the hazards of floodplain development, construction within the 50-year floodplain remains an immensely popular enterprise. The

---

[19]U.S. Dept. of Agriculture, Soil Conservation Service, *Sediment: It's Filling Harbors, Lakes and Roadside Ditches*, Agriculture Information Bulletin No. 325, p. 3.

questions concerning an ordinance's legal status begin with the data used in the documentation of the floodplain. This is the most critical, and often the most expensive, phase of a regulatory flood program. The development of base maps and flood data is a prerequisite to the preparation of a floodplain management program. Although various federal agencies will have information affecting the delineation of a regulatory flood and discharge, the first source agencies will be:

1. The U.S. Corps of Engineers
2. The U.S. Geological Survey
3. The Soil Conservation Service
4. The National Weather Service

When a project involves any changes or improvements along existing water routes, tributaries to navigable waters, or wetlands, the jurisdiction of the Corps of Engineers must be consulted. The U.S. Army Corps of Engineers has been regulating the nation's water activities since 1890. Up until the 1960s, the primary purpose of the Corps was to protect navigation. After the 1960s, as a result of laws and court decisions, the Corps began to regulate both the protection and utilization of water resources.

The Corps of Engineers has the responsibility and authority to regulate based on the following laws:

Section 10 of the Rivers and Harbors Act of 1899 (33 U.S.C. 403) prohibits the obstruction or alteration of navigable waters of the United States without a permit from the Corps of Engineers.

Section 404 of the Clean Water Act (33 U.S.C. 1344). Section 301 of this Act prohibits the discharge of dredged or fill material into waters of the United States without a permit from the Corps of Engineers.

Section 103 of the Marine Protection, Research, and Sanctuaries Act of 1972, as amended (33 U.S.C. 1413) authorizes the Corps of Engineers to issue permits for the transportation of dredged material for the purpose of dumping it into ocean waters.[20]

Any changes or improvements to a site that might include such areas could involve Corps approval through a standard individual permit. These permits are filed with the Corps of Engineers by the owner or consultant and are outlined in detail in Corps of Engineers Regulatory Program Pamphlet No. EP 1145-2-1, May 1985. This pamphlet reviews the typical procedure and stipulates the evaluation factors used to determine permit approval or denial. Failure to consult the Corps and obtain proper approval is in violation of federal law.

Since the vocabulary of floodplain management can be confusing, an overview of a few concepts is essential to an understanding of the process of delineating the various intervals of the flood. First, for every flood discharge or flood frequency, there is a different floodplain, flood fringe, and floodway. A flood discharge is essentially the translation of a flood into that quantity of water which flows past a specific point in 1 second and is expressed in cubic feet per second. A flood frequency is the translation of a storm's intensity (inches of rainfall/hour) into a probability factor. This probability is based on the documented rainfall for the region, as well as the hydrological characteristics of the water course. A rain of n inches per hour in one region may occur so infrequently that it may happen only 5% of the time. This 5% occurrence can be translated into a frequency term and in doing so is then expressed as a 20-year storm (Fig. 7-9).

Two things are important to remember. First, these intensity levels will vary widely from one region to the next. Second, it is possible for any storm (20-year, 25-year, 50-

---

[20]U.S. Corps of Engineers, Regulatory Program Pamphlet No. EP 1145-2-1, May 1985.

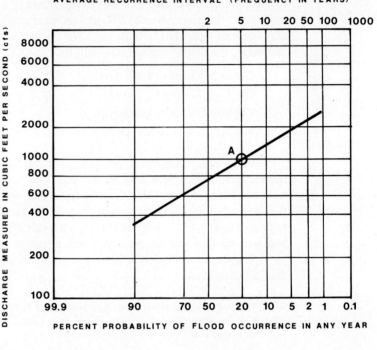

Example: Use a curve at point ˙A˙.   Discharge= 1000 cfs
Percent Probability = 20   Average Recurrence Interval = 5 year frequency

Figure 7-9   Flood discharge versus frequency curve.

year, etc.) to occur more often than once every 20, 25, or 50 years. Recall that this is a probability index and is based on existing data. To recapitulate, a storm of such intensity that it would occur 50% of the time is considered a 2-year storm. Figure 7-10 illustrates the conditions that might occur under a variety of storms within the same natural channel. One final aspect of the frequency/discharge ratio is that the intensity (inches/hour) is not a geometric relationship. The 10-year storm is not double the intensity of the 5-year storm. Knowing the precipitation rates and intervals, then, provides the community with the first level of information necessary to document its various flood-prone areas. Figures 7-11 and 7-12 are maps published by the U.S. Department of Agriculture which portray regional variances of rainfall for both 5- and 10-year storms of 30-minute durations.

There is often confusion as to the difference between the definition of a floodplain and a floodway. First, the floodplain is that area beyond the natural flow of the water course that is necessary to accommodate the flow of water for a known frequency (10-year, 20-year, etc.). The limits of this floodplain line are a function of two primary variables: the amount of water in the floodplain and the configuration or form of the floodplain. Obviously, the more concave the section in the floodplain, the larger its holding capacity.

The floodway is that zone of the floodplain that would be required to pass an amount of water equal to a flood of the same period at an elevation 1 ft above the line of the floodplain (Fig. 7-13). This interrelationship between the floodplain and floodway prescribes, for example, that the flow capacity of the 100-year floodway, with its additional 1 ft above the elevation of the natural 100-year floodplain, is equal in capacity to that of the 100-year floodplain. The effect of this in various communities has been to

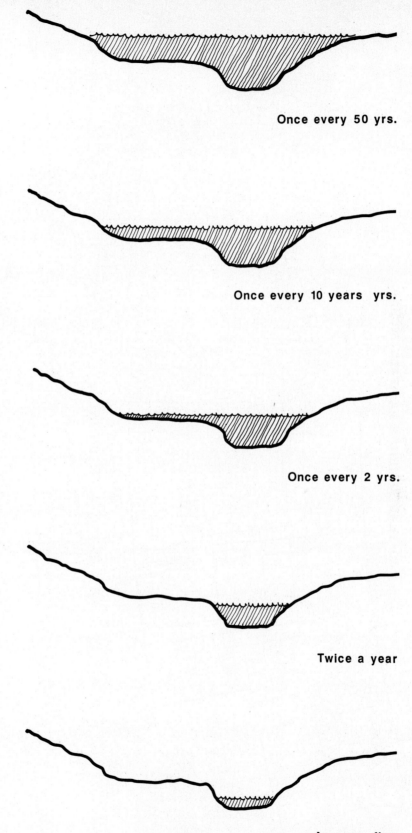

Once every 50 yrs.

Once every 10 years yrs.

Once every 2 yrs.

Twice a year

Average flow

Figure 7-10 Diagram of flood plains.

Figure 7-11 Ten year–30 minute rainfall.

Figure 7-12 Five year–30 minute rainfall.

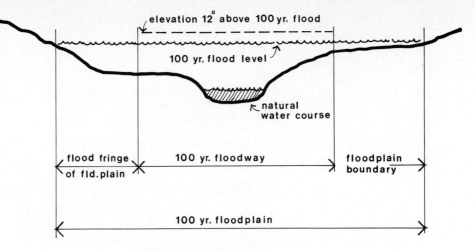

Figure 7-13 Floodplain/floodway section.

permit filling and construction in the 100-year floodplain as long as new structures maintained finish floor elevations 1 ft above the 100-year floodplain. This policy would conceptually permit the normal 100-year flood to pass through the floodway without physically entering buildings. The only problem is, as we know, that floodplains tend to expand as development continues. Unless a community has an active program to maintain the runoff at current levels, the extent of the floodplain is likely to increase.

Table 7-2 is a summary of Flood Data Classifications criteria, hydraulic factors, and applicability. This information is particularly useful in evaluating the accuracy of a floodplain. Since classes B and C are based on extrapolated data, the delineation of the floodplain with either method may invite a legal challenge. Common sense should prevail. The experienced site planner approaches with caution any development near a known floodplain. In those circumstances where the floodplain is undocumented, development in areas that have characteristics similar to the following should be reviewed extensively for flooding before site planning.

1. Relatively low, gentle-sloping terrain confined by a valley wall
2. Soils of high water table and poor drainage
3. Healthy vegetation of the species that flourish in wet, flooded soil conditions
4. Land areas adjacent to water courses with:
   (a) Outer edges of steep slopes
   (b) Traces of "oxbow" lakes
   (c) Natural terraced benches against valley walls

Local and regional history can sometimes help determine the extent of an inundated area. The lack of intense agriculture in a flood-prone area may be the result of several generations of farmers. Remote sensing involves infrared satellite photography which can be used to identify areas of standing water. Although the scale of this photography is very large and detailed information will require enlargement, in the absence of other documentation, remote sensing may be the only source of hard facts. The Earth Observation Satellite Company (EOSAT) is the source of remote-sensing photography.

Most urban communities have identified and delineated both 50- and 100-year floodplains. However, knowing the boundary lines has not necessarily retarded the sale or purchase and ultimate development of properties within either the 50- or 100-year floodplain. Some municipalities permit development in a floodplain provided that the developer increase, by dredging or other earthworks, the capacity of the floodplain in

TABLE 7-2 Summary of Flood-Data Classifications and Applicability

CLASSIFICATION	DETERMINATION OF THREE HYDRAULIC FACTORS ESSENTIAL TO REGULATIONS			DESIRABLE AREAS OF APPLICATION	DISADVANTAGES	ADVANTAGES	SUGGESTED ZONING DISTRICTS
	Profile	Floodway	Floodplain				
Class A: exact flood data based on hydraulic calculations	Determined initially from engineering study	Determined initially from engineering study	Determined initially from engineering study	Areas of high development for urban growth; Areas of intense existing development; Areas of high land values; Areas where zoning is the only management tool	Very costly and sometimes takes many years before studies are complete	Provide sound legal base for zoning; Expedites evaluation of proposed developments or amendments to adopted plans; Minimize hardships to applicant of proposed development; Contribute to flood emergency preparedness plan	Floodway; Flood fringe; Basement
Class B: interpreted flood data based on known high-water marks	Extrapolation from past floods records	Normal depth analysis on a case-by-case basis	Location by elevations from extrapolated profile on Topographic maps; Street-sewer maps that show ground elevations or Field surveys	Small amount of existing development affected; Little development pressure; Strong sanitary subdivision controls and public policy; Much land under public ownership; Ongoing program to acquire class A data	Legal base questionable; Requires technical assistance to evaluate floodway; Applicant has greater burden to provide survey information	Low cost; Discourage land speculation; Valuable river basin; Guide to public facilities and transportation; Can be made available in short time to serve immediate need	General floodplain district
Class C: interpreted flood data based on nonhydraulic calculations	Determined case-by-case	Determined case-by-case	Experienced flood maps, aerial photo examination, or detailed soil maps that have been correlated with engineering studies on similar streams	Rural areas little potential for development; Large portion of area under public ownership; Land-easement or acquisition program; Strong sanitary and subdivision regulations; Ongoing program to acquire class A data	Frequency of mapped flood unknown; All three hydraulic factors unknown; Weak legal base; Source of technical assistance is needed; Burden to applicant to furnish surveys	Low cost; Readily expected by local people; Identifies pressure areas; Discourages land speculation	General floodplain district

Source: Jon A. Kusler and Thomas M. Lee, "Regulations for Flood Plains," American Society of Planning Officials, Report No. 277, February 1972, p. 33.

an equal amount. This concept is based on the assumption that floodplain levels are fixed and unchanging. Depending on the community and its land development policies, this may or not have been a well-founded assumption. Although many local governments have stringent controls concerning "fill" in a 50-year floodplain, others are silent and consider floodplain "fill" as a land reclamation enterprise.

To reiterate the point made earlier, the prevalant methods used by local governments to control land uses and hazards in flood-prone areas are the following:

1. Zoning
2. Subdivision regulations
3. Building and housing codes
4. Sanitary and water well codes[21]

These methods are independently successful, and collectively they provide local government with a comprehensive package of implementation procedures. But regardless of what methods are adopted, the regulations should work to protect adjacent upstream and downstream landowners from direct and indirect increases in flood damage.

Zoning is considered first because it addresses the problem of land use, coverage (impervious surfaces), and density comprehensively and at the site source. Zoning is employed to restrict from the floodplain development uses which, when inundated by water, could create health or safety hazards either by chemical decomposition or floating debris. Although the constitutionality of some floodplain ordinances has been challenged, those that are upheld usually have the following qualities in common:

1. Similar situations are treated equally.
2. The regulation is based on solid data.
3. The threat of flood damage is balanced with land use needs.
4. Some realistic private economic land use is permitted.

An additional quality of zoning is that it can be applied in river or coastal zones to regulate what uses may be permitted and under what set of conditions. Subdivision regulations are also to be employed to control the parameters under which development might occur in a floodplain.

Since a building code is limited by ordinance to the structure and site, codes can only focus on limiting the flood damage and property loss. A building code for construction in the floodplain will have established standards to prevent flotation of building by:

1. Specifying minimum anchorage systems or methods
2. Imposing material restrictions to exclude those which deteriorate when exposed to water
3. Imposing structural design standards which reflect anticipated water pressures and flood velocities[22]

Sanitary and water well codes are also ordinances that can be tailored to reflect the specific conditions of a flood-prone environment. In areas of high water table or susceptible to flooding, sanitary codes commonly prohibit the use of on-site waste disposal facilities in areas of high groundwater and flooding.

Good floodplain management is critical to the development health of many communities, and thus legislation adopted must reflect each community's unique physical, social, economic, and environmental conditions. The difficulty occurs in developing a

---

[21]Kusler and Lee, p. 8.
[22]Ibid., p. 9.

Figure 7-14 Woodlands: 100-year flood plan.

balance between the public's interest and the environment, on the one hand, and private property rights and economics, on the other.

An excellent example of that balance was achieved in the development of the Woodlands community north of Houston, Texas. The 18,000-acre site was a serious challenge to the developer. On the positive side of the ledger, the existing pine–oak forest, streams, and abundant wildlife could be undeniably attractive to potential home buyers. On the negative side, approximately one-third of the site was within the 100-year floodplain of three major streams; the site was so flat that drainage patterns depended partially on prevailing wind direction, and much of the soil had a very slow percolation rate (Fig. 7-14).

Conventional development practices would have eliminated much of what made the Woodlands such an attractive place to live. Prevailing development standards would have required the construction of an extensive artificial drainage system complete with concrete drainage channels. The alternative was to analyze the existing ecology in an effort to discover what level of development the existing natural systems could support. The research was very productive. A feasible natural drainage system of existing swales, ponds, and pockets of permeable soil provided the basis for the plan to follow. Although the natural system needed some redirection and additional capacity, the developer's willingness to invest in the research without knowing the results was commendable.

The payoff was at two levels: one economic and one environmental. Utilizing the existing drainage patterns permitted the developer to reduce runoff, protect the natural vegetation, retard erosion and siltation, maintain water quality, enhance scenic amenities, recharge groundwater supply, and reduce maintenance. The ubiquitous economic "bottom line" is equally as good. 1972 estimates of the engineering and construction costs for the artificial drainage system that would have been used under conventional circumstances totaled $18,679,300. By comparison, the alternative to supplement the natural drainage system to accomplish the same development objectives cost $4,200,400.[23] Making the process produce these types of dramatic results will not always be possible, but be assured that it always pays. Although the circumstances for alternative comparisons will never be the same, the experienced site planner begins with the assumption that the natural environment is a collection of systems that can be integrated and positively supplement urban settlement.

[23]Wallace, McHarg, Roberts, and Todd, "Woodlands New Community; Phase One: Land Planning and Design Principles" (Philadelphia: WMRT, December 1973), p. 6.

An Environmental Inventory and Assessment

chapter 8

Climate and Site

by George Truett James

INTRODUCTION

The process of planning a site to accommodate buildings and exterior spaces should involve an analysis of climate with a focus on comfort and building energy conservation. In this chapter we focus on the nature of human thermal comfort, the climatic elements that affect the site and buildings, and how the analysis of these elements may inform the site planning process. Later, in Chapter 17, the focus shifts to how the analysis of external thermal loads (created by the climatic elements) and internal thermal loads (created inside the building by people, lights, and equipment) can provide the site planner with useful information for the preliminary siting, massing, and orientation of buildings. By using these analytic techniques, the site planner will be able to anticipate the impact of climate on exterior spaces and the thermal loading problems that will be encountered by a proposed building, thereby permitting the inclusion of comfort and energy-conscious design criteria during the earliest possible stages of the design process.

COMFORT

A realistic discussion of climate and building energy conservation cannot occur without considering human thermal comfort. It is a premise of this book that through careful analysis, the site planner can:

1. Develop exterior spaces which are sensitive to local climatic norms and extremes, thereby expanding the opportunities for thermally comfortable outdoor experiences
2. Reduce the thermal loads imposed on the site's buildings, thereby promoting thermally comfortable indoor conditions for a minimum expenditure of energy

Although human thermal comfort will not be discussed in great detail here, one should not minimize the importance of comfort as an issue in the design process. It has been estimated that over the normal 40-year life span of a commercial office building, for every dollar invested in building construction, operation, and maintenance, as much as $20 may be expended on wages, salaries, and benefits for the people who occupy the building. Assuming that there is a connection between comfort and productivity, anything that can be done to promote comfort can produce significant financial benefits. Similar benefits may accrue to industrial and retail establishments which provide comfortable conditions for employees and customers. If, through sensitive planning and design, people are provided with comfortable, stimulating places to live, work, and play, and business realizes some economic benefit, the designer partially fulfills his social responsibility to the community and his professional obligation to the client.

What, then, is this commodity that we call "comfort"? Perhaps the surest definition of comfort is "the lack of discomfort." This may seem trite, but it indicates the uncertainty of defining comfort in a generalized sense. Comfort is a function of individual perception, expectation, and need. It depends on our physiological and psychological responses to the environment—a world composed of thermal, luminous, auditory, olfactory, gustatory, and tactile stimuli. All of these elements are important in terms of our sense of comfort, but because we are dealing specifically with climatic issues and building energy use, our discussion of comfort will focus on the thermal environment and, to a limited extent, the luminous environment.

Studies suggest an upper and lower limit for man's existence, where prolonged exposure results in hypothermia.[1] The ideal combination of environmental conditions can be assumed to occur approximately midway between these two extremes—a set of conditions where thermal stress is minimized and the body's thermal balance is most easily maintained. This suggests that a "zone" can be identified which would represent conditions of thermal comfort in a general sense. A "comfort zone" was postulated in

Figure 8-1 Bioclimatic chart.

[1]American Society of Heating, Refrigerating and Air-Conditioning Engineers, Inc., *ASHRAE Handbook—1981 Fundamentals* (Atlanta: ASHRAE, 1981), Chap. 8.

1963 by Victor Olgyay in *Design with Climate* and has recently been updated.[2] As indicated in Fig. 8-1, a zone of comfort is identified in what Olgyay calls the "bioclimatic chart." It should be noted that the bioclimatic chart refers to conditions in the exterior environment, and that the comfort zone defines a range of temperature and humidity conditions where a person in normal indoor clothing, doing sedentary or light work in the shade, and with no wind blowing, will presumably be comfortable. The chart indicates the requirements to remedy discomfort when temperature and relative humidity do not fall within the comfort zone. For example, when temperatures are below the comfort zone, the addition of radiation can produce conditions of comfort. With high temperature and high humidity levels, air movement is required to achieve comfort. The chart indicates that the elements which influence thermal comfort are: air temperature, humidity, radiation, and air movement. Clothing and activity levels also have a profound effect on thermal comfort.

The preceding discussion has been a brief introduction to thermal comfort. An enormous amount of detailed information is available on this subject. For a more thorough discussion, the reader is directed to *Design with Climate* by Victor Olgyay; *Man, Climate and Architecture* by Baruch Givoni; *Climatic Design* by Donald Watson and Kenneth Labs; *Thermal Delight in Architecture* by Lisa Heschong; Chapter 1 in *Building Control Systems* by Vaughn Bradshaw; Chapter 8 in the *1981 ASHRAE Handbook of Fundamentals*; and "A New Bioclimatic Chart for Passive Solar Design" by Arens, McNall, Gonzales, Berglund and Zeren.

THE CLIMATIC ELEMENTS

The four basic climatic elements that influence thermal comfort, building energy use, and the site planning process are *solar radiation*, *air temperature*, *relative humidity*, and *air movement*. To familiarize the site planner with these elements, each will be discussed in terms of:

1. Its physical description
2. The effects that it produces or its behavior
3. Basic strategies for its control or modification
4. The access and interpretation of related data concerned with measuring its magnitude, intensity, or effects

General climatic analysis related to site planning will then be discussed. Attention will also be focused on the difference between normal and extreme climatic conditions. In a general sense, location of exterior spaces, building orientation, massing, and architectural design should be based on normal climatic conditions—the seasonal conditions that can be expected to occur normally or most frequently. Knowledge of the extreme or worst-case conditions that can occur (those conditions with which the mechanical engineer must deal in determining the proper size for mechanical air-handling systems) allows the site planner or architect to compensate for those conditions in order to minimize their impact on exterior spaces and buildings.

Before proceeding with the discussion of climatic elements, it is important to distinguish between the three basic climatic regimes: macroclimate, mesoclimate, and microclimate. Macroclimate refers to the general climatic conditions of a region, while mesoclimate relates to the climate of a particular area or city. An understanding of these regimes is important in any planning process. However, the site planner's influence is exerted most notably on the microclimate—the climate of a specific site.[3] Anytime a

---

[2]E. Arens, P. McNall, R. Gonzales, L. Berglund, and L. Zeren, "A New Bioclimatic Chart for Passive Solar Design," *Proceedings of the 5th National Solar Conference* (American Section of the International Solar Energy Society, 1980).

[3]C. Thurow, *Improving Street Climate through Urban Design*, Planning Advisory Service Report No. 376 (Chicago: American Planning Association, 1983), p. 2.

building is constructed, a variety of new microclimates are created in and around the building within the existing microclimate of the site. The ensuing discussion will focus primarily on how climate-responsive site planning decisions can ameliorate adverse microclimatic conditions, providing thermally pleasant outdoor spaces and reducing climatic loads on buildings.

SOLAR RADIATION

> Radiation is undoubtedly the most important of all meteorologic elements. It is the source of power that drives the atmospheric circulation, the only means of exchange of energy between the earth and the rest of the universe, and the basis for organizing our daily lives.
> *Rudolph Geiger*[4]

Description.   The sun is the driving force for the earth's climate. A giant fusion reactor, the sun emits electromagnetic energy in three broad ranges of frequencies: the ultraviolet, the visible, and the infrared. The portion of this energy with which we will be concerned is physically perceived as light (the visible frequencies) and heat (the infrared frequencies). Generally, light is referred to as shortwave radiation and heat as longwave radiation.

Solar radiation reaches us in the form of direct, diffuse, and reflected radiation. Direct radiation arrives directly through our atmosphere. Diffuse radiation results from the scattering of light by particulate matter and moisture in the earth's atmosphere. Once solar radiation has reached the earth's surface it is absorbed, transmitted, or reflected. When shortwave radiation (light) is absorbed, it is converted to longwave radiation (heat). In this manner, the sun heats the earth's surface, driving the climatic cycles of air movement, temperature, evaporation, and precipitation. In addition, the sun's light enables sight and the photosynthetic processes that occur in plants.

The constancy of the earth's rotation and its planetary orbit allow us to predict precisely the location and ''apparent'' movement of the sun relative to the earth's surface. An understanding of the seasonal variations of solar angles has informed planning decisions for at least two millennia. The ancient Greeks and Romans exploited their knowledge of solar geometry in architecture, site planning, and urban planning.

> Modern excavations of many Classical Greek cities show that solar architecture flourished throughout the area. Individual homes were oriented toward the southern horizon, and entire cities were planned to allow their citizens equal access to the winter sun.[5]

Vitruvius, the Roman architect, advised in the first century B.C.:

> If our designs for private houses are to be correct, we must at the outset take note of the countries and climates in which they are built . . . it is obvious that designs for houses ought similarly to conform to the nature of the country and to diversities of climate.[6]

History is replete with examples of cultures that took advantage of the seasonal differences in the sun's position in planning settlements and designing buildings. Although our knowledge of solar geometry may be more precise than that of our predecessors, and our computational devices more sophisticated, the guiding principles are still the same. In the northern hemisphere during the winter months, the sun travels a low path across the southern sky. In the summer, the sun travels a much higher overhead path (Fig. 8-2).[7] The sun's position relative to any terrestrial location can easily be

---

[4]R. Geiger, *The Climate Near the Ground* (Cambridge, Mass.: Harvard University Press, 1975), p. 5.

[5]K. Butti and J. Perlin, *A Golden Thread: 2500 Years of Solar Architecture and Technology* (New York: Van Nostrand Reinhold Company, Inc., 1980), p. 3.

[6]Vitruvius, *The Ten Books on Architecture*, M. H. Morgan, trans. (Cambridge, Mass.: Harvard University Press; New York: Dover Publications, Inc., 1960), p. 170.

[7]D. Watson and R. Glover, *Solar Control Workbook* (prepared for the U.S. Department of Energy Passive Solar Curriculum Project, *Teaching Passive Design in Architecture*, November 1981), p. 6.

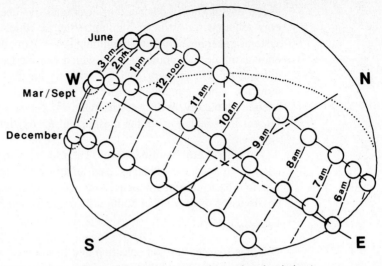

Figure 8-2 Seasonal sun paths (northern hemisphere).

determined, and is described by its altitude angle (angle "A") and azimuth (bearing) angle (angle "B") at any given time (Fig. 8-3). Sources and application of solar angles are presented later in the chapter.

Effects.   The sun provides light and heat for both our exterior and interior environments. Sunlit exterior spaces are welcomed in the winter. On hot summer days, we seek relief from the sun in cool, shaded exterior spaces. Solar radiation heats the interior spaces of our buildings when it passes through glass and is absorbed and converted to thermal energy by the various surfaces inside the building. This causes a local heating of the air in contact with these surfaces, and the "sealed" nature of the building inhibits the escape of the warmed air. This is commonly referred to as the "greenhouse effect."[8] Solar radiation also heats the opaque surfaces of a building, and additional heat is conducted through these materials into the building.

Passive solar heating of buildings can be beneficial during cold weather, reducing our reliance on mechanical heating systems. However, the solar loads imposed on our buildings during warm periods of the year can greatly increase our dependence on mechanical cooling systems.

The sun provides us with an abundance of natural light, even on overcast days. In addition to the suggested psychological and physiological benefits of natural light,[9] the

Figure 8-3 Sun angles.

[8]D. Watson and K. Labs, *Climatic Design* (New York: McGraw-Hill Book Company, 1983), p. 20.
[9]"Light as Nutrition," *Progressive Architecture*, April 1981, pp. 176–177.

use of daylighting in our buildings can conserve energy by reducing the amount of energy required for artificial lighting systems, which can be the most energy-intensive systems in certain commercial building types. Parenthetically, lighting systems also generate a signficant amount of heat, which can increase a building's air-conditioning requirements. The primary goal in designing for daylighting "is to provide natural illumination while effectively blocking direct solar radiation, since it usually carries uncomfortable levels of heat and light."[10] Generally speaking, diffuse, reflected, and filtered solar radiation are the most useful for daylighting buildings.

Control and Modification.   The following discussion focuses on the use of vegetation, architectural elements, and landforms or hardscape to control solar radiation. The four basic control strategies—admission, obstruction, filtration, and reflection—will be discussed as they affect both outdoor spaces and buildings.

Vegetation:

Outdoor spaces.   Proper selection and location of vegetation can ameliorate microclimatic conditions by providing exterior spaces with access to solar radiation when temperatures are below the comfort zone, and shade when they are not.

Vegetation produces shade and can intercept and absorb 60 to 90% of incident solar radiation.[11] Dense foliage, multiple foliage layers, or dense canopies obstruct solar radiation, whereas plants with open, loose foliage filter it. The temperatures of surfaces in shade (and consequent air temperatures) can be reduced significantly by shading. During the summer, it is not uncommon for unshaded dark-colored "hard" surfaces to reach temperatures in excess of 160°F. Oppressive levels of radiant heat generated by such surfaces even after sunset, in addition to their ability to raise the temperature of the proximate air mass, can have a profound impact on perceptions of comfort. The bioclimatic chart (Fig. 8-1) indicates that under calm wind conditions and depending on relative humidity levels, shading is desirable when air temperatures exceed the range 68° to 72°F (the "shade line"). Obviously, shading can be an extremely productive comfort strategy during periods of overheating.

Conversely, exterior spaces that have access to solar radiation can improve or produce conditions of comfort even during very cold conditions. The bioclimatic chart (Fig. 8-1) indicates that a person in normal street clothing exposed to full solar radiation (100%, 45° solar altitude) will feel comfortable when it is calm and the temperature is 44°F. Increasing clothing insulation or actively levels can produce comfort at even lower temperatures with sunshine. It is therefore possible for properly oriented, unshaded exterior spaces which are protected from the wind to be comfortable when ambient air temperatures are well below the comfort zone.

At this point, it is appropriate to examine the distinction between deciduous and evergreen vegetation. Deciduous vegetation normally becomes foliated in the spring and provides shade during the overheated periods in summer and fall. As fall defoliation occurs, solar radiation is no longer obstructed and can be used to warm exterior spaces during winter months. (It should be noted that deciduous trees with dense branching structures can produce a significant amount of shading (greater than 50%) when defoliated). These selective shading characteristics can be particularly useful in temperate climates with hot summers and cold winters. Evergreen vegetation maintains its foliage throughout the year and can be useful for shading exterior spaces in tropical climates where warm temperatures and sunshine occur throughout the year. Shade trees can be selected with foliation periods that correspond approximately to the times of overheating

[10]"Through a Glass Brightly," *Progressive Architecture*, November 1981, p. 138.

[11]W. E. Reifsnyder and H. W. Lull, *Radiant Energy in Relation to Forests*, U.S. Department of Agriculture Forest Service Technical Bulletin No. 1344 (Washington, D.C.: U.S. Government Printing Office, 1965) cited by E. G. McPherson, "Planting Design for Solar Control," *Energy Conserving Site Design* (Washington, D.C.: American Society of Landscape Architects, 1984), p. 144.

TABLE 8-1 Foliation Periods for Various Trees

COMMON NAME	FOLIATION	DEFOLIATION	REFERENCE
Amur maple	March	October	3
Norway maple	April	November	1
Red maple	April	October	3
Silver maple	May	November	2
Sugar maple	May	October	3
European birch	April	November	1
European hackberry	March	November	1
Common hackberry	April	November	2
English hawthorn	May	December	2
Carrier hawthorn	April	December	3
European beech	May	December	3
European ash	May	November	2
Moraine ash	March	November	1
Green ash	April	October	3
Honey locust	April	October	3
Black walnut	May	October–November	2
Sweetgum	April	November	1
Sweetgum	May	December	3
California sycamore	March	December	1
Cottonwood	April	November	2
Quaking aspen	April	November	2
Pin oak	April	December	1
English oak	May	December	3
Chinese tallow tree	March	November	1
American elm	May	November	2
Siberian elm	April	November	2

Source: E. G. McPherson, ''Planting Design for Solar Control,'' *Energy Conserving Site Design* (Washington, D.C.: American Society of Landscape Architects, 1984), pp. 144–146 citing (1) J. Hammond, J. Zanetto, and C. Adams, *Planning Solar Neighborhoods* (Sacramento: California Energy Commission, 1981); (2) E. G. McPherson, *The Use of Trees for Solar Control in Utah* (Salt Lake City: Utah Energy Office, 1981); and (3) R. L. Ticknor, ''Selecting Deciduous Trees for Climatic Modification,'' *American Nurseryman*, 153(1), 1981, pp. 10–88.

at a specific site. Table 8-1 lists the foliation periods for a variety of trees. (The observations listed in the table were made in California, Utah, and Oregon, and therefore may not be applicable to your site. Local plant guides, experts, or observation can provide information on the foliation characteristics of trees indigenous to your area.) Determining when overheated periods occur is discussed in the section ''General Climatic Analysis.''

Vines, used in conjunction with architectural elements (such as arbors), and shrubs are also useful for shading exterior spaces. Ground covers and grasses are useful for shading ground surfaces, and in the summer, grass surfaces can be 10 to 14°F cooler than bare soil[12] and 50°F cooler than pavement.

Buildings.   As with exterior spaces, vegetation can be used to reduce solar radiation loads on buildings by shading walls, roofs, and glazed openings. Figure 8-4 indicates the varying seasonal impact of solar radiation on different building surface orientations. It is apparent that south-facing vertical surfaces receive the most solar radiation during winter months, whereas horizontal, west, and east orientations receive more radiation during summer months. Surface temperatures of walls and roofs exposed to the sun can be more than 40°F warmer than shaded surfaces during the summer.[13] Therefore, resi-

[12]V. Olgyay, *Design with Climate* (Princeton, N.J.: Princeton University Press, 1963), p. 51.

[13]E. G. McPherson, ''Planting Design for Solar Control,'' *Energy Conserving Site Design* (Washington, D.C.: American Society of Landscape Architects, 1984), p. 146 citing E. G. McPherson, *The Use of Plant Materials for Solar Control*, unpublished master's thesis, Utah State University, 1980.

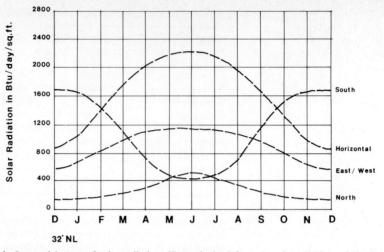

Figure 8-4 Seasonal impact of solar radiation. [Data obtained from American Society of Heating, Refrigerating and Air-Conditioning Engineers, Inc., *ASHRAE Handbook-1981 Fundamentals* (Atlanta: ASHRAE, 1981), Table 22A, p. 27.32.]

dential buildings in temperate climates are often prudently oriented with a long wall facing south to maximize collection of solar radiation in the winter while minimizing summer heat gain. If properly designed, vegetative shading provided for horizontal, west-, and east-facing surfaces can reduce summer solar radiation loads, improve comfort, and reduce air-conditioning requirements. Shrubs or vines used to shade a wall also retard air movement across the wall surface, effectively increasing its thermal resistance and reducing convective heat flow.

Vegetation can have a significant impact on visual comfort in exterior spaces and on the use of daylighting in buildings. Shade trees, which obstruct or filter sunlight, can reduce brightness levels and visual discomfort due to glare, both in exterior and interior spaces. However, reduction of light levels can reduce the amount of daylight in building interiors. Figure 8-5 indicates that light transmission can be significantly reduced by trees.

Shrubs, ground covers, and grasses are also useful for brightness and glare control. The ability of a surface to reflect shortwave radiation is referred to as its albedo rate. Surfaces with low albedo rates are useful for reducing contrast and controlling glare, whereas those with high albedo rates can help reflect useful daylight deep into building interiors. Table 8-2 lists the albedo rates for a variety of common ground surfaces.

Architectural Elements. Like vegetation, architectural elements can obstruct or filter solar radiation and selectively provide shading for exterior spaces and buildings. Architectural elements are defined in the broadest possible terms and include buildings. Small, free-standing or detached elements, such as gazebos and arbors, have long been used to

Figure 8-5 Light-transmission reduction by trees.

TABLE 8-2 Albedo Rates for Common Ground Surfaces

SURFACE	ALBEDO RATE (% REFLECTIVITY)
Fresh snow cover	75–95
Clean, firm snow	50–65
Old snow cover	40–70
Dirty, firm snow	20–50
Light sand dunes, surf	30–60
Sandy soil	15–40
Meadows, fields	12–30
Dark, cultivated soil	7–10
Water surfaces, sea	3–10
Bare ground	10–25
Rock, gravel	12–15
Dry grass	32
Grass fields, lawns	6
Asphalt	15
Concrete	55

Sources: G. Robinette, ed., *Plants/People/and Environmental Quality* (Washington, D.C.: National Park Service, U.S. Department of the Interior, 1972), p. 70, and *How to Predict Interior Daylight Illumination* (Toledo, Ohio: Libbey-Owens-Ford Company, 1976), p. 11.

modify microclimate through shading. Similar shelters are often used at bus stops to provide shade for waiting passengers, as well as protection from wind and rain.

There is also a long history of attached architectural elements which provide seasonal shading of exterior spaces, as well as building surfaces—from the porticoes, arcades, and courts of ancient Egyptian, Greek, Roman, and Islamic architecture, to the outdoor living porches of southern plantation architecture, the exaggerated prairie-style overhang, and brise-soleil of more recent times. The similar effect of all of these elements is to provide transitional exterior spaces which can ameliorate microclimatic conditions, increasing the opportunities for comfortable outdoor experiences.

Buildings, as single or collected objects in the landscape, will produce shading in adjacent exterior spaces. Obviously, building shadow patterns will vary both daily and seasonally. Outdoor activities around buildings often tend to migrate with either sun or shade, depending on individual comfort requirements. These migrations can be observed at locations such as the American town-square courthouse and in many urban parks and plazas. There are numerous examples of settlements in hot, arid climates where buildings are used to provide shade for exterior spaces (Fig. 8-6). However, building shadows produce an interesting set of problems in modern urban high-rise districts, as in the following hypothetical example. Consider the effects produced by a 50-story (600 ft high) reflective glass tower on the surrounding environs. At 32° north latitude (Dallas), the shadow cast by our building, on December 21 one hour after sunrise (8 A.M. solar time), extends over 3400 ft (0.64 mile). Figure 8-7 indicates the extent of building shadows for the day of December 21. During winter months, our building casts a shadow across the adjacent park to the north during much of the day, as well as the street-level plaza located on the north side of our building. Shortwave radiation reflected from our building creates glare and visual discomfort in adjacent exterior spaces, but may reduce the heating requirements of buildings in the path of the reflections. Air-conditioning requirements for buildings in the path of summer reflections may be significantly increased by the additional radiation loads imposed by our building, and law suits have occurred in similar situations. Figure 8-8 indicates the areas affected by June 21 reflec-

Figure 8-6   Buildings in hot arid climates.

Figure 8-7   Shadows from 50 story building.

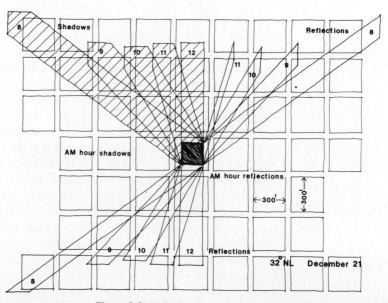

Figure 8-8   Reflections from 50-story building.

Figure 8-9   Solar radiation, slope gradient, and orientation.

tions. Parenthetically, dense high-rise districts such as those in New York City can have a significant impact on the amount of daylight reaching the street, which has prompted zoning legislation concerning building form.[14]

In summary, architectural elements and vegetation can be useful devices for controlling or modifying solar radiation. However, their design and location must be carefully considered and must be based on a thorough analysis of microclimatic conditions.

Landforms and Hardscape.   In the following discussion, the entire site will be considered a landform, as will smaller landscape elements. "Hardscape" refers to "hard" surfaces constructed in contact with the ground in the exterior environment.

In the site planning process, the selection of appropriate locations for exterior spaces and buildings related to solar access or shading can be affected by slope direction and gradients on the site. A slope inclined toward the south will receive more winter radiation than will a "flat" area of equal size, and with a gradient of 20%, can expedite the arrival of spring and delay the onset of winter by as much as 3 weeks.[15]

Surface A in Fig. 8-9, normal to the sun's rays, receives maximum radiation. As surfaces rotate away from normal (surfaces B), they receive increasingly less radiation. At 90° of rotation (surface C), the surface receives no direct radiation. Therefore, different slope aspects or orientations produce different microclimatic conditions, as delineated by Robinette in *Energy Efficient Site Design*:[16]

Southeast slope	Most desirable
South slope	Preferred: warm winter, early spring, late fall
East slope	Acceptable: warm winter mornings, cool summer evenings
West slope	Undesirable: hottest summer slope
North slope	Least desirable: coldest in winter

When the slope gradient approaches 100%, the slope becomes essentially a vertical "wall." South-facing cliff walls were used to shelter the Indian settlements at Canyon de Chelly in northeast Arizona (Figs. 8-10 and 8-11). As noted earlier (Fig. 8-4), south-facing vertical surfaces maximize winter radiation while minimizing summer radiation. The Indian settlements are recessed into the cliff face, which improves summer shading characteristics. Similar settlements also existed in southern Tunisia and Shensi province in China.[17] Although this is not ordinarily a feasible site planning option, an understanding of the principles will inform any planning process.

[14]H. Bryan and S. Stuebing, "Natural Light as an Urban Amenity," *Lighting Design and Application*, June 1986, pp. 44–48.

[15]Olgyay, *Design with Climate*, pp. 49–50.

[16]G. Robinette, ed., *Energy Efficient Site Design* (New York: Van Nostrand Reinhold Company, Inc., 1983), p. 13.

[17]J. M. Fitch and D. P. Branch, "Primitive Architecture and Climate," *Scientific American*, December 1960, p. 140.

Figure 8-10   Canyon de Chelly. (Photo courtesy of National Park Service, Department of the Interior.)

Finally, at a smaller scale, landforms and hardscape exposed to solar radiation affect comfort in several ways. Hardscape can be effectively used to collect, store, and radiate thermal energy, ameliorating cold microclimatic conditions. However, during the summer, unshaded hardscape surface temperatures can be significantly higher than those of vegetated landforms, increasing discomfort through the generation of oppressive

Figure 8-11   Canyon de Chelly. (Photo courtesy of National Park Service, Department of the Interior.)

levels of radiant heat and by further warming of the air. These surfaces continue to radiate heat well after sunset. This effect is commonly experienced in urban environments and in large paved areas such as parking lots. Landforms and hardscape also reflect some percentage of the light striking them, depending on the surface albedo rate. That reflected light can be used to daylight buildings but must be controlled to minimize glare.

In summary, the sun provides us with light and heat, drives the earth's climatic cycles, and significantly affects our perception of comfort. Its position relative to the earth's surface is precisely predictable. If properly designed, vegetation, architectural elements, landforms, and hardscape can be used to modify microclimates by admitting, obstructing, filtering, and reflecting solar radiation. Site planning decisions have an enormous impact on how solar radiation affects the exterior spaces and buildings we create. A thorough understanding of solar radiation principles and effects is therefore prerequisite to an effective site planning effort.

AIR TEMPERATURE

Description. The second climatic element with which we are concerned is air temperature. Dry-bulb temperature, commonly referring to air temperature, is the most common climatic reference when describing weather or feelings of comfort. It is the relative measure of the thermal energy (sensible heat) content of the air, as indicated by an ordinary thermometer.

Temperature differences are the driving force behind the heat-transfer processes of conduction, convection, and radiation which occur between the environment and our bodies and buildings. When a temperature differential exists between two masses (either solid or fluid), thermal energy is transferred *from* the area of higher temperature *to* the area of lower temperature.

Effects. Simply stated, temperature affects our sense of comfort, which in turn affects the amount of energy required to heat and cool our buildings. Disregarding other environmental factors, the relative effect of air temperature can be seen in the bioclimatic chart (Fig. 8-1), where comfort conditions exist in a fairly narrow range of temperatures. It is therefore important for the site planner to understand the dynamic behavior of air temperature. An air temperature profile for March 25, 1979, recorded at the Dallas–Fort Worth Regional Airport (DFW), is shown in Fig. 8-12. This was a day with cloudless skies, and it will be used to illustrate certain points concerning daily air temperature fluctuations.

The lowest temperature of the day occurs shortly before dawn. After the sun rises, the earth's surface is heated by solar radiation and the surface air layer is warmed by convection. Air temperature rises rapidly and peaks during mid-afternoon. From this high point, the temperature drops at a more gradual rate. As the earth's surface reradiates thermal energy to the clear night sky, the surface air layer slowly cools and temperatures drop until dawn. By contrast, the temperature profile for March 29, 1979, an overcast day, is quite different (Fig. 8-12). The cloud cover inhibits solar radiation from reaching the earth's surface. Some radiation does penetrate, however, which accounts for the slight warming trend in the afternoon. Cloud cover also inhibits night reradiation, which keeps the temperature of the earth's surface and the surface air layer relatively constant. Although general in nature, this overview of daily (diurnal) temperature fluctuations should provide an insight into air temperature dynamics. Methods for analyzing air temperature variations over longer periods of time are discussed in the section "General Climatic Analysis."

Control and Modification. The site planner has few opportunities to control or

Figure 8-12 Temperature profiles at D/FW.

modify air temperature directly. However, air temperature and comfort can be affected indirectly through control of solar radiation and air movement.

Vegetation.   As water changes to water vapor at leaf surfaces (transpiration), an energy exchange occurs. Thermal energy is extracted from the air during the evaporative process, lowering air temperature but raising humidity levels. Studies have suggested that this process can produce a significant amount of cooling in air temperature, and this may be true in the mesoclimatic regime with large, heavily vegetated parcels of land. However, due to the rapid mixing that occurs in the surface air layer caused by wind and temperature differences, the transpirational cooling produced at the microclimatic level by smaller areas of vegetation or individual trees is negligible.[18] The effects of shading, wind shielding, soil-moisture retention, transpiration, and night reradiation from the canopy in stands of vegetation do combine to alter air temperatures substantially, particularly those at ground level (Fig. 8-13). Although temperatures and humidities in the

Figure 8-13 Vegetation and temperature/humidity changes.

[18]McPherson, "Planting Design for Solar Control," p. 147 citing B. A. Hutchinson, F. G. Taylor, R. L., Wendt, and The Critical Review Panel, *Use of Vegetation to Ameliorate Building Microclimates: An Assessment of Energy Conservation Potentials* (No. 1913) (Oak Ridge, Tenn.: Oak Ridge National Laboratory, 1982), pp. 17–18.

Figure 8-14 The Alhambra: Granada.

canopy and understory fluctuate markedly, they remain relatively constant near the ground.[19]

Architectural Elements.   Fountains and other water features can have a beneficial impact on air temperature in hot, arid climates. The evaporative cooling process lowers air temperature and raises humidity levels, both of which promote comfort in hot, dry conditions. Water features are often located in courtyards protected from the wind, where they generate a ''pool'' of cool, heavy air which is retained by the court's walls (Fig. 8-14). In cold climates, building surfaces exposed to sun and protected from cold winds can create a ''sun pocket'' which is capable of raising localized air temperatures as much as 40°F (Fig. 8-15).[20]

Landforms and Hardscape.   Other than the effects produced by solar radiation, landforms and hardscape have limited influence on air temperature. However, it is important to note that topographical features on the site, such as valleys, ravines, or natural depressions, have the ability to collect cold air. Cold air flows downhill and will settle in low

Figure 8-15 Sun pocket.

[19]G. Robinette, ed., *Plants/People/and Environmental Quality* (Washington, D.C.: U.S. Department of the Interior, National Park Service, 1972), pp. 89 and 96.

[20]Robinette, *Energy Efficient Site Design*, p. 42 citing W. Langeweische, ''How to Fix Your Private Climate,'' *House Beautiful*, October 1949, p. 150.

spots on the site. These areas can be useful for collecting cooler air in predominantly warm climates, but pose problems in colder climates.

HUMIDITY

Description. The third climatic element to be discussed is humidity. Although it is referred to and measured in a variety of ways, relative humidity is the climatic reference with which most of us are familiar. It is defined as "the ratio of the actual vapor pressure of the air-vapor mixture to the pressure of saturated water vapor at the same dry-bulb temperature."[21]

Effects. Human tolerances for humidity variations are greater than for temperature variations. When air temperatures are elevated, high relative humidities limit the air's ability to evaporate moisture from our bodies, thereby increasing thermal stress and our sense of discomfort. High humidity also produces a significant thermal load on a building's air-conditioning equipment, which expends energy to remove moisture (latent heat) from the air. If high humidities are not sufficiently reduced, mildew problems can occur in buildings. In cold weather, high indoor humidity may result in condensation, usually on interior glass surfaces, which can damage materials and deteriorate finishes.

Low relative humidities can also create problems in buildings. Direct air-heating systems (without humidity control) significantly reduce the percentage humidity of circulating air. In addition to the drying effect on human respiratory passages, low humidities contribute to static electricity problems, which are of particular concern in the computerized work environment. Humidity control in buildings, such as hospitals, can be extremely important. Studies have indicated that the propagation of bacteria is minimized in the relative humidity range 50 to 55%.[22]

Like air temperature, relative humidity is cyclic in nature. In a very general sense, the maximum relative humidity during the course of a day without precipitation coincides with the minimum temperature, and the minimum relative humidity is coincident with the daily maximum temperature. This is certainly not always true but serves as a general model of the relationship between relative humidity and air temperature. If the moisture content of the air remains constant over the course of a day, as the air temperature rises the relative humidity decreases. When the air temperature falls, the relative humidity increases. This type of pattern is illustrated in Fig. 8-16, which shows the

Figure 8-16 Air temperature and humidity interrelationship.

[21]V. Bradshaw, *Building Control Systems* (New York: John Wiley & Sons, Inc., 1985), p. 26.

[22]M. D. Egan, *Concepts in Thermal Comfort* (Englewood Cliffs, N.J.: Prentice-Hall, Inc., 1975), p. 9.

temperature and relative humidity profiles at Dallas–Fort Worth Regional Airport on March 25, 1979. With the exception of 12 midnight on March 26, the correlation holds true.

As indicated earlier in the bioclimatic chart (Fig. 8-1), comfort conditions span a fairly wide range of relative humidity levels (between 18 and 77%). The desirable range exists on the chart between 30 and 65% relative humidity.[23] Analysis of the effects of relative humidity are discussed further in the section "General Climatic Analysis."

Control and Modification.   As with air temperature, the site planner's options for significant modification of relative humidity are limited. The primary concern with humidity is when air temperatures occur above the comfort zone. In hot, dry conditions, moisture can be added to the air (evaporative cooling or evapotranspiration from plants) to induce comfort (Fig. 8-1, upper left portion of bioclimatic chart). In hot, humid conditions, air movement is the only means to alleviate discomfort (Fig. 8-1, upper right portion of the bioclimatic chart).

Vegetation.   As indicated previously (Fig. 8-13), relative humidities often exceed ambient levels and air temperatures are diminished in dense stands of vegetation close to the ground. This situation could produce beneficial effects in hot, arid climates, but it is often difficult to maintain dense vegetation in such climates. In hot, humid climates, dense vegetation may be detrimental to comfort by increasing relative humidity and inhibiting air movement. Therefore, planning solutions using vegetation should be designed to provide effective shading which does not significantly retard air movement. Thinning underbrush and removing lower limbs of trees to a height of 8 to 10 feet promotes comforting airflow.

Plants are natural humidifiers and can be used to provide supplementary humidity in buildings. This is an appropriate strategy when air-heating systems reduce humidity levels in buildings during cold periods.

Architectural Elements.   When properly designed and protected, water features can raise humidity levels and lower temperature. This is essentially an adiabatic process where heat is not gained or lost but transformed from sensible to latent heat. Consider a hypothetical, perfectly protected courtyard with a fountain in a hot, arid climate, where the temperature is 90°F and the relative humidity is 20%, a point above Olgyay's comfort zone (Fig. 8-1). If enough moisture is evaporated from the fountain to raise the relative humidity of the air mass in the courtyard to 40%, the air temperature theoretically will drop to approximately 79°F, a point almost in the comfort zone. At 50% relative humidity, the temperature would drop to 75°F. (These temperature–humidity combinations occur along a line of constant enthalpy on the psychrometric chart. Refer to the discussion of psychrometric processes in *Mechanical and Electrical Equipment for Buildings*, 6th Ed., Chap. 5, for a detailed discussion.)

Because of the number of variables involved and the dynamic nature of the climatic elements, the effects of elevating humidity levels in exterior spaces are extremely difficult to quantify. For the purposes of this discussion, it is sufficient to understand that evaporative cooling can be useful in hot, arid climates. Increasing humidity levels in hot, humid conditions will increase discomfort, although active water features may offset this by providing "psychological cooling." Finally, it should be noted that areas of the site with poor drainage or low areas with standing water can elevate localized humidity levels, adversely affecting comfort in hot, humid climates.

---

[23]Olgyay, *Design with Climate*, p. 18.

Figure 8-17 Flow of air from forest to plain.

AIR MOVEMENT/WIND

Description. The final climatic element requiring discussion is air movement or wind. The site planner should be familiar with how specific site characteristics affect air motion and how local wind patterns vary seasonally. Knowledge of the speed and direction of the air mass close to the ground and its associated temperature can provide valuable information for siting buildings and planning exterior spaces, so as to protect against winds that are undesirable while taking advantage of those which are useful.

The distribution and characteristics of air movement over a region are affected by both global and local factors:[24]

1. The seasonal global distribution of air pressure
2. The earth's rotation about its axis
3. The daily variations in the heating and cooling of the land and sea
4. The topography of the region and its surroundings

Temperature and pressure differences affect local air movement and the microclimate of the site. Air flows from high-pressure areas to low-pressure areas. G. Z. Brown[25] describes an example of a meadow surrounded by a forest. As solar radiation heats the meadow air, its density and pressure decrease, causing it to rise. This air is replaced by cooler air flowing from the higher pressure zone of the forest (Fig. 8-17). Similarly, sun-warmed air in a valley flows uphill during the day (Fig. 8-18). The airflow is reversed at night as cold, dense air falls down the valley slopes (Fig. 8-19).[26]

Large bodies of water also affect daily air movement patterns, because they are normally cooler during the day and warmer at night than the adjacent land surface. Consequently, during the day as the warmed air over land rises, it is replaced by breezes of cooler air off the water (Fig. 8-20). The land surface and adjacent air mass cool rapidly at night, and the airflow reverses (Fig. 8-21).[27] Parenthetically, large bodies of water are cooler in summer and warmer in winter than inland areas, and therefore moderate seasonal temperature extremes of coastal sites.[28]

Figure 8-18 Air movement uphill—day.

---

[24]B. Givoni, *Man, Climate and Architecture*, 2nd ed. (New York: Van Nostrand Reinhold Company, Inc., 1981), p. 8.

[25]G. Z. Brown, *Sun, Wind, and Light* (New York: John Wiley & Sons, Inc., 1985), p. 26.

[26]Ibid., p. 27.

[27]Olgyay, *Design with Climate*, p. 51.

[28]Ibid.

Figure 8-19 Air movement shoreline, downhill—night.

Figure 8-20 Air movement shoreline—day.

Figure 8-21 Air movement shoreline—night.

Moving air behaves like a fluid and will take the path of least resistance as it flows over, under, around, and through objects in the landscape. Air flows smoothly around a streamlined object (Fig. 8-22). As illustrated in Figs. 8-23 and 8-24, when moving air encounters a nonstreamlined or "bluff" object, a high-pressure area and pressure eddies are created on the windward side of the object. As the air moves over or around the object, it compresses and its speed increases. A low-pressure area is created on the leeward side of the object, producing suction eddies and a turbulent wake. Having passed the object, the air mass begins to resume its original pattern of flow. The area of protection between the object and the point where the wind resumes its normal flow is referred to as the "wind shadow." The highest wind speeds occur at the windward corners and along the sides of the object parallel to the flow, while a relatively calm area is produced at the leeward side. Any modification or addition to the object will alter

Figure 8-22 Air movement around streamlined object.

Figure 8-23 Air movement around rectangular object.

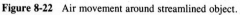

Figure 8-24 Air movement around rectangular object.

the pattern of airflow around it. The object under discussion could be dense vegetation, a building, landform, or hardscape. The general principles of air motion apply to all.

Effects

Cold winds are disagreeable, hot winds enervating, moist winds unhealthy.
Vitruvius, The Ten Books on Architecture[29]

Air movement affects both our perception of thermal comfort and the amount of energy required to maintain thermally comfortable conditions in buildings. Cold winds increase our sense of discomfort by increasing the rate of heat loss from our bodies. This effect is commonly described by the wind chill factor, which combines the effect of wind and air temperature to produce an ''apparent'' air temperature lower than the actual air temperature. For example, at 30°F, a wind velocity of 25 mph produces a wind chill temperature of 0°F.[30] Cold winds can also affect comfort-energy requirements in buildings by increasing heat loss rates through the building ''skin'' and by increasing infiltration or air-leakage rates.

Temperate winds can be useful in promoting thermal comfort in both outdoor and indoor settings. In the outdoor environment, air movement promotes the evaporative cooling of our bodies and is essential for reducing discomfort when high temperatures are associated with high relative humidities. As indicated by the bioclimatic chart (Fig. 8-1), a wind speed of approximately 2.5 miles per hour can produce comfort when the temperature is 80°F with 80% relative humidity. It is also apparent that air movement is important even when relative humidities are not high (Fig. 8-1, e.g., 90°F, 30% relative humidity). Temperate winds are also useful for ventilating buildings and cooling occupants, thereby reducing mechanical cooling requirements.

Control and Modification.   When discussing the control or modification of air movement, it is important to understand the nature of air motion and how it can be affected by design decisions and various site features. Seasonal wind patterns are fairly predictable, and effective site planning for wind control can divert discomforting winds while admitting or channeling useful winds. The identification of seasonal wind patterns is discussed in the section ''General Climatic Analysis.''

Figure 8-25   Vegetation as windbreak. (Photo by Kenneth Roemer.)

---

[29]Vitruvius, *Ten Books on Architecture*, p. 24.
[30]ASHRAE, p. 8.17.

Figure 8-26 Vegetation as windbreak. (Photo by Kenneth Roemer.)

Vegetation. Vegetation can control or modify wind by obstruction, diversion, guidance, and filtration. When vegetation is used to protect exterior spaces and buildings from cold winter winds, it is referred to as a *shelterbelt* or *windbreak* (Figs. 8-25 and 8-26). The direction of seasonal winds and those winds associated with cold weather events, such as winter cold fronts, are predictable with some certainty, allowing the site planner to determine the most effective location for shelterbelts.

Airflow is affected by the geometry and density of the shelterbelt. Figure 8-27 indicates the general effects on air flowing perpendicular to a moderately dense shelterbelt 30 feet tall. Airflow can be affected for a distance 5 to 10 times the barrier height on the windward side, and up to 30 times the barrier height on the leeward side.[31] When airflow is oblique to the barrier, the area of protection will be reduced.

The relative density or penetrability of the shelterbelt affects leeward wind speeds and the size of the wind shadow. The suction eddies on the leeward side of a barrier pull the airflow back toward the ground. Dense barriers produce more suction than penetrable barriers. Dense vegetation provides a greater reduction of wind speeds close to the shelterbelt but a shorter wind shadow. The effects of more penetrable vegetation extend farther beyond the shelterbelt because airflow through the barrier reduces the suction pressures on the leeward side. The graph in Fig. 8-28 indicates the effects of shelterbelt density on airflow.[32]

Evergreen vegetation is effective for year-round wind control, while deciduous vegetation is effective when foliated. It should also be noted that a shelterbelt that is open near the ground, such as a screen of high-branching trees, measurably increases wind velocity immediately beneath and just beyond the screen.[33] A detailed discussion of shelterbelts can be found in *Plants, People, and Environmental Quality* by G. O. Robinette.

Figure 8-27 Windbreak: effects on airflow.

---

[31]Robinette. *Plants/People/and Environmental Quality*, p. 78.

[32]Ibid., pp. 78–79.

[33]Ibid., p. 77 citing R. F. White, *Effects of Landscape Development on the Natural Ventilation of Buildings and Their Adjacent Areas*, Texas Engineering Experiment Station Research Report 45 (College Station, Tex.: Texas Engineering Experiment Station, 1945), p. 25.

Shelterbelt Density vs Wind Velocity

----- Open

— — Moderately Dense

——— Very Dense

Figure 8-28 Shelterbelt density versus wind velocity.

In addition to diverting discomforting winds, properly designed windbreaks can direct desirable winds through exterior spaces. The windbreak illustrated in Fig. 8-29 is designed for a site where cold winds arrive primarily from the north and northwest, and temperate winds are from the south. The windbreak protects the building and yard space from cold winter winds while helping to channel southerly winds through the side and rear yards.

Smaller screens of vegetation can also be used to direct airflow through exterior spaces and buildings. Figure 8-30 illustrates how two different dense hedge placements produce essentially the same effects on airflow through a small building.[34]

Architectural Elements.   The primary architectural elements that influence airflow are buildings, walls, and fences. Like vegetation, buildings, or groups of buildings, can be used for wind control. In cold climates and hot, arid climates, buildings and exterior

Figure 8-29 Windbreak designed for seasonal wind patterns.

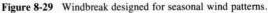

[34]Olgyay, *Design with Climate*, p. 102.

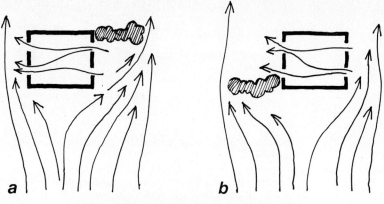

Figure 8-30 Diversion of airflow through building.

spaces often huddle together, avoiding discomforting winds (Fig. 8-31). In hot, humid climates, buildings can be spaced apart to admit comforting winds (Fig. 8-32). Small elements like gazebos are usually designed to provide access to comforting winds as well as shade.

Large urban structures can produce extremely discomforting, even dangerous winds at street level. The urban pedestrian is often faced with wind gusts that may make walking difficult, and with airborne dust and debris. An excellent discussion of urban wind and its control can be found in *Improving Street Climate through Urban Design* by Charles Thurow.

Walls and fences, as objects in the airstream, can be used to divert or channel winds and produce effects similar to the shelterbelts discussed previously. Again, the

Figure 8-31 Settlement in hot-arid climate.

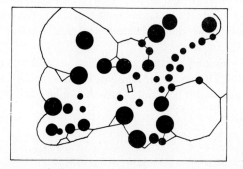

Figure 8-32 Settlement in hot-humid climate.

Figure 8-33 Berm deflecting airflow.

effects on airflow are dependent on barrier geometry (height and length) and penetrability.[35]

Landforms. As wind flows over and around hills, the highest wind velocities occur at the crest and on the windward side of the hill. Protected areas occur on the leeward side. Landforms such as berms also affect airflow and can be used to divert or channel winds (Fig. 8-33).

INFORMATION SOURCES AND INTERPRETATION

Information on the climatic elements is readily available, and an analysis of local climate can be used to inform decision making in the site planning process. Initial site planning decisions which consider the impact of climate can eliminate some difficult compromises that might otherwise occur in later stages of the design process. The acquisition of climatic information is discussed in this section. Discussion of the analysis of this information follows in the section "General Climatic Analysis."

Ideally, instrumentation would be set up on the site to monitor the microclimate for an extended period of time prior to the site planning process. The expense and time requirements make this an impractical approach, and the site planner must rely on other sources of information. The climatic information the site planner often ends up using has been recorded somewhere quite remote from the site being analyzed. Often referred to as "macroclimatic data" and representing the general climatic characteristics of a region, it is recorded in or close to many major urban areas. It is in reality a record of the microclimate at the weather recording station. Data may therefore require some adjustment to more closely reflect actual conditions at the building site.

Table 8-3 indicates the general climatic differences between urban and rural sites at a similar elevation and latitude. As site elevation increases above the weather station, air temperature decreases. A rule of thumb for estimating these effects is that temperature will drop 1°F for each 330 ft of elevation increase in the summer and each 400 ft in the winter.[36]

Coastal sites and sites located only a few miles inland may experience significant differences in temperature, wind flow, radiation, and humidity levels.[37] Due to the unpredictability of these differences, local experts should be consulted.

Wind instruments at weather stations are usually located well above ground level (22 ft at Dallas–Fort Worth Regional Airport, as indicated in *Local Climatological Data*). Since wind velocity generally increases with elevation, the wind velocity close to the ground at a nearby building site is generally less than weather station data would indicate.

The primary source of climatic information used in this text is the National Climatic Data Center (NCDC) under the National Oceanic and Atmospheric Administration (NOAA) in Asheville, North Carolina. Data should be obtained for a recording station

---

[35]For more information, see Robinette, *Energy Efficient Site Design*, pp. 68–70.
[36]Olgyay, *Design with Climate*, p. 44.
[37]Ibid., p. 45.

TABLE 8-3 Climatic Alterations Produced by Cities

ELEMENT		COMPARED TO RURAL ENVIRONS
Contaminants	Particulates	10 times more
	Gaseous admixtures	5–25 times more
Radiation	Total on horizontal surface	0–20% less
	Sunshine duration	5–15% less
Cloudiness	Clouds	5–10% more
	Fog, winter	100% more
	Fog, summer	30% more
Precipitation	Amounts	5–15% more
	Thunderstorms	10–15% more
	Snowfall, inner city	5–10% less
	Snowfall, lee of city	10% more
Temperature	Annual mean	1–5°F more
	Winter minima (average)	2–3.5°F more
	Summer maxima	2–5°F more
	Heating degree days	10% less
Relative humidity	Annual mean	6% less
	Winter	2% less
	Summer	8% less
Wind speed	Annual mean	20–30% less
	Extreme gusts	10–20% less
	Calm	5–20% more

Source: C. Thurow, *Improving Street Climate through Urban Design.* Planning Advisory Service Report Number 376 (Chicago: American Planning Association, 1983), p. 2 citing H. E. Landsberg, *The Urban Climate* (New York: Academic Press, Inc., 1981), pp. 119–120.

close to the building site, or a station with similar climatic characteristics. A list of weather-recording stations for which local climatological data can be obtained from NOAA/NCDC is contained in Appendix A.

SOLAR GEOMETRY

The sun's position relative to any point or object on the earth's surface is described by its altitude angle (angle A) and azimuth (or bearing) angle (angle B) (Fig. 8-3). The altitude angle indicates the vertical position of the sun, while the azimuth angle describes the horizontal position of the sun relative to *true south.* (It should be noted that magnetic orientation and solar orientation are different. Magnetic north is different from true north.[38] All ensuing references to orientation will relate to solar orientation.) Solar angles can be obtained from the *sun angle calculator*, a "tool" that provides a quick graphic method for determining altitude and azimuth angles for various latitudes. It also provides other useful information on profile and incidence angles. It can be obtained for a modest price from Libbey–Owens–Ford Company (811 Madison Avenue, Toledo, OH, 43695). Because of the graphic format, the sun angle calculator provides an "image" of solar geometry and seasonal sunpaths which is not readily apparent from solar angle tables. This device is extremely useful for determining shadowing and designing sun-shading devices for buildings.

The altitude and azimuth angles can be used to project plan shadows to determine the location and extent of daily and seasonal shadows on the building site. Figure 8-34 illustrates the determination of shadowing on a flat site from a 30-ft-tall cone-shaped tree and a square building of the same height, when the azimuth angle is 30° west of

---

[38]*Sun Angle Calculator* (Toledo, Ohio: Libbey-Owens-Ford Company).

Figure 8-34 Shadow projections.

true south and the altitude angle is 59° (32° north latitude, September 11, 1:00 P.M.). The length of the shadow is determined by the equation

$$SL = \frac{H}{\tan{(Alt)}}$$

where

SL = shadow length
H = height of the object or edge casting the shadow
Alt = sun's altitude angle

$$SL = \frac{30}{\tan{(59°)}} = \frac{30}{1.6643} = 18.02 \text{ ft}$$

The shadow length of 18 ft is then scaled along the azimuth lines projected from the objects (Fig. 8-34).

Figure 8-35 Sun peg.

(a)   (b)

Figure 8-36 Solar transit.

This process is normally complicated by topographical changes and shadows falling across other objects. When this occurs, plan/section/elevation projections are often required to determine the precise location of shadows. It is critical for the site planner to understand solar geometry and its implications for site design, and seasonal shading comparisons for a site can be developed using the techniques that have been described. However, even relatively simple sites require a tedious series of calculations and drawings to produce seasonal shading comparisons. A simplified method for determining seasonal site shading is available—the *sun peg* (Fig. 8-35). This tool, when used in conjunction with a site model, quickly indicates site shading for each hour of the twenty-first day of each month of the year.

Sun pegs are simple to construct and use. Photocopy the sun peg chart from Appendix B which most closely corresponds to your latitude. Attach it to a stiff piece of cardboard or foam core and "erect" a gnomon peg to the height indicated on the chart. Place the sun peg on your site model, with the north arrow aligned to true north on the site, making sure that the sun peg lies "flat." By tilting the site model and sun peg in the sunlight, the gnomon's shadow can be manipulated to indicate the time of day and month of the year, and seasonal shading comparisons can quickly be developed.

One final tool will be mentioned. An inexpensive, home-made *solar transit* was developed by Charles Benton, James Akridge, and Scott Wright (Georgia Institute of Technology) (Fig. 8-36). This is a very useful instructional device which provides a good sense of seasonal solar geometry, and can be used to establish solar access and shading for specific points on the site.[39]

---

[39]Instructions for constructing and operating the solar transit can be found in the following document, which was distributed to schools of architecture as part of a curriculum development package: C. Benton and J. Akridge, "Solar Site Analysis," *Laboratory Exercises* (prepared for the U.S. Department of Energy Passive Solar Curriculum Project, *Teaching Passive Design in Architecture*, June 1981).

CLIMATOLOGICAL DATA

There are a number of publications that can be used for climatic analysis, available from the National Environmental Satellite, Data, and Information Service at the National Climatic Data Center (NCDC), Asheville, NC 28801-2696, (704)259-0682. Telephone ordering is recommended, and rush delivery can be purchased.

Local Climatological Data—Annual Summary with Comparative Data
Information on normal climatic conditions is available for individual locations listed in Appendix A. In addition to the one-page ''Narrative Climatological Summary'' included in the *Annual Summary*, ''Normals, Means, and Extremes'' for the weather recording station are identified (Table 8-4) and are the source of information dealing with normal ranges of temperature, and humidity, and sky conditions.

As shown in Table 8-4, normal temperature information is presented under ''temperatures (°F)'' in the second, third, and fourth columns. For the month indicated, the second column represents the normal daily maximum temperature, the third column the normal daily minimum temperature, and the fourth column the normal daily average temperature. Under ''relative humidity (%)'' are listed normal relative humidity values for midnight, 6 A.M., 12 noon, and 6 P.M. (listed in military time). Finally, in the first three columns, under ''mean number of days'' (''sunrise to sunset''), information on sky conditions is presented (the mean number of ''clear,'' ''partly cloudy,'' and ''cloudy'' days for the month indicated). The application of this information is discussed in the section ''General Climatic Analysis.''

Comparative Climatic Data for the United States
For our purposes, this publication provides essentially the same temperature and sky condition information as that in *Local Climatological Data*, with less humidity information. Information is listed for over 250 locations around the country. A typical format is shown in Table 8-5.

Airport Climatological Summary—(CLIM90)
In addition to temperature, relative humidity, and sky condition information, Table 11.A in this publication provides information on wind direction and coincident wind speed for each month of the year as well as totals for the year. Table 8-6 indicates the format of the information. The percentage of observations occurring for a given direction and individual wind speed group is given. The total percentage of observations for a given wind direction is listed under ''total.'' This information will be used to construct wind roses for climatic analysis.

SMOS—Summary of Meteorological Observations, Surface: Part E—Psychrometric Summaries
This publication provides data on wind direction and associated air temperature, as illustrated in Table 8-7, in addition to a great deal of other psychrometric information. Data is recorded at present and former military installations.

The first three publications can be considered interchangeable, and provide all the temperature, humidity, and sky condition information required for general climatic analysis. One of these inexpensive publications should be ordered from NCDC. The third publication provides necessary wind information and should be ordered for the weather station nearest your site. The last publication listed is used in this book to clarify certain issues regarding the bivariate frequency analysis of wind direction and temperature and is not essential for climatic analysis as described herein.

The preceding discussion has focused on a range of climatic information sources. During analysis, it is important to remain aware of the differences between the building

TABLE 8-4 Normals, Means, and Extremes[a,b]

Month	Temp Normal Daily Max	Temp Normal Daily Min	Temp Normal Monthly	Extremes Record Highest	Year	Extremes Record Lowest	Year	Degree Days Heating	Degree Days Cooling	Precip Water Equiv Normal	Precip Max Monthly	Year	Precip Max 24 hr	Year	Precip Min Monthly	Year	Snow Max Monthly	Year	Snow Max 24 hr	Year	RH 00	RH 06	RH 12	RH 18	Wind Mean Speed	Prevailing Dir	Fastest Mile Speed	Dir	Year	Mean Sky Cover	Clear	Partly Cloudy	Cloudy	Precip .01+	Snow 1.0+	Thunderstorms	Heavy Fog	Max 90+	Max 32 below	Min 32 below	Min 0 below	Avg Sta Pressure
(yrs of record)				12		12					22		22		22		22		22		12	12	12	12	22	10	22	22	22	22	22	22	22	22	22	22	22	12	12	12	12	3
J	55.7	33.9	44.8	88	1969	4	1964	626	0	1.80	3.60	1968	2.39	1971	0.19	1968	12.1	1964	12.1	1964	75	82	61	59	11.5	S	46	36	1957	6.1	10	6	15	7	1	1	3	0	1	14	0	998.4
F	59.8	37.6	48.7	87	1969	12	1971	456	0	2.36	6.20	1965	4.06	1963	0.15	1965	3.7	1975	3.7	1975	71	80	57	52	12.3	S	51	36	1962	5.6	10	7	12	7	1	2	2	0	T	10	0	997.9
M	66.6	43.3	55.0	96	1974	19	1965	335	25	2.54	6.39	1968	2.99	1972	0.10	1968	2.5	1962	2.5	1962	74	80	57	51	13.3	S	55	29	1954	5.8	9	7	14	7	T	4	1	T	0	4	0	992.2
A	76.3	54.1	65.2	95	1972	30	1973	88	94	4.30	12.19	1957	4.55	1959	0.92	1957	0.0		0.0		75	85	59	54	13.1	S	55	32	1970	6.1	9	7	14	8	0	7	T	1	0	T	0	993.9
M	82.8	62.1	72.5	96	1967	42	1971	0	236	4.47	12.64	1957	4.86	1961	1.06	1957	0.0		0.0		80	88	62	59	11.4	S	55	14	1955	5.8	8	11	12	8	0	7	T	3	0	0	0	991.5
J	90.8	70.3	80.6	105	1972	51	1964	0	468	3.05	6.94	1962	3.11	1964	0.40	1962	0.0		0.0		74	86	57	52	11.0	S	52	32	1955	4.8	11	11	8	6	0	6	T	19	0	0	0	992.8
J	95.5	74.0	84.8	106	1974	59	1972	0	614	1.84	11.13	1973	3.76	1965	0.09	1973	0.0		0.0		68	81	50	45	9.7	S	65	36	1961	4.3	15	9	7	5	0	5	0	27	0	0	0	994.6
A	96.1	73.7	84.9	108	1964	56	1967	0	617	2.26	6.85	1970	3.30	1973	0.01	1970	0.0		0.0		70	83	53	48	9.3	S	73	36	1959	4.3	15	10	6	5	0	5	T	25	0	0	0	994.8
S	88.5	66.8	77.7	102	1963	46	1971	0	381	3.15	9.52	1964	4.76	1956	0.23	1964	0.0		0.0		79	88	60	58	9.7	S	53	11	1961	4.8	13	8	9	7	0	4	1	11	0	0	0	995.3
O	79.2	56.0	67.6	96	1963	37	1966	60	141	2.68	9.22	1959	2.83	1970	0.20	1959	0.0		0.0		76	85	56	57	9.9	S	44	27	1957	4.5	14	7	10	5	0	3	1	2	0	0	0	997.6
N	67.5	44.1	55.8	88	1965	22	1975	287	11	2.03	6.23	1964	3.10	1955	0.21	1971	g	1974	g	1974	75	82	56	58	10.9	S	50	34	1957	5.0	13	5	12	6	T	2	1	0	0	3	0	997.4
D	58.7	37.0	47.9	84	1966	10	1963	530	0	1.82	6.99	1971		1963			2.6	1963	2.5	1963	76	81	60	60	11.2	S	53	32	1968	5.6	12	6	13	7	T	1	3	0	T	9	0	997.8
YR	76.5	54.4	65.5	108	Aug. 1964	4	Jan. 1964	2382	2587	32.30	12.64	Oct. 1957	5.91	Oct. 1975	g	May 1957	12.1	Jan. 1964	12.1	Jan. 1964	74	83	57	55	11.1	S	73	36	Aug. 1959	5.2	140	93	132	79	1	45	11	88	2	39	0	995.4

Elevation 525 ft m.s.l.

[a] Means and extremes are from existing and comparable exposures. Annual extremes have been exceeded at other sites in the locality as follows: Highest temperature 112 in August 1936; lowest temperature −8 in February 1899; maximum monthly precipitation 17.64 in April 1922; minimum monthly precipitation 0.00 in November 1903; maximum precipitation in 24 hours 9.57 in September 1932.

[b] Normals, based on record for the 1941–1970 period.

[c] Prevailing wind direction, record through 1963; wind direction, numerals indicate tens of degrees clockwise from true north, 00 indicates calm; fastest mile wind, speed is fastest observed 1-minute value when the direction is in tens of degrees.

[d] 70°F and above at Alaskan stations.

[e] Length of record, years, through the current year unless otherwise noted, based on January data.

[f] Less than one-half.

[g] Trace.

Source: National Climatic Data Center, *Local Climatological Data—Annual Summary with Comparative Data* (Asheville, N.C.: National Oceanic and Atmospheric Administration).

TABLE 8-5   Normal Daily Maximum Temperature (°F)

NORMALS 1951–1980	YEARS	JAN.	FEB.	MAR.	APR.	MAY	JUNE	JULY	AUG.	SEPT.	OCT.	NOV.	DEC.	ANNUAL
Birmingham C.O., Ala.	30	51.7	56.6	64.8	75.0	81.7	88.2	90.6	89.8	84.1	73.5	62.3	54.5	72.7
Birmingham AP, Ala.	30	52.7	57.3	65.2	75.2	81.6	87.9	90.3	89.7	84.6	74.8	63.7	55.9	73.2
Huntsville, Ala.	30	49.4	53.9	61.9	73.0	79.9	86.8	89.4	89.2	83.5	73.4	61.6	53.0	71.2
Mobile, Ala.	30	60.6	63.9	70.3	78.3	84.9	90.2	91.2	90.7	87.0	79.4	69.3	63.1	77.4
Montgomery, Ala.	30	57.0	60.9	68.1	77.0	83.6	89.8	91.5	91.2	86.9	77.5	67.0	59.8	75.9
Anchorage, Alaska	30	20.0	25.5	31.7	42.6	54.2	61.8	65.1	63.2	55.2	40.8	27.9	20.4	42.4
Annette, Alaska	30	37.3	41.3	43.3	49.1	55.7	60.5	64.1	64.6	60.0	51.8	44.2	39.9	51.0
Barrow, Alaska	30	−8.0	−13.8	−9.7	5.4	23.6	37.4	44.6	42.4	33.8	18.9	4.6	−7.0	14.4
Barter Is., Alaska	30	−8.5	−14.3	−9.5	7.0	26.1	38.1	45.3	43.7	35.0	20.4	5.7	−6.7	15.2
Bethel, Alaska	30	11.8	13.1	19.3	31.7	48.7	58.9	62.1	59.4	52.0	35.6	23.7	11.3	35.6
Bettles, Alaska	30	−6.5	−0.6	12.1	31.6	52.5	67.2	69.0	62.7	48.8	25.5	6.2	−4.7	30.3
Big Delta, Alaska	30	0.8	11.0	23.0	40.5	56.5	66.7	69.4	65.0	52.7	31.7	14.6	2.3	36.2
Cold Bay, Alaska	30	32.8	32.2	33.6	37.7	44.3	50.0	54.9	55.4	52.0	44.2	38.8	33.9	42.5
Fairbanks, Alaska	30	−3.9	7.3	21.7	40.8	59.2	70.1	71.8	66.5	54.4	32.6	12.4	−1.7	35.9
Gulkana, Alaska	30	0.2	13.8	27.2	41.8	54.6	64.9	68.4	64.8	54.0	35.7	14.7	1.8	36.8
Homer, Alaska	30	27.0	31.2	34.4	42.1	49.8	56.3	60.5	60.3	54.8	44.0	34.9	27.7	43.6
Juneau, Alaska	30	27.4	33.7	37.4	46.8	54.7	61.1	64.0	62.6	55.9	47.0	37.5	31.5	46.6
King Salmon, Alaska	30	20.0	22.9	27.6	38.7	50.8	58.9	62.9	61.3	54.7	40.5	30.0	19.7	40.7
Kodiak, Alaska	30	36.6	34.8	38.3	43.3	48.4	56.1	59.3	61.0	55.9	47.1	39.9	35.2	46.3
Kotzebue, Alaska	30	3.7	1.3	8.0	21.5	38.6	49.8	58.7	56.9	46.9	27.8	13.6	2.2	27.4
McGrath, Alaska	30	−1.1	9.1	21.5	37.5	54.9	65.5	68.0	63.5	52.7	31.8	13.4	−0.8	34.7
Nome, Alaska	30	13.4	11.8	15.7	25.8	42.1	52.0	56.6	55.7	48.5	33.8	22.7	12.0	32.5
St. Paul Island, Alaska	30	30.4	26.4	28.2	32.0	38.6	45.1	49.4	50.8	48.4	41.7	37.2	32.2	38.4
Talkeetna, Alaska	30	17.9	25.3	32.0	43.7	55.9	64.8	67.8	64.5	55.6	39.8	26.3	17.7	42.6
Unalakleet, Alaska	30	10.3	12.0	18.0	30.1	45.5	55.3	60.5	58.3	50.5	33.1	19.3	8.2	33.4
Valdez, Alaska	30	29.3	30.0	36.2	43.9	51.1	57.5	62.1	61.5	54.1	43.2	33.8	25.1	44.0
Yakutat, Alaska	30	30.1	34.8	37.2	43.2	49.7	55.6	59.5	59.7	55.3	47.2	38.4	32.7	45.3
Flagstaff, Ariz.	30	41.7	44.5	48.6	57.1	66.7	77.6	81.9	78.9	74.1	63.7	51.0	43.6	60.8
Phoenix, Ariz.	30	65.2	69.7	74.5	83.1	92.4	102.3	105.0	102.3	98.2	87.7	74.3	66.4	85.1
Tucson, Ariz.	30	64.1	67.4	71.8	80.1	88.8	98.5	98.5	95.9	93.5	84.1	72.2	65.0	81.7
Winslow, Ariz.	30	45.0	53.2	60.7	70.0	79.9	91.0	94.5	91.1	85.2	73.1	57.9	46.0	70.6
Yuma, Ariz.	30	68.6	73.9	78.5	85.7	93.6	102.9	106.8	105.3	101.4	90.9	77.4	69.1	87.8
Fort Smith, Ark.	30	48.4	53.8	62.5	73.7	81.0	88.5	93.6	92.9	85.7	75.9	61.9	52.1	72.5
Little Rock, Ark.	30	49.8	54.5	63.2	73.8	81.7	89.5	92.7	92.3	85.6	75.8	62.4	53.2	72.9
North Little Rock, Ark.	30	48.6	53.6	62.0	73.1	80.3	87.5	91.6	90.7	84.0	74.5	61.2	51.9	71.6
Bakersfield, Calif.	30	57.4	63.7	68.6	75.1	83.9	92.2	98.8	96.4	90.8	81.0	67.4	57.6	77.7
Bishop, Calif.	30	52.9	58.2	63.4	70.9	80.2	90.4	97.5	95.2	88.2	77.1	63.5	55.1	74.4
Blue Canyon, Calif.	30	43.5	44.9	45.3	51.3	60.3	69.2	77.7	76.5	72.4	62.8	51.4	46.3	58.5
Eureka, Calif.	30	53.4	54.6	54.0	54.7	57.0	59.1	60.3	61.3	62.2	60.3	57.5	54.5	57.4
Fresno, Calif.	30	54.2	61.2	66.5	73.7	82.7	91.1	97.9	95.5	90.3	79.9	65.2	54.4	76.1
Long Beach, Calif.	30	66.0	67.3	68.0	70.9	73.4	77.4	83.0	83.8	82.5	78.4	72.7	67.4	74.2
Los Angeles AP, Calif.	30	64.6	65.5	65.1	66.7	69.1	72.0	75.3	76.5	76.4	74.0	70.3	66.1	70.1
Los Angeles C.O., Calif.	30	66.6	68.5	68.7	70.9	73.2	77.9	83.8	84.1	83.0	78.5	72.7	68.1	74.7
Mount Shasta, Calif.	30	42.1	47.3	50.9	57.9	67.0	75.4	85.1	83.3	77.5	65.4	50.9	43.9	62.2
Red Bluff, Calif.	30	53.9	60.0	64.0	71.2	81.2	90.3	98.2	95.7	90.4	78.8	63.6	55.2	75.2
Sacramento, Calif.	30	52.6	59.4	64.1	71.0	79.7	87.4	93.3	91.7	87.6	77.7	63.2	53.2	73.4
San Diego, Calif.	30	65.2	66.4	65.9	67.8	68.6	71.3	75.6	77.6	76.8	74.6	69.9	66.1	70.5
San Francisco AP, Calif.	30	55.5	59.0	60.6	63.0	66.3	69.6	71.0	71.8	73.4	70.0	62.7	56.3	64.9
San Francisco C.O., Calif.	30	56.1	59.4	60.0	61.1	62.5	64.3	64.0	65.0	68.9	68.3	62.9	56.9	62.5
Santa Barbara, Calif.	30	63.3	64.4	65.0	66.6	68.4	71.1	73.6	74.8	75.0	72.5	69.0	64.8	69.0

Source: National Climatic Data Center, *Comparative Climatic Data for the United States* (Asheville, N.C.: National Oceanic and Atmospheric Administration).

site and the weather recording station. Following is a discussion of climatic data analysis as it relates to the site planning process.

GENERAL CLIMATIC ANALYSIS

In this section we focus on planning for thermal comfort in exterior spaces. In this regard, the purpose of climatic analysis is to identify those areas on the site which are most appropriate for the location of exterior spaces and buildings. During the initial site microclimate analysis, it is important to remember that at least six new submicroclimates

TABLE 8-6 Wind Direction versus Wind Speed (Percent Frequency of Observations) All Weather[a]

| WIND DIRECTION | WIND SPEED (KNOTS) | | | | | | | | | | |
	0–3	4–6	7–10	11–16	17–21	22–27	28–33	34–40	Over 40	Total	Average Speed
N	0.4	2.7	2.5	1.9	0.2					7.6	8.3
NNE	0.3	1.4	1.7	1.1	0.2					4.7	8.6
NE	0.4	1.1	1.6	0.7						3.8	7.7
ENE	0.5	0.8	0.9	0.1						2.3	6.2
E	0.5	2.7	1.8	0.5						5.5	6.7
ESE	0.3	3.2	1.6	0.6						5.6	6.6
SE	0.4	2.9	3.8	1.5	0.0					8.7	7.7
SSE	0.3	2.7	5.7	4.2	0.7	0.0				13.7	9.6
S	0.6	3.3	7.0	9.2	2.1	0.3				22.4	11.0
SSW	0.1	1.8	2.9	3.1	0.6	0.0				8.6	10.2
SW	0.4	1.0	0.8	0.5	0.2					2.9	7.6
WSW	0.2	0.4	0.5	0.2						1.2	6.9
W	0.2	0.8	0.4	0.1	0.0					1.5	6.3
WNW	0.1	0.4	0.3	0.3	0.1					1.1	8.9
NW	0.1	0.8	0.6	0.5						2.0	8.0
NNW	0.2	1.7	1.4	1.0						4.4	7.9
CALM	4.2									4.2	
Total	9.0	27.6	33.4	25.5	4.1	0.4				100.0	8.5

[a]*All weather: all wind observations.*

Source: National Climatic Data Center, *Airport Climatological Summary—(CLIM90)* (Asheville, N.C.: National Oceanic and Atmospheric Administration).

will be created in, on, and around a building when it is placed on the site. Therefore, the initial analysis should always be reevaluated when locating buildings on the site.

The initial site microclimate inventory should establish the general climatic conditions of the building site. The first step is to identify normal temperature and humidity conditions and plot them on the bioclimatic chart (Fig. 8-1). This provides the site planner with an "image" of local temperature and humidity ranges and roughly identifies those times of the year when conditions of thermal comfort are likely to exist. In addition, appropriate remedial measures are suggested by this analysis for those conditions occurring outside the comfort zone.

As discussed previously in the section "Humidity," the lowest daily temperature and highest daily humidity can be considered to occur at the same time of day. Similarly, it can be assumed that the maximum daily temperature coincides with the minimum relative humidity. (These assumptions apply to a day without precipitation.) Using the temperature and relative humidity data obtained from either *Local Climatological Data* or *Comparative Climatic Data* (see "Information Sources and Interpretation"), plot the point representing normal daily maximum temperature and the lowest relative humidity for January on the bioclimatic chart. Then plot the normal daily minimum temperature and the highest relative humidity value. A "line" representing the temperature–humidity conditions for a normal day of the month in question is produced by connecting these two points. Repeat this process for each month, or every other month, to generate a picture of the normal temperature–humidity conditions over the course of a year. Figure 8-37 represents the normal conditions at Dallas–Fort Worth Regional Airport (DFW). The temperature–humidity data used to plot the month of January were obtained from *Local Climatological Data*—"Normals, Means, and Extremes" (Table 8-4). For example, the points representing January are:

Point 1:   55.7°F   59% relative humidity
Point 2:   33.9°F   82% relative humidity

TABLE 8-7   Percentage Frequency of Air Temperature versus Wind Direction

93901	Dallas, Texas		Jan. 1973-Dec. 1977		All	All
Station	Station Name		Years		Month	Hours

TEMP.	WIND DIRECTION								Calm	Total Freq.	Percent of Total
	NNW & N	NNE & NE	ENE & E	ESE & SE	SSE & S	SSW & SW	WSW W	WNW & NW			
122+											
117–121											
112–116											
107–111			50.0						50.0	2	.0
102–106			23.5	29.4	17.6	5.9	5.9		17.6	17	.1
97–101	4.8	1.6	11.1	19.0	46.0	7.1	4.0	.8	5.6	126	.9
92–96	1.3	3.9	5.8	16.4	57.0	8.4	2.0	1.9	3.4	537	3.7
87–91	3.7	4.7	9.5	19.4	48.0	6.4	2.8	1.7	3.8	811	5.6
82–86	3.7	4.6	8.9	17.2	49.6	8.6	2.3	1.4	3.7	1247	8.5
77–81	4.8	4.3	7.6	17.3	45.5	9.5	2.4	2.0	6.7	1739	11.9
72–76	7.9	4.6	7.5	15.9	41.8	10.3	2.0	2.2	7.9	1833	12.5
67–71	9.4	7.3	7.3	12.8	38.0	7.9	3.8	5.3	8.2	1426	9.8
62–66	12.3	4.9	7.6	12.8	33.3	8.1	4.2	7.0	9.7	1338	9.2
57–61	17.2	6.5	5.9	9.8	27.4	8.9	6.5	7.9	9.7	1133	7.8
52–56	15.9	6.3	6.8	9.5	24.7	10.1	5.1	11.5	10.1	1087	7.4
47–51	18.9	6.4	7.3	7.3	17.2	9.5	7.2	14.4	11.8	977	6.7
42–46	23.6	6.6	5.8	9.2	15.2	8.5	5.4	14.1	11.6	850	5.8
37–41	22.7	6.7	6.1	4.9	12.3	10.4	6.1	16.0	14.8	656	4.5
32–36	32.3	8.1	1.5	2.3	6.4	13.5	3.3	15.8	16.8	393	2.7
27–31	33.9	7.0	3.5	1.6	7.8	12.8	3.9	17.1	12.5	257	1.8
22–26	47.7	5.5	.9		6.4	10.1	.9	22.9	5.5	109	.7
17–21	56.3	6.3	2.1		2.1	10.4		8.3	14.6	48	.3
12–16	26.3					26.3		47.4		19	.1
7–11									100.0	1	.0
2–6					100.0					1	.0
−3–1											
−8–−4											
−13–−9											
−18–−14											
−23–−19											
−28–−24											
−33–−29											
−38–−34											
−43–−39											
−48–−44											
−53–−49											
−58–−54											
−59 and lower											
Totals	12.4	5.6	7.1	12.6	33.8	9.2	3.9	6.9	8.6	14607	100.0

Source: National Climatic Data Center, *SMOS—Summary of Meteorological Observations, Surface: Part E—Psychrometric Summaries* (Asheville, N.C.: National Oceanic and Atmospheric Administration).

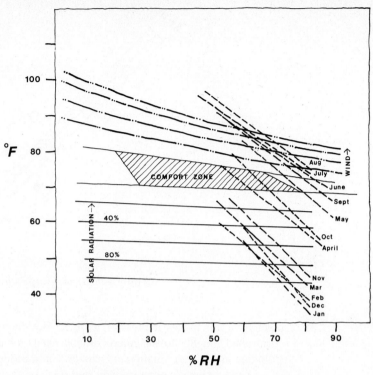

Figure 8-37   Normal conditions at Dallas–Fort Worth.

Whichever data source is being used, associate the lowest relative humidity value listed with the daily maximum temperature, and the highest humidity with the lowest temperature. (Four daily humidity values are listed in *Local Climatological Data*; only two are listed in *Comparative Climatic Data.*)

The DFW example (Fig. 8-37) suggests a temperate climate with periods of overheating on summer and fall days, where wind and shade are necessary to improve thermal comfort. The underheating that occurs on winter and spring days can be remedied with solar radiation. Since each normal day "line" represents 24 hours, the line can be subdivided to indicate time of day in order to understand when solar radiation will be available. It is assumed that the maximum temperature on the January day occurs in the afternoon at 4:00 P.M. and that the minimum temperature occurs 12 hours before, at 4:00 A.M. These two times can be assigned to opposite ends of the "line" as illustrated in Fig. 8-38. Here the line is represented as a double "bar" and daylight hours are differentiated from night by the crosshatching. Sunrise and sunset times can be estimated from the sun angle calculator for any month. This permits the visualization of time along the normal day line.

The results of this analysis are interpreted in Table 8-8, which indicates the desirable conditions for exterior spaces in the Dallas–Fort Worth area under normal temperature and humidity conditions. By grouping "like" conditions, two primary categories emerge: times when sunny, calm conditions are desirable; and times when shade and wind are desirable. From a practical standpoint, it is important to remember that this analysis is based on "normal" conditions, and that daily conditions can vary considerably. (The record high temperature for January in the Dallas–Fort Worth area is 88°F.) Therefore, site planning solutions should be able to accommodate varying microclimatic conditions, such as the provision for shady areas in January in Dallas–Fort Worth.

A knowledge of solar geometry, a sun peg, and a site model allow precise determination of those areas of the site which will have access to the sun when it is desirable. Areas with desirable shading characteristics can also be identified. Knowledge of local

Figure 8-38 January temperature as "bar."

plant materials makes it possible to select deciduous trees with foliation periods that correspond roughly to the microclimatic needs which were identified in the analysis (foliation in April, defoliation in October would be ideal in the Dallas–Fort Worth area).

The bioclimatic analysis indicated that comforting winds should be admitted during periods of overheating, and that winds should be blocked during underheated periods. The primary source directions of both comforting and discomforting winds should be determined in order to develop responsive design solutions for exterior spaces.

The information found in Table 11.A of the *Airport Climatological Summary* (see Table 8-6) can be used to construct what is commonly referred to as "wind rose" diagrams. These diagrams graphically depict the directional frequency of winds for each month of the year. The percent frequency of observations listed in the "total" column (Table 8-6) is graphed for the appropriate direction. The monthly wind roses for Dallas–Fort Worth are shown in Fig. 8-39. (The percentage of observations that were "calm" is shown in the center of the wind rose.)

The January wind rose indicates that the majority of winds arrive from the south and north. Moving toward the summer months, the northerly components steadily decrease. The southerly components increase to a peak in July. In August, the hottest Dallas–Fort Worth month, the winds undergo a transition toward the east. Beginning in September, the northerly components begin to resume some relative prominence, until

TABLE 8-8   Bioclimatic Analysis Results for Dallas–Fort Worth

Month	Sun	Shade	Wind	Calm
May		×	×	
June		×	×	
July		×	×	
August		×	×	
September		×	×	
October	×	×	×	×
November	×			×
December	×			×
January	×			×
February	×			×
March	×			×
April	×	×	×	×

Jan   Feb   Mar   Apr

May   Jun   Jul   Aug

Sept   Oct   Nov   Dec

Figure 8-39 Wind roses.

the northerly and southerly components again approach a "balance" in December and January.

As seasonal temperatures increase (from winter to spring and summer), the percent frequency of winds from southerly directions increases. It can be inferred, with some certainty, that the source of warm, temperate winds is from these southerly directions. As seasonal temperatures decrease (from summer to fall and winter), the percent frequency of winds from northerly directions increases, even though the prevailing wind direction is still from the south. It can be surmised, perhaps with less certainty, that the northerly directions may be the source of cold, discomforting winds. Information from the "Narrative Climatological Summary" contained in *Local Climatological Data*, personal knowledge of area climatic patterns, or information provided by local experts or residents can usually verify the primary source directions of cold and temperate winds.

A more precise determination is possible using *Summary of Meteorological Observations: Part E—Psychrometric Summaries*, which contains percent frequency observations relating wind direction to air temperature (see Table 8-7). Wind roses for discrete air temperature "ramps" or "bins" (Fig. 8-40) clearly indicate that the coldest winds (2 to 31°F) arrive primarily from northerly directions. (Note that only 3% of all observations occur in the 2 to 31° temperature bin.) Comfort and ventilating winds (62

Figure 8-40 Wind roses for discrete temperature bins.

to 86°F bin, 51.9% of observations) arrive primarily from southerly directions. The trend from warm-south to cold-north is clearly identifiable in this sequence of diagrams.

The bioclimatic analysis (Fig. 8-37 and Table 8-8) indicated that wind is desirable from May through September. The prevailing direction for winds during these months is primarily out of the south, south-southwest, and south-southeast. These winds can be useful in improving thermal comfort and should be admitted to exterior spaces. The cold, northerly winds that occur during winter months should be blocked. It should be recognized that most but not all discomforting winds (2 to 31°F bin) come from the northerly directions, and that most but not all temperate winds arrive from the southerly directions.

The site planner's focus in the Dallas–Fort Worth area should be the provision of sunny exterior spaces protected against cold, northerly winds during underheated periods (November into April), shady exterior spaces which admit winds during overheated periods (May through September), and a variety of in-between spaces that accommodate the other-than-normal climatic conditions which will occur and the varying comfort criteria of the people who will be using the spaces. In other words, exterior spaces should be planned that will accommodate a variety of climatic conditions and provide a range of opportunities to locate thermally comfortable places to inhabit.

SITE-MICROCLIMATE MAPPING

Having completed an analysis of normal climatic conditions, the site planner is equipped with the necessary information to analyze the microclimates of a specific site. This process, which will be referred to as site-microclimate mapping, was demonstrated in *InsideOut* by Brown, Reynolds, and Ubbelohde, and again by Brown in *Sun, Wind and Light*. It will indicate which areas of the site are most suitable for the location of exterior spaces.

The bioclimatic analysis indicates seasonal requirements for sun and wind. As defined by *InsideOut* and illustrated in Fig. 8-41, four general conditions can exist on a site at any given time:

   A: areas with sun and wind
   B: areas with sun protected from the wind
   C: areas with shade and wind
   D: areas with shade protected from the wind

Category B was identified as the desirable combination during underheated periods, while category C was desirable during overheated periods. Using a site plan gridded to some convenient scale (15- to 30-ft cells or greater, depending on drawing scale or the site), this identification system can be used to "map" site microclimates. The initial mapping should identify the predominant conditions existing in each cell for winter and summer extremes (January and August for Dallas–Fort Worth conditions). A B

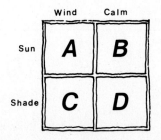

Figure 8-41 Bioclimatic analysis matrix. [From G.Z. Brown, J.S. Reynolds, and M.S. Ubbelohde, *InsideOut: Design Procedures for Passive Environmental Technologies* (New York: John Wiley & Sons, Inc., 1982) pp. 3–12.

condition (sun with wind protection) is desirable for exterior spaces in the winter, while a C condition (shade and wind) is desirable during summer. A cell on the gridded site plan which is mapped as B/C (winter/summer) would most likely have characteristics promoting comfort year-round. A C/B cell would be least suitable for exterior spaces. Keep in mind that the grid lines do not represent absolute cell boundaries. The grid is simply a device used to identify general areas on the site.

Figure 8-42 illustrates a small, hypothetical "flat" site in the Dallas–Fort Worth area. There are dense screens of evergreen vegetation at the northwest and southeast corners of the site which will be effective windbreaks. There are four mature deciduous trees (branching begins 8 ft above the ground) providing shade in summer and admitting sunshine in winter. All trees are 30 ft tall. Cold winds come from the north and northwest. Ventilating winds come from the south.

Figure 8-43 illustrates the microclimate mapping of the site based on the climatic analysis discussed previously. Some of the cell conditions may be uncertain or imprecise, and qualified judgments are often necessary. Cells F-2, F-3, G-2, and G-3 (B/C cells) define the area most suitable for developing exterior space, while cells H-7, and H-8 (C/B cells) are least suitable. Figure 8-44 shows these areas as well as other areas which are seasonably suitable. A site model with a sun peg can clarify which areas are predominantly sunny or shady.

With intervention, any or all of these conditions of course can change. A conditions can be changed to desirable B or C conditions using architectural elements and/or vegetation. For example, the placement of a wall or fence along the north property line in concert with deciduous trees can convert cells E-4 through E-8 from an A/A to a B/C designation (Fig. 8-45). This wall and the vegetation can be designed to provide not just a continuous B/C set of conditions, but a range of microclimatic conditions, thereby increasing the opportunities for comfort with "other-than-normal" climatic conditions. Figure 8-46 illustrates an "environmental option wall" which is designed to produce a range of microclimatic conditions.

Figure 8-42 Hypothetical site.

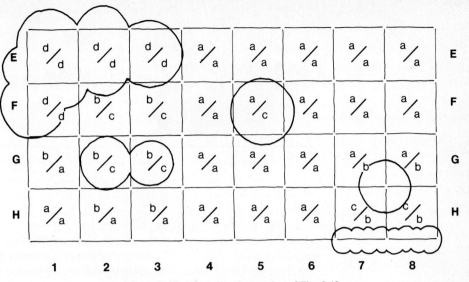

Figure 8-43 Microclimatic mapping of Fig. 8-42.

Figure 8-44 Area suitability of hypothetical site.

Figure 8-45 Modifications to hypothetical site.

Shady and Calm   Sunny and Calm   Sunny and Windy   Shady and Windy

Figure 8-46 Environmental options wall.

The site-microclimate mapping process identifies general areas that may be appropriate for the location of exterior spaces, and indicates what must be done to alter the microclimate of other areas on the site to increase comfort opportunities. Finally, when buildings are being located on the site, the microclimates should again be mapped to reflect changes created by the buildings. The process of determining the appropriate location for a building on the site is similar, but in addition to comfort the focus must include building energy conservation. A building responds not only to the climatic elements (external thermal loads) but also to heat generated inside the building (internal thermal loads). Methods for anticipating the thermal loading problems of buildings are discussed in Chapter 17. These methods provide the site planner with information that can be used for preliminary siting, massing, and orientation decisions.

chapter 9

Earthworks: Shaping the Site

INTRODUCTION

Adapting a site's form to accommodate structures is a principal objective of most site plans. Where the quality of the work will vary, the primary intent of the plan is to direct the changes in the site's character to integrate man-made uses. Although this integration is accomplished primarily through grading, the English term ''earthworks'' appears to be more appropriate, as it includes drainage and erosion control as well. Grading, erosion control, and drainage are all part of the same process to find that compromise which accepts the change with a minimal amount of environmental damage. Although grading is often considered as a perfunctory exercise of site planning, an ill-conceived grading plan often reflects basic flaws in reconciling the scope of issues associated with earthworks.

The purposes of grading fall into four basic categories. First, it involves the effort to model the topography to accept a structure and its immediate land area. Buildings naturally require that some areas must be made level, but only those areas to receive buildings should be level, as other parts of the site without slope would not drain properly.

Second, grading for drainage involves the manipulation of the topography into a coordinated system that directs water away from those areas that need to be kept dry. Erosion control is a concomitant element of this task.

The third most common problem in earthworks is the grading associated with the access and location of those facilities to accommodate the automobile. This would include roads as well as parking, since location and configuration of these facilities are some of the most problematical for site planners. Grading associated with pedestrian movement, recreational activities, or special design issues make up the last category of earthworks problems. This would include, but not be limited to, sidewalks, ramps, stairs, retaining walls, berms, parking, drives, and field games.

The notion of architecture without architects generates an image and quality of buildings and communities worth a second look in terms of site planning and earthworks.

There are numerous examples of vernacular architecture where the building and site appear as an integrated, unpretentious achievement. These are often the result of cultural precepts associated with the site, or simply the fact that the technology to change the site radically was unavailable. Unlike today, where Gulliveresque equipment is everywhere, the ancients were not only apprehensive of radical change to the earth, but the methods or techniques by which the land could be reshaped were limited. Indeed, more careful and sensitive site planning would probably occur tomorrow if every cubic yard of soil were to be moved by human hands. This is not to say that technological advancement has been counterproductive to the development of a humane environment; but didn't we recently rediscover the value of the 'low-tech' operable window and the ceiling fan?

CONCEPTS AND VOCABULARY

THE CONTOUR LINE

To understand grading, one begins with an understanding of contours and the contour line. Although the principles associated with the contour line are simple, their manipulation in the grading process is one that continues to be a source of consternation to the novice. This is due, in part, to the nature of contour lines, as they are a two-dimensional device used to represent three dimensions. Nothing in architectural drawing is similar to contour lines, and although the contour line as a concept may be easy to grasp, it seems that the ability to visualize the vertical distance (contour interval) on a map lies at the base of the enigma.

Although the technique was abandoned in favor of contour lines, hachures still provide the site planner with a valuable graphic technique. Hachures are drawn perpendicular to a contour line, and the closer that two contour lines are to each other, the more frequent the number of hachure lines (Fig. 9-1). Hachures are a valuable tool, as they provide the planner with an image of the site as well as an understanding of the drainage pattern. Since the hachure line is the shortest distance between two contour

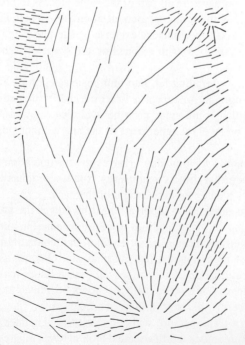

Figure 9-1 Hachure plan.

lines, it also represents the flow of water across the site. The darker area depicts the steeper slopes and rapid flow of water, the lighter areas, the shallow slopes and gradual runoff.

The contour line was apparently first used as a method to record the edge of a river. The various levels of water in the river were probably obvious to the observer and hence provided the basis for the notion that a line at the water's edge at a given elevation also existed in dryland forms (Fig. 9-2). Compared to the use of hachures, the contour line was much less time consuming to delineate. Furthermore, the necessity to locate buildings, roads, orchards, and vegetation on a map with hachures was not always the clearest of drawings (Fig. 9-3). The role and function of the contour line are such that they must be understood completely to comprehend site planning and the grading process properly.

Since, by definition, the contour line is a line on a plane that connects all points of the *same* elevation, the first rule is that contour lines never cross (Fig. 9-4). The only exception to that rule is a natural topographic overhang or natural bridge. The second rule is that a contour line will either close on the site plan or run to the edge of the site. They never exist as a line that begins at a point *a* and ends at a point *b* on the plan (Fig. 9-5). The third rule is that they never fork or merge, as in Fig. 9-6. There are, however, common occasions in which contour lines of the same elevation may be represented side by side (Fig. 9-7). The fourth holds that the interval between contour lines is constant. This is to say that a topographic map of a specific scale will represent the contour lines at a constant interval, for example: 1 ft, 2 ft, 5 ft, and so on. This constant vertical interval is necessary to avoid circumstances in which varying intervals would develop a distorted picture and an inaccurate interpretation of a site's physical form. Only in unusual circumstances in which contour lines are omitted because they are too close to be drawn and visualized is this rule compromised (Fig. 9-7).

An additional note is necessary here concerning very flat sites. On those occasions in which the topographic change is very modest, consider interpolating between the

Figure 9-2

Figure 9-3 Road, buildings, and orchard on hachure map.

Figure 9-4 Contour lines crossing.

Figure 9-5 Contour lines beginning and ending *a* to *b*.

1-ft interval to locate an intermediate 6-in. contour. This additional interval provides a much sharper picture of the site whose physiography is subtle and visual topographic relief is absent. During the regrading process, this additional interval will become invaluable as change to the site and the design of a positive drainage pattern becomes a challenge.

Figure 9-6 Contour lines forking.

Figure 9-7 Contour lines at same elevation and omitting contour lines.

TOPOGRAPHY

On the topographic map, all existing contour lines are dashed and every fifth contour is drawn darker. The darker lines provide an additional interval level and assist in the visual interpretation of the site. During the site planning process the contour lines that need to be changed (proposed contour lines) are drawn solid. This change between existing and proposed contours becomes easy to read and identifies areas of topographic "cut" or "fill."

Contour lines provide a picture of the site's topographical relief. Contour lines delineate areas that appear similar, such as:

1. Ridge (Fig. 9-8), valley (Fig. 9-9)
2. Depression or hill (Fig. 9-10)
3. Convex or concave slopes (Figs. 9-11 and 9-12)

Sections through these landforms reveal not only the dramatic differences but also the essential importance of the section. Just as no architect or engineer would attempt to design a structure with plans or elevations alone, the section is equally as important to the site planner. The section is of immense value in reconciling the perceived vertical distance illustrated on the plan to the real change that occurs on the site.

Although the vocabulary of landforms and topographic features varies, all are variations on basic forms, and the best way to understand their function is to draw them. When possible, build a model. That "a picture is worth a thousand words" and "a

plan

RIDGE/ Ridge Line

section

Figure 9-8

plan

VALLEY

section

Figure 9-9

plan

HILL

section

Figure 9-10

plan

CONVEX SLOPE

section

Figure 9-11

CONCAVE SLOPE

Figure 9-12

model is worth a thousand pictures'' are never more true than when dealing with topography. Although the experienced site planner has developed a sense of understanding topography, laypersons have serious problems visualizing a site's character. For that reason, models are highly recommended as a method to ensure better communication between planner and client (Fig. 9-13).

Summits and depressions are spot elevations of the landform and identified with an ✕ on the topographic map (Fig. 9-14). The hachure lines on the low side of the contour line graphically define the depression. Spot elevations are also used to identify man-made elements on a site such as the top of a curb, a slab, a wall, or a drainage structure. A ''bench mark'' is a primary spot elevation or reference point. Bench marks are located on U.S. Geological Survey maps as well as on topographic surveys made for site-specific problems (Fig. 9-15). Spot elevations are also used to define critical elevations for drainage patterns. As an example, an 8-in. swale is often very important to the development of a system and can only be identified with spot elevations. Natural features such as trees and rock outcroppings are also often identified with spot elevations, as they influence design and grading decisions.

SLOPE ANALYSIS

Quantifying the character of any design problem is an appropriate step in the process of finding a solution. Each site has a number of qualities and characteristics that can be quantified, and among those is its relative slope. Since describing an area as steep or flat is both insufficient and simplistic, slope analysis is a method that permits the graphic identification and illustration of various slopes on a site.

The term ''slope'' will be used in two ways in this section on earthworks; the first will be as a function of slope analysis. The process of slope analysis is necessary to

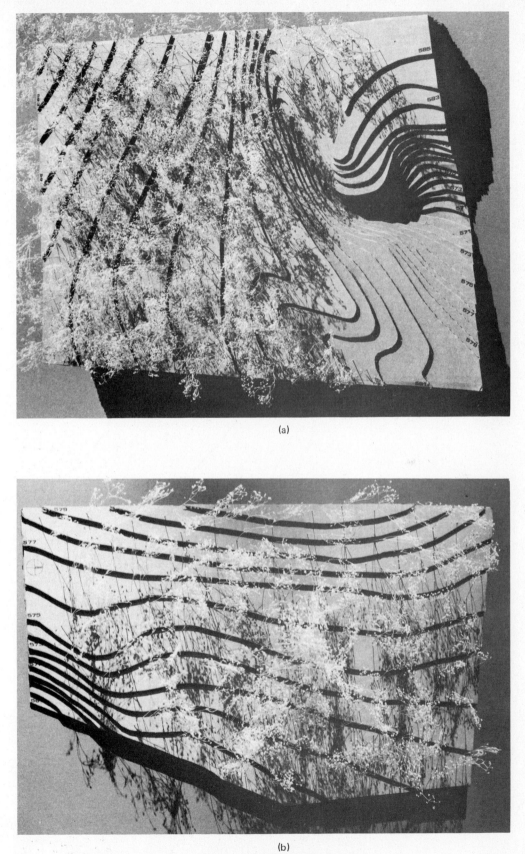

(a)

(b)

Figure 9-13 Topographical model.

Figure 9-14 Summit and depression.

Figure 9-15 Benchmark.

AREA	FUNCTION	SLOPE IN PERCENT	
		MAX.	MIN.
Streets & Drives		5%	1% [a]
		8%	.05% [b]
Ramps		10%	1% [a]
		15%	NA [b]
Walkways Approaches and Entrances		4%	1% [b]
		5%	0.5% [a]
Service Areas and Collector Walks		8%	0.5% [a]
		10%	0.5% [b]
Terrace and Sitting Areas		2%	1%
		2%	0.5% [b]
Lawn Area and Playgrounds		3%	2% [a]
		4%	0.5% [b]
Swales		10%	1% [a]
Grassed Banks		33% [3:1] [a]	NA
		25% [4:1] [b]	NA
Planted Banks (unmowed vines or ground cover)		50% [a]	NA
		2:1 [b]	NA

[a] Richard Untermann, *Grade Easy* (Washington, D. C.: Landscape Architecture Foundation, 1973), p. 73.
[b] Public Housing Design, National Housing Agency (Washington, D. C.: Federal Public Housing Agency, 1946).

Figure 9-16 Slope criteria.

make certain that there is some general agreement between the character of the man-made improvements and the quality of the topography. Figure 9-16 illustrates some acceptable design criteria for various site activities. Slope analysis essentially expresses the change in vertical elevation over a horizontal distance of 100 ft expressed as a percentage. As an example, a vertical change of 2 ft across a 100-ft distance is a 2% slope. A 4-ft vertical change across a 100-ft distance is a 4% slope. It follows that a 4-ft vertical change in a horizontal distance of 50 ft is an 8% slope. This change in vertical distance is commonly measured from one contour line directly to the next.

It appears, however, that there are no uniform percentages employed for slope analysis. If the only topography available is at a 5-ft interval, it's easy to see that the ratios for slope analysis will be simpler to identify in 5% increments, that is 0 to 5%, 5 to 10%, 10 to 15%, and so on. If the topographical interval is at 2 ft, the slope analysis is easier to break down into 0 to 4%, 4 to 8%, 8 to 12%, and so on.

It also needs to be mentioned that slopes are sometimes analyzed relative to the scale of the problem and topographic interval combined. Instead of a slope analysis developed as the percentage of slope between two contour lines, the slope analysis might be developed for some constant distance. As an example, on a 200-acre site with topography at 2-ft contour intervals and at a scale of 1 in. = 100 ft with high topographic relief, the site planner may choose to execute the slope analysis as a change across 50 ft, not from one contour line to the next. This method has some validity, as it permits the slope analysis to reflect the scale of the problem as well as the existing resources.

On a smaller site the opposite may be more appropriate. Figure 9-17 is just such a case. This is a 20.8-acre site where the topographic interval is 2 ft, the map scale was 1 in. = 50 ft, and the slope analysis was executed from one contour line to the next. The level of detail is much finer, and for most site planning problems, this is the preferred methodology.

Following the determination of the various slope categories, the development of a map that depicts a site's slopes becomes the next step. Since the basis for determining

Figure 9-17 Slope analysis of 20.8-acre site.

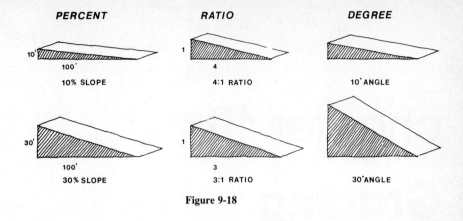

Figure 9-18

the slope is a function of contour interval and the distance between two contour lines, that relationship can be expressed by the following formula:[1]

$$\text{Distance between contours} = \frac{\text{contour interval}}{\text{the percent of slope}} \times 100$$

As an example, if the slope category is 4 to 8% on a map with a 2-ft contour interval, the distance between two contour lines for these respective slopes would be

$$\text{Distance} = \frac{\text{contour interval}}{\text{the percent of slope}} \times 100$$

$$D = \frac{2 \text{ ft}}{4\%} \times 100 \qquad\qquad D = \frac{2 \text{ ft}}{8\%} \times 100$$

$$= 50 \text{ ft} \qquad\qquad\qquad = 25 \text{ ft}$$

Therefore, for an area to be in a 4 to 8% slope category, the distance between two contour lines (with a 2-ft interval) could not be *more* than 50 ft to be a minimum of 4% slope, nor *less* than 25 ft to be a maximum of 8% slope.

Slope analysis is one of the most basic components of site analysis and no research is complete without it. This information is a crucial step in determining the appropriate location for all site improvements and thus is an essential part of intelligent decision making.

The second way in which "slope" is used as a term is to describe vertical change in small areas, particularly as a design criterion for cut and fill. In areas where the site planner must maintain a specific angle of repose, slope as a percentage of change over 100 ft is inappropriate. Another common expression refers to the slope as a ratio between a horizontal dimension and 1. In Chapter 10 reference is made to an unstabilized "cut" of 3:1. This translates to mean that the length of the slope (perpendicular to the contours) will be 3 horizontal feet for every foot of vertical change. Figure 9-18 illustrates the difference between the slope ratio of 3:1, a slope of 30%, and an incline of 30°.

Since substantial quantities of grading outside a building's perimeter will occur in less than 100 ft, the value of the slope as a percentage has little applicability. The key to remembering the differences between the two types of slope is to understand that each serves an entirely different function: one in site analysis, the second in grading. Second, because of those differences, each is expressed in two entirely different mathematical forms.

---

[1]Harvey Rubenstein, *A Guide to Site and Environmental Planning*, 2nd ed. (New York: John Wiley & Sons, Inc., 1980), p. 17.

chapter 10
Grading

GRADING BASICS

By its very nature, site planning implies change. The question comes down to how that change can be accomplished with minimal economic costs and environmental damage. As mentioned earlier, the grading plan is discovered or emerges as a result of good research, careful documentation, detailed analysis, creative synthesis, and patience. Grading does not lend itself to the quick-fix, big idea.

An evaluation of a site's more buildable areas must be based on an understanding of its topography, and the quantitative character of that is slope analysis. Since grading involves the modification of existing contours, the location of a building site or parking lot should reflect the information developed in the slope analysis. Before beginning any grading, review the slope analysis discussion in Chapter 9. If during the grading process, it appears that the results will create major environmental damage or loss of vegetation, consider relocating the structure. With the slope analysis, a locational decision concerning roads, parking, or building site can be made within a more enlightened framework. Grading may now be considered within the context of all site constraints.

Keeping water from draining into the building is the obvious, primary mission of the grading plan. Since grading and drainage must be thought of in a symbiotic way, each must be considered as a function of the other. In a pursuit to shape the site to accommodate an activity, a positive drainage pattern must be an integral aspect of the plan. The development of a site for a building implies that at least parts of the area must be level, and any topographical change must reflect earthworks that will induce water to run away from the immediate building area. To reiterate a point made earlier, the two characteristics of water that need to be remembered are that it always runs downhill and perpendicular to the contour line (Fig. 10-1).

Richard Untermann in *Grade Easy* suggests three basic topographical forms that might be employed in grading.[1] The sloping plane is the first and most common landform

---

[1]Richard Untermann, *Grade Easy* (Washington, D.C.: Landscape Architecture Foundation, 1973), pp. 52–53.

Figure 10-1 Contour lines and flow of water.

used because of its infinite varieties (Fig. 10-2). The sloping plane may also emerge as a convex or concave slope. Although it is possible that a site can be graded using the sloping plane alone, one must realize that the water will eventually accumulate at the bottom of the "plane" and cannot, in all cases, simply become someone else's problem.

When the case is such that the water must be restricted to a site, a partial answer may be the use of a valley as a method to control the runoff (Fig. 10-3). This is the second basic form and is used in situations where the valley is as shallow as a swale (Fig. 10-4) or as pronounced as a creek (Fig. 10-5). Although the swale is a common method of carrying water around a building, it must be designed so that the water has a positive flow. Critical to the success of the swale is remembering that the minimum recommended slope to achieve positive drainage in turf is 1%.

The funnel (Fig. 10-6) is the third form normally considered as a primary grading configuration. This shape is an aggregation of the two discussed earlier, but it has one characteristic that the others do not have. A graded funnel form will, in most cases, require the inclusion of a drainage structure at the base of the funnel. Although the

Figure 10-2 Sloping plane.

Figure 10-3   Valley.

addition of an area drain is not a monumental endeavor, it must be noted that its omission could create a very undesirable condition. Later we address in more detail the various drainage structures ordinarily used in the development of a grading plan.

The grading process requires a careful change of the contours so that they support the integration of building and site. Smooth grades and convex earth forms are methods used to develop a site planning quality that reflects a natural aesthetic. Geometric lines, harsh angles, and steep grades make the hand of man more evident and sometimes create difficult transitions between site and building. Urban environments often require an architectural response, especially when the development program demands a highly articulated hardscape (Fig. 10-7). The message here is that the site planner must be cognizant of the context wherein each of those methods would be appropriate and intelligent.

In a review of earthworks, the site planner needs a working knowledge of grading to save a tree. Grading in this sense means: Do not fill (add soil) or cut soil or roots back within the drip line (Fig. 10-8). Respecting this first rule and using common sense will go a long way toward keeping most vegetation out of harm's way. This criterion is based on the knowledge that a tree's health is, in large part, determined by the health

Figure 10-4   Swale.

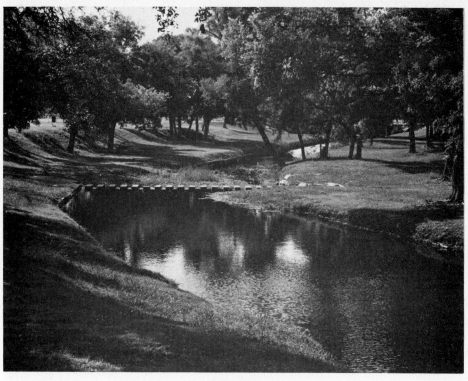

Figure 10-5

of its roots. If the roots are damaged or impaired, the leaf and limb systems will reflect that damage (Figs. 10-9 and 10-10). If regrading inside a tree's drip line is unavoidable, the limbs on the same side should be cut back proportionally to reduce the possibility of disease attacking any withering branches. If changing the grade within the drip line appears imminent, use stacked stone walls at the edge of the drip line to ensure a tree's access to moisture (Fig. 10-11). The technique is not only a functional alternative to save vegetation, but it also adds to the aesthetic quality of the earthworks as well. Before the process gets to the problem stage, check to see if the building's location can be

Figure 10-6   Funnel.

Figure 10-7 Articulated hardscape.

adjusted and, with it, the grading plan. If the area is being graded to accommodate pedestrian traffic, try to use wood decking and avoid grading (Figs. 10-12 and 10-13). A more extensive examination of trees in the urban environment is covered in Chapter 6 and should be consulted in the event that more complex problems with trees arise.

The importance of topsoil to a site also needs to be emphasized. Topsoil is rich with the nutrients that foster and maintain healthy plant growth. Although some parts of the continent are still rich with the resource, other areas have had topsoil stripped by

Drip Line

Figure 10-8 Grading near tree.

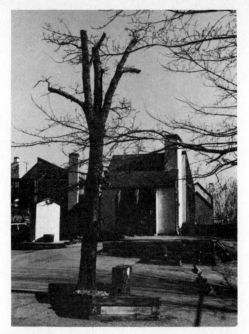

Figure 10-9 Trees lost due to paving inside the drip line.

erosion or the development processes. When the topsoil depth is too shallow to support revegetation, sandy loam or an equivalent substitute is introduced to the site. Needless to say, when an area must be regraded, the topsoil stripped from that area needs to be retained on the site and utilized in the regrading process. The distribution of topsoil across the site is obviously crucial to the site's ability to support new vegetation.

Every site will have its own set of restrictions, whether physical or legal. Physical

Figure 10-10 Trees lost due to paving inside the drip line.

Figure 10-11 Stacked stone wall at drip line.

restrictions must be acknowledged. When possible, rather than changing the site, consider modifying other design parameters to resolve conflicts between building and site. As an example, consider reducing the area of the site to be regraded. Sometimes a client's program is sufficiently flexible to permit reducing a building's "footprint" by increasing its height. A design solution that is two stories instead of one can, in some cases, favorably accommodate a site's natural attributes. Reducing the area to be graded also implies an examination of the paving area committed to the automobile. Auto access and parking can create an enormous demand for paving. A careful examination of the design criteria for auto circulation should be made and every effort expended to keep the amount of paving to a minimum without jeopardizing safety.

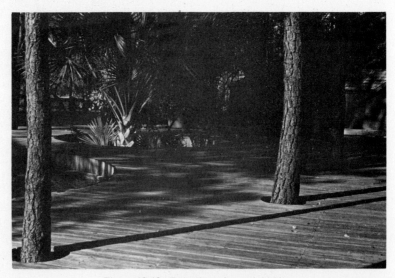

Figure 10-12 Trees through wood decking.

Figure 10-13 Trees through wood decking.

THE GRADING PROCESS

The grading process begins with establishing the parameters of the grading problem. In addition to the known, existing spot elevations that control and/or influence every grading plan (roads, curbs, sewers, easements), each site has a property line beyond which *no* regrading may be done. These "givens" should identify significant vegetation, rock outcroppings, or problems such as depressions or drainage pockets. The site planning checklist in Chapter 4 will provide some guidance to this research. Secure with a knowledge of contours and topography, the implications of change are next. Some site modifications become part of a project when the program implies change. Normally, that change means that the contour configuration will be modified by a "cut," a "fill," or a combination of the two. Just as the nomenclature suggests:

1. A cut is the removal of a portion of a site's natural topography (Fig. 10-14).
2. Fill is the process of blending additional earth into a site's existing topography (Fig. 10-15).
3. A combination of the two is shown in Fig. 10-16.

The preferred method of solving grading problems is to balance cut and fill. The

Figure 10-14 Cut (section).

Figure 10-15 Fill (section).

emphasis is on *preferred* because, in some cases, the combination is not appropriate. There are some distinctive advantages and disadvantages of cut and fill. One positive aspect of cutting is that the bank from which the cut was made was relatively stable. Undisturbed earth is generally stable, as it has had years to compact and, as a result, often permits more economical grading solutions.

Balancing the cut and fill also resolves the question of acquisition of new fill or the disposal of any residual. Since either acquisition or disposal has a dollar cost associated with it, the financial benefits of balancing the cut and fill are obvious. The balancing concept by its nature implies that any fill will use soils from the same site; as such, the bonding action is often more successful. There will, however, be circumstances in which a site plan may need to be developed using only a cut or fill, and attempts at balancing may only create problems. Certainly, any time that topographical modifications are excessive, destroy major trees, or create drainage problems, the grading plan should be changed.

In those situations in which the topography is too steep for a fill, a cut may be the only legitimate alternative. Under those circumstances where a cut is required on a steep slope, the grading plan may also necessitate a retaining wall to avoid erosion or spalling. A disadvantage to the cut lies in the need to dispose of the residual. Although in some communities, fill may be sold, in other municipalities, finding a place to dump fill has become a serious problem. Some local and state governments have adopted very stringent ordinances concerning fill, and for that reason, consultation with local authorities is highly recommended. Small sites can be a problem in balancing cut and fill, and generally, lend themselves to regrading by cutting alone. Opportunities for filling on small sites are obviously limited, as indiscriminate fill can create serious problems for

Figure 10-16 Combination of cut and fill.

existing trees. Often, grading by fill is done simply to make an area usable. Low or poorly drained areas are commonly filled to develop positive drainage patterns for a site, but there are a few guidelines that should be recognized before regrading by fill. First, some caution must be exercised in filling on a slope. Because of the lack of long-term bonding between the existing grade and the new fill, the potential for erosion is very high. Second, any construction on fill must be designed to respect the quality of the fill.

Following the decisions associated with the location of the structure and the documentation of all known fixed or controlling elevations, the next step involving the grading of a site begins with identification of the finish floor elevation. Make note of the fact that the process began by establishing a spot grade on the slab from which other decisions were made. A site is planned and graded based on spot grades. Contours are then changed to reflect the spot-grading decisions. The following chart can be used to determine the various decimal intervals of 12 in.

Decimal Equivalents (Inches to Feet)

1 in. = 0.083 ft	5 in. = 0.416 ft	9 in. = 0.75 ft
2 in. = 0.166 ft	6 in. = 0.5 ft	10 in. = 0.833 ft
3 in. = 0.250 ft	7 in. = 0.583 ft	11 in. = 0.916 ft
4 in. = 0.333 ft	8 in. = 0.667 ft	12 in. = 1.0 ft

If the site is to be graded using a cut alone, specify an elevation for the finish floor 0.5 ft above the nearest contour line on the low side of the building (Fig. 10-17). This requires that all contours above the finish floor elevation of the building be "wrapped" around the building. Where each of the new contour lines crosses an existing contour line of higher elevation, we know that a "cut" occurs. Figure 10-17 illustrates the cut necessary as the new contour line 6 crosses the existing contour 7, and 7 moves up toward 8. Note that the proposed contours are carefully curved and shaped back into the existing contour lines. This is referred to as "meeting the grade." While an effort must be made to merge the proposed contour with the existing contour as soon as possible to minimize the extent of the cut, some care must be taken that merging does not result in an abrupt or harsh topographical change.

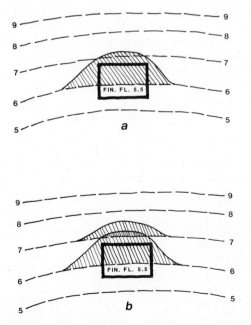

Figure 10-17 Cut in plan.

The contour change and its relationship to the slab must also conform to some accepted slope criteria. Remember that "slope" is the relationship between horizontal distance and vertical rise and is also expressed as a ratio (i.e., 3:1 or 4:1). This concept is critical to the grading process, for without established criteria, the relationship between contour lines becomes arbitrary and will vary between unnecessarily shallow and inappropriately steep. Accepted criteria for grading an unstabilized cut are a maximum 3:1 slope and 4:1 fill. Since the fill is not as secure in its bonding to the existing soil, the slope must necessarily be more gradual. Since stabilized cut and fill slopes are a function of the techniques employed, they are addressed more extensively later (Chapter 13). For now, however, stabilized cuts can be as steep as 1:1 and stabilized fill 2:1. These guidelines will permit the site planner to develop a grading plan knowing that there are alternatives and base criteria for these options.

Following the established criteria, subsequent contours can be located beginning with the lowest and, in turn, progressing to the higher contour elevations. When complete, the plan should identify each existing and proposed contour line, as well as all spot elevations critical to the grading effort. The necessity of identifying the spot elevations surrounding the structure in sufficient detail to know that the grade slopes away from the building is a common oversight. Remember, leave nothing to chance.

To grade an area level using fill only, the process is simply the reverse of the cut. A finish floor elevation is identified which is 0.5 ft above the highest contour line that passes through the area to be graded level. Having established that elevation, the highest contour line in the area to be graded is "wrapped" around the slab over the lower contour lines at a distance that reflects the slope criteria mentioned earlier (Fig. 10-18). Similar considerations concerning meeting the grade are still applicable and, in some cases, more obvious when executed poorly on a fill. Buildings that appear to be rising out of the topography, demanding dramatic alterations in a site's character, detract not only from the total aesthetic quality of a building and site, but also become maintenance problems when soils are given to spalling under heavy moisture.

Make note of the fact that in the examples of both cut and fill, the long sides of the rectangular slabs were oriented parallel to the contours. This is a basic corollary associated with a structure's location on a slope and should be considered as a primary criterion in the process. The location of any structure on a site should take into account

Figure 10-18 Fill in plan.

Figure 10-19 Cut and fill.

its orientation relative to the direction of the contours, as the implications of cut and fill can be significant.

Having reviewed the methods of cut and fill separately, the third alternative, which combines the two techniques, needs to be examined. Pursuing the concept that the best method is to balance the cut and fill, the finish floor level is established at 6.5 ft above the contour line that appears to be midway between the highest and lowest elevations covered by the slab (Fig. 10-19). This median elevation implies that half of the area to be graded will be accomplished by a cut and the other half by a fill. After determining the desired elevation of the slab and those of the surrounding grade, the contour lines are then "wrapped" above (cut) or below (fill) the slab to reflect the new elevations. Figure 10-19 illustrates the extent of the cut and fill. The same criteria concerning slopes and meeting the grade are still in effect. Additional earthworks techniques associated with retaining walls, stairs, ramps, and terracing will all be explored but will also rely on the basic concepts of cut and fill.

Two important aspects of the process need to be mentioned now. First, it has been suggested that good grading is discovered, not imposed. If, in the grading process, it appears that the results cause major environmental damage or radical loss of vegetation, consider relocating the structure. Another part of the site may be more accommodating. Solutions to site planning problems that require extensive grafting or extensive removal might need reevaluation. Second, if holding or maintaining one elevation for the slab in every direction creates large areas of cut or fill, consider breaking or separating the slab vertically (Fig. 10-20). Keep in mind that this must be done in conjunction with the spatial planning of the building. Properly executed, the change in vertical dimensions can emphasize or define the limits or functions of a particular area of the architectural plan and greatly add to its aesthetic quality. This concept applies to building as well as site scale. This technique could be applied to tennis courts, parking lots, or any situation where the change in elevation would reduce the amount of site grading. The bifurcated

Figure 10-20   Plan of slab on sloping topography.

road is an example of a two-way thoroughfare that has been separated in sections to reduce the amount of cut and fill (Fig. 10-21). The value of this strategy is not only one in which large parking areas may be broken and their nuisance quotient reduced, but also one in which there is the potential to enhance the character of an architectural space (Fig. 10-22).

To summarize cut and fill, remember that when proposed contour lines cross existing contour lines that are numerically higher, the change is a cut (Fig. 10-17). When the proposed contour lines cross existing contour lines that are numerically lower, the change is a fill (Fig. 10-18). Both techniques, individually and compositely, must become a working part of the site planner's lexicon of skills.

For some reason there is an overwhelming desire for many to think of grading as the movement of contours. Invariably, when presented with a grading problem, students begin drawing contour lines instead of developing the site with spot elevations first. This

Figure 10-21 Bifurcated road.

was mentioned earlier but bears repeating, as the urge to draw overpowers the necessity to think.

To facilitate the grading process, Table 10-1 is a matrix of distance and slope. The left margin is distance; the horizontal line is slope. To determine the change in grading necessary for a particular problem, identify the slope at the top of the chart; read down the column to locate the distance that corresponds to the problem. Use combinations of even numbers: 50 plus 4 for 54 ft. The chart can eliminate a lot of time-consuming math while respecting good grading practice.

The final step in the process requires a review of those circumstances in which no grading should be done. Richard Untermann in *Grade Easy* has suggested that the following conditions be avoided or reevaluated.

1. Grading that results in radical loss of vegetation and/or topsoil

Figure 10-22 Section illustrating slab vertically separated to accommodate sloping topography.

TABLE 10-1 Percent of Slope

DISTANCE (ft)	0.5	0.75	1.0	1.25	1.5	0.75	2.0	2.5	3.0	3.5	4.0	4.5	5.0
							SLOPE (%)						
1	0.005	0.08	0.01	0.013	0.015	0.018	0.02	0.025	0.03	0.035	0.04	0.045	0.05
2	0.01	0.015	0.02	0.025	0.03	0.035	0.04	0.05	0.06	0.07	0.08	0.09	0.10
3	0.015	0.023	0.03	0.38	0.045	0.05	0.06	0.075	0.09	0.105	0.12	0.135	0.15
4	0.02	0.03	0.04	0.05	0.06	0.07	0.08	0.10	0.12	0.14	0.16	0.18	0.20
5	0.025	0.04	0.05	0.063	0.075	0.09	0.10	0.125	0.15	0.175	0.20	0.225	0.25
6	0.03	0.05	0.06	0.075	0.09	0.105	0.12	0.15	0.18	0.21	0.24	0.27	0.30
7	0.035	0.05	0.07	0.088	0.10	0.123	0.14	0.175	0.21	0.245	0.28	0.329	0.35
8	0.04	0.06	0.08	0.10	0.12	0.14	0.16	0.20	0.24	0.28	0.32	0.36	0.40
9	0.045	0.064	0.09	0.113	0.14	0.158	0.18	0.225	0.27	0.315	0.36	0.405	0.45
10	0.05	0.75	0.10	0.125	0.15	0.175	0.20	0.25	0.30	0.35	0.40	0.45	0.50
15	0.075	0.11	0.15	0.188	0.23	0.265	0.30	0.375	0.45	0.53	0.60	0.655	0.75
20	0.10	0.15	0.20	0.25	0.30	0.35	0.40	0.50	0.60	0.70	0.80	0.90	1.0
25	0.125	0.19	0.25	0.31	0.38	0.44	0.50	0.63	0.75	0.88	1.0	1.12	1.25
30	0.150	0.23	0.30	0.376	0.45	0.53	0.60	0.75	0.90	1.05	1.2	1.35	1.50
35	0.175	0.26	0.35	0.409	0.53	0.62	0.70	0.88	1.05	1.24	1.4	1.58	1.75
40	0.20	0.30	0.40	0.50	0.60	0.70	0.80	1.0	1.2	1.4	1.6	1.71	2.0
45	0.225	0.34	0.45	0.56	0.68	0.79	0.90	1.13	1.35	1.58	1.8	2.03	2.25
50	0.250	0.38	0.50	0.62	0.75	0.88	1.0	1.25	1.5	1.76	2.0	2.24	2.50
55	0.275	0.41	0.55	0.68	0.83	0.97	1.1	1.38	1.65	1.94	2.2	2.47	2.75
60	0.30	0.45	0.60	0.75	0.90	1.06	1.2	1.5	1.8	2.12	2.4	2.7	3.0
65	0.325	0.48	0.65	0.81	0.98	1.15	1.3	1.63	1.95	2.30	2.6	2.93	3.25
70	0.350	0.53	0.70	0.82	1.0	1.24	1.4	1.76	2.10	2.48	2.8	3.16	3.50
75	0.357	0.57	0.75	0.94	1.1	1.33	1.5	1.89	2.25	2.66	3.0	3.39	3.75
80	0.40	0.60	0.80	1.0	1.2	1.4	1.6	2.0	2.4	2.8	3.2	3.6	4.0
85	0.425	0.64	0.85	1.06	1.3	1.49	1.7	2.13	2.55	2.98	3.4	3.83	4.25
90	0.45	0.676	0.90	1.12	1.35	1.58	1.8	2.26	2.7	3.16	3.6	4.06	4.5
100	0.50	0.175	1.0	1.25	1.50	1.75	2.0	2.5	3.0	3.5	4.0	4.5	5.0

Source: Richard Untermann, *Grade Easy* (Washington, D.C.: Landscape Architecture Foundation, 1973), p. 75.

2. Grading that interrupts the natural drainage
3. Grading that results in aesthetic degradation
4. Grading on difficult slopes (excess of 25%), in floodplains, estuaries, or bogs, or in other environmentally unique conditions
5. Grading in areas susceptible to natural disasters, such as mud slides or along earthquake fault lines[2]

Each of these circumstances is obviously the harbinger of future problems to either client, user, or community. Although the values of some communities are such that development would not be permitted in any of these conditions, others perceive development in any form as a means to expand the tax base. What we often fail to realize is that if communities and professionals abdicate the responsibility to define the limits to development, private self-interest never will.

GRADING AND DRAINAGE

GRADING PRINCIPALS

Two of the principal goals in the development of a grading plan are:

1. Keep unwanted water from entering a building
2. Keep surface runoff from creating damage to property or people during periods of heavy rainfall and subsequent runoff

For those good and sound purposes, the site planner must begin by considering drainage a function of grading, just as the architect considers structure an integral part of architecture. The scope of problems to resolve in every grading plan will range widely, as much depends on a site's ecology and context. Regardless of whether the site's context is an urban area, where 80 to 90% of a site may be impervious surfaces, or a suburban area, where those percentages can drop from 90% to 40%, decisions relative to on-site runoff cannot be dismissed casually.

To avoid the problems associated with drainage and runoff, the site planner needs to recognize that nothing can be left to chance. While each set of site circumstances is different, each has a common set of criteria and concepts. The first criterion is that water always flows downhill, from a higher to a lower elevation, and perpendicular to the contours. Although this may be an elaboration of the obvious, faulty drainage diagrams and ridge-line identification are not limited to student site planning exercises; mistakes associated with analysis errors have also been built.

Although the natural methods by which rainfall might be removed from a site might also appear obvious, it is important that they be identified, as they combine and become part of the hydrological cycle.

1. Surface runoff is the first and most visible method of removing water from a site. Just as the name implies, the precipitation that is not absorbed into the soil accumulates across the surface of the site and is collected in swales or into subsurface storm sewer systems. Ultimately, all of the runoff in a watershed is combined into freshwater tributaries which find their way to the sea. The development process almost invariably creates additional runoff. As such, some consideration must be given to the direction of the flow as well as the quantity of the impending runoff.

---

[2]Ibid., p. 87.

2. Subsurface runoff is the second method by which water is removed from a site. This is the process in which water permeates the surface, is absorbed by the soil, and becomes part of the groundwater supply or an aquifer. Since subsurface runoff is a very important contributor to the quantity of water in both groundwater and aquifers, it is particularly important for the site planner to consider ways in which the runoff may be transferred into subsurface systems. As mentioned in Chapter 7, subsidence, or the settling of the earth's crust, follows the extraction of groundwater at a rate faster than replenishment of the resource. This particular environmental malady is the result of public policies that permit water removal as a priority, without guidelines as to groundwater or aquifer replenishment. Obviously, any effort that is cognizant of the potential environmental problem and facilitates the natural processes should be pursued.

3. Evaporation of water from plants or bodies of surface water (lakes, creeks, etc.) is the third method by which water is removed from a site. The notion of utilizing plant life to retain water molecules on a site may appear as a rather modest means of removing negligible amounts of water. When the alternatives to be considered are vegetation vis-à-vis an impervious surface, there is no question which contributes more to the elimination of surface water and reinforces the natural systems.

4. Transpiration from vegetation is the fourth method of removing rainfall from a site. Plants and vegetation absorb water in photosynthesis, contributing to the hydrological cycle. Like evaporation, although the amount of water absorbed through transpiration may be negligible, the process is still preferred to an impervious surface. Although the primary method that will be employed to remove rainfall will generally be surface runoff, evaporation and subsurface infiltration should be considered as potential contributors to that process.

In the design of a grading plan for the site, the principal objective of the plan is to collect, transfer, and dispose of surface water.[3] Within that framework, there are two basic methods: open and closed systems. Surface water can be accommodated in low density/minimal coverage situations with "open" surface systems which control the water through the shape and form of the topography. Although more expensive, "closed" systems (subsurface piping) are sometimes necessary due to a site's location, off-site drainage, or land use. In many cases, the most cost-effective method will be one that employs a combination of open and closed systems. Just as in grading, where cut and fill are often part of the same plan, the same applies to drainage. There are always those conditions where one method or another could prove to be the only appropriate solution. There is also a set of circumstances in which closed systems would need to be used in spite of the site's appearance. In some places where the topographical relief is too slight or shallow, closed systems are almost mandatory. Recall that there are minimum slopes to accommodate positive drainage. If the natural gradient is less than the criterion, water will pond, creating a nuisance and hazard to health.

DRAINAGE: CONSIDERATIONS AND PLAN

The grading and drainage process begins with three primary considerations. Determine, first, where the water is coming from; second, where it needs to go; and third, how it traverses the site. Just as the site planner knows that the context of every site mandates an examination of the land beyond the property line, that requirement is never more obligatory than in the case of drainage. An analysis of the site and its context relative to the development of a grading plan should document, as a minimum:

1. The topographical characteristics, identifying high and low points, drainage swales, ridge lines, and the extent of the immediate water shed

---

[3]Ibid., p. 47.

2. Any unusual soil types such as gravelly or sandy soils, which percolate satisfactorily, as well as clay or silty soil, which do not

3. Fixed elevations or points on the site, such as roads, trees, adjacent buildings, or rock outcroppings

4. All areas that need to be kept dry and their corresponding elevations

5. The location and extent of the existing sewer systems

Finally, develop a drawing that illustrates the existing drainage pattern from the areas adjacent to the site, across the site, and beyond. It is imperative to look beyond today. Recognize that undeveloped sites will change and could, in that process, create problems for those who did not anticipate the potential for change. The factors that need to be considered in addressing drainage problems on-site are (1) topography, (2) soil types, (3) vegetation, (4) size of property, (5) land use, and (6) precipitation rates. Land use should give some insight as to the amount of impervious surfaces or open space that would probably occur on a site. A knowledge of the site's soil and vegetation can provide an index of absorption attainable by the natural systems. The size of the area and amount of rainfall are statistical quantities that provide the site planner with the final two parameters necessary for an understanding of drainage and surface runoff. See Chapter 13 for an explanation of storm water management methods and runoff analysis.

No development question can be resolved without an understanding of its economic implications. The financial considerations of a grading/drainage plan need to be understood, as they are a part of the entire building budget. As an example, surface drainage systems which permit water to flow across sloping planes of planted or paved areas are often more cost-effective than a closed system of catch basins and subsurface pipes. On occasion, the rate of runoff can be ameliorated with on-site detention ponds (Fig. 10-23). On-site retention often results in a reduction in the amount and size of the

Figure 10-23 On-site detention pond.

Figure 10-24 Riprap or stone at edge of creek.

pipes, which can be translated into lower financial costs. Although more environmental objectives can be attained through the use of retention ponds, the site planner must also be aware of the economic implications.

Since erosion control is an integral part of the grading/drainage plan, there are a few necessary precautions that must be taken concerning the plan in the construction process. Water can be a genuine problem and create substantial erosion damage. For that reason, avoid stripping an entire site of its natural vegetation. Some thought should be given to regarding the site in stages, where erosion can be controlled in a more effective way. Finally, all slopes should be replanted immediately following regrading.

Listed here are a few widely accepted guidelines to follow in the development of the grading plan and design of the drainage system.[4]

1. New runoff must never be purposefully redirected from its natural course on one property so as to become a nuisance on another property. It is acceptable in most communities to continue that process or system that occurs naturally, but do not increase the flow artificially.
2. Always consider some method to retard the velocity of the water so that it might be absorbed into the soil. Riprap or stone lining are often employed as techniques to dissipate the force of the water in swales or creeks. In reducing the rate of flow, the technique dramatically reduces the scouring action of water and increases the rate of absorption (Fig. 10-24).
3. Design the grading and drainage plan so as to respect, reinforce, and duplicate the existing natural systems.

[4]Ibid., p. 48.

4. While on occasions there are few alternatives, a drainage plan with more than one outlet course is considered good planning.

5. Avoid draining large paved areas across pedestrian paths. Catch basins and trench drains can be used to collect the substantial quantities of runoff created by parking lots or pedestrian plazas.

6. Identify any areas that appear to be appropriate for drainage structures. Sinks, depressions, or long channels are always primary candidates for catch basins or drains.

7. In the design of subsurface systems, begin at the higher elevations of the site and work toward the lower. This method should result in a drainage system that resembles a tree form, with its smaller branches (pipe size) at the ends and higher elevations progressing to larger sizes as it approaches major limbs (mains), or the trunk, at the bottom of the water shed or drainage area. The pipe size should increase as the system collects and transfers the runoff to the lower elevations.

Surface drainage systems are generally preferred to underground systems for two reasons: cost and ecology. Since surface systems are more preferred and gravity is the vehicle, some minimal grades must be respected. Water will move downhill only if there is enough change in elevation to permit that movement. Figure 9-16 identifies some of those minimum and maximum grades.

Avoid the design of a system that necessitates the location of a drainage line through a foundation or under a slab. The problems associated with a drainage line that ruptures or leaks are the ingredients of an architect's bad dream. One should avoid cutting a hole in a grade beam for a pipe; for similar reasons, one avoids cutting holes in floor beams to accommodate air-conditioning ducts. The process suggests that some criteria be established which will facilitate objective decisions. As a minimum, that criteria might include:

1. The minimum grades to drain, taking into account the natural and man-made character

2. The maximum grades for cut or fill without stabilization

3. The maximum grades for a cut or fill with stabilization

4. The stabilization methods

Basic Subsurface Systems and Structures.   Having established those conditions under which the plan will be developed, some mention of drainage structures and their function is in order. Subsurface systems are designed to resolve the same objectives as those of surface systems: collect, transfer, and dispose. Surface runoff is collected in area drains (Fig. 10-25), catch basins (Fig. 10-26), and trench drains (Fig. 10-27). The area drain should be located at the lowest point in a drainage area. It is conceptually like a big shower drain through which all of the water falling in a specified area passes. "Trench drain" is a term that has been given to any linear drain. This structure is often used at the bottom of a slope where water needs to be collected to protect an adjacent area.

The catch basin is also an area drain, but it has been designed to "catch" debris in its base below the pipe that transfers the water to a point of disposal. When the lid of the catch basin is lifted, the debris and sediment that would otherwise have clogged the drainage system can be removed. Curbs and gutters supplement the area drains and catch basins as methods of collecting surface runoff.

Subsurface collection is often accomplished with perforated pipe set in ditches filled with gravel. The holes are on one side of the pipe and are pointed "up" to catch the water that seeps down through gravel ditches (Fig. 10-28a). A minimum percent slope on the pipe is necessary to provide positive drainage. By reversing the orientation

Figure 10-25 Area drain.

Figure 10-26 Catch basin.

Figure 10-27 Trench drain.

Figure 10-28 ''French'' drain —perforated pipe.

of the perforations, the runoff collected can be transferred in the same system and disposed of on-site (Fig. 10-28b). Water runs through the system, draining through the pipe and gravel, recharging the groundwater. The system is environmentally sound and keeps runoff and erosion at a minimum, but it is an expensive way to control on-site runoff. All alternatives have both economic and environmental costs. The problem for the site planner is to develop a grading and drainage plan that respects a site's unique ecology while minimizing the obligations of capital costs.

GRADING FOR STREETS AND ROADS

Grading for a road or any circulation system relies on the basic concepts discussed in Chapter 9. The road appears to be a more complex grading problem because it has a constant slope and is a continuous system. The function of roads is such that they serve first as an auto path and second as an adjunct to a drainage system. A road must be designed in conformance with strict design standards, maintaining appropriate grades, curvatures, and sight distances. Since most communities have established street and road design criteria, these important variables will be discussed only conceptually.

As the character of natural topography is such that it is almost never level, for safety purposes, roads should be designed to minimize the fluctuations across variable terrain. Keep in mind that neither the road nor the pedestrian path is really level; both are designed to permit movement on constant slope or grade (Figs. 10-29 and 10-30). Both systems simply require design considerations that will permit travel horizontally and vertically. One common and sensible objective for any system is the design of a route that is as short and direct as possible. Accepting that as a worthy objective must be balanced against the implications of that decision. Although the shortest route may have certain desirable advantages, sometimes the change in the natural topography is so great that a road alignment of the ''shortest distance'' approach could result in extensive cutting (Fig. 10-31). A road designed in an alignment that is at or nearly perpendicular to the topographical fall is described as ''bucking the grade.'' The road, like any other site ''improvement,'' must be designed so as to minimize the cut and fill necessary, while responding to prescribed design criteria. For that reason, unless the natural topographical slope is very shallow and requires only minimal grading, a common design guide is to align the road's centerline with or parallel to the contour lines (Fig. 10-32). This method can keep large cut or fill areas to a minimum while the alignment changes vertically. In those circumstances in which the technique may demand ''switchbacks'' in the alignment, care must be taken to make certain that the outside of the curve is elevated to accommodate the centrifugal force of the vehicle through the curve (Fig.

Figure 10-29 Road on slope.

10-33). The common crown section would only exacerbate the problem created by the centrifugal force developed by the vehicle moving through the turn.

Because of a road's section and length, the grading problem for roads often creates genuine consternation for the beginner. Some thought must be given to considering the design of the road, first, as the function of the road's centerline. If the road is initially thought of as a centerline, the decisions associated with its slope, curvature, or connections may be simpler to achieve. By reducing the road to a line, the question of cut or fill can also be evaluated in a very straightforward way. If the objective is to balance the cut and fill, the point at which the centerline of the road and the contour line cross simply becomes the center of the road (Fig. 10-34). The "high" side to the centerline is a cut and the "low" side is a fill.

If the topography is too steep for a successful fill, the point at which the outer edge of the road crosses the contour is used as the control point on the low side (Fig.

Figure 10-30 Pedestrian path on slope.

Figure 10-31 Plan of road "bucking the grade."

Figure 10-32 Plan of road parallel to contours.

Figure 10-33 Elevated section of switchback.

Figure 10-34 Centerline of road: cut and fill.

Figure 10-35 Centerline of road: cut only.

Figure 10-36 Centerline of road: fill only.

10-35). The contour line is then adjusted to reflect the crown of the road and the extent of the cut. If the road must be graded on fill, the point at which the high side of the road crosses the contour line becomes the control point (Fig. 10-36). The contour line is adjusted accordingly to meet the grade of the existing topography.

Most often, "What do I do now" problems occur when the road alignment or configuration does not match the examples in the text. Three problems are not uncommon and need to be mentioned: (1) the road crosses a series of contours; (2) the road crosses a drainage swale; and (3) the road crosses a steep slope.

In the design of the road across a series of contours, the site planner needs to keep in mind the criteria established for the road. One of those criteria reflects the need for a constant slope (Fig. 10-37). This is critical to its design, as a road that might continu-

Figure 10-37 Road in plan with spot elevations.

Figure 10-38 Road in plan with new contour lines.

ously rise or fall with the natural contour could create problems with sight distances and intersections. So, to respect the uniform slope design criteria, the decisions concerning the road's alignment would begin as they did earlier with the road's centerline, the slope, and the first contour. The criteria determine the specific elevations of the road's centerline and, as such, the locations of each new contour line in the series (Fig. 10-38).

The second problem mentioned considers those circumstances in which the road crosses a drainage swale and the question concerning the intersection between the road and the topographical depression. Depending on the length and depth of the swale, the road may necessitate either a culvert or a bridge. Modest topographical changes that accommodate minor amounts of water can be resolved with a culvert (Fig. 10-39). If substantial amounts of water are visible on the site in a natural water course, a bridge may be necessary. Additional riprap to reduce the erosion probability in a water course could also be an important adjunct to the design. These are considerations to support an

Figure 10-39 Culvert.

Figure 10-40 Small vehicular bridge over creek.

enlightened response to the role of both creek and road and to separate their functions (Fig. 10-40).

The third problem involves the encounter between the road and radical topographical slope. Even though the road's centerline is "running" with the contour lines, the road's section across the slope can sometimes create problems. One alternative is a bifurcated section (Fig. 10-21). The technique can be employed where the number of moving lanes are four or more (two each way). It would be inappropriate to separate a two-lane street and create a situation where a stalled vehicle in either lane would render a section of the road impassable. The other alternative is to consider the road's section in typical cut and/or fill terms. Although a cut is more stable than a fill, caution should be exercised, as heavy rainfall can induce mud slides and create disastrous problems. As mentioned earlier, fill is more unstable than cut, and soils with any history of bonding problems should be avoided. Often in these cases, the only way to resolve the situation is with a retaining wall on the high side of the slope (Fig. 10-41). Although it is not an inexpensive device, the retaining wall is a very positive method of resolving a situation that is potentially dangerous. In resolving those situations, there is an old canard in offices that bears repeating: "Why is it that we always find the time and money to do it right the second time?"

The road also serves as a drainage system and there are some basic configurations with which the site planner needs to be familiar. First, the typical cross section (Fig. 10-42) has a "crown" in the center, with the curb and gutter at the edges. The high crown forces the water to the edges and keeps standing water out and away from the path of moving vehicles. This is a primary criterion for the design of any street or thoroughfare. If water is trapped and left to stand on a road, it can induce hydroplaning in auto/truck tires, which reduces the basic adhesion necessary for control of a vehicle. Although a crown of 6 in. is common, always check with the appropriate governmental authority, as their design standards will vary to reflect local climate and environmental conditions.

On occasions, the road may be sloped from side to side (Fig. 10-43). This is sometimes necessary to accommodate a natural topographical slope where use of the typical crown section cannot produce the necessary positive drainage. Under some circumstances, the road may be designed in a concave shape, eliminating all together the need for a curb. The example in Fig. 10-44 is an illustration of a private road in a small (60-dwelling-unit) subdivision. There are two important variables associated with this

Figure 10-41 Retaining wall on high side of bifurcated road.

Figure 10-42 Section through road with crown.

Figure 10-43 Road sloped from side to side.

Figure 10-44 Road with concave section.

sidewalks

traffic signs
and light standards

utilities

Private Property   Public Right·Of·Way   Private Property

Figure 10-45 Section through road, illustrating location of utilities.

design. The first is the shape and the absence of the traditional curb. The second is the paving material. This material has an ''open'' joint and, as such, ''accepts'' the runoff from adjoining lots and paving. The total runoff from the development and the street to the sewer is significantly smaller than that of concrete or asphalt.

It must be recognized that this particular solution is uniquely appropriate to the conditions associated with this site. Although the concave section contains and controls surface runoff for this community, it is successful because the entire site, including roads and paving material, was considered as an integrated system.

The negative aspects of this example required that the sewer be located under the paving section. Under most conditions today, utilities are located in either the public right-of-way or easements at the edge of the paving section. Figure 10-45 depicts a utility location which recognizes the fact that utility systems often need both repair and expansion. As such, a separate right-of-way is a more cost-effective alternative to the traditional thinking, which required removing the paving to gain access to the utilities.

chapter 11

Retaining Walls

by Ernest Buckley

Significant differences in finished surface elevations are frequently a part of the design, sometimes as an unavoidable consequence of the topography and sometimes as a means of dramatizing features for purely aesthetic reasons. In all cases, retaining walls must be properly designed to resist the lateral loads imposed by soil over the long term. All too often, too little attention is given to the structural requirements and the soil's characteristics, and retaining wall failures are the result.

Properly designed and constructed retaining walls are relatively expensive; therefore, their use should be avoided whenever possible. Differences in elevation can be accommodated more inexpensively by graded slopes. Slopes are, however, contingent on a soil's stability and thus can become subject to erosion. The expense of retaining walls is frequently justified to accommodate abrupt changes of grade and reduce the potential for erosion.

Where a change of grade must be made vertically, the retaining wall is, in effect, a dam. Although soil normally appears to be a hard, stiff, and stable material, it is important to recognize that under some conditions of saturation or near saturation the soil mass will slide, slip, or flow. The soil can act as a viscous fluid, and the retaining wall must be able to prevent the sliding or flowing action under all foreseeable conditions.

The retaining wall design is, in some respects, analogous to a building foundation (see Fig. 11-1). Basement walls restrain the earth outside by lateral reactions produced by the footing and by the structural elements at the ground level. Free-standing walls are designed to be stiff enough to transfer lateral loads to the reaction at the footing. In either case, the design of the wall and footing must take into account active earth pressure and, where it exists, passive earth pressure. Figure 11-2 provides a further explanation.

Active earth pressure exerts horizontal force against any structural element that prevents the soil from sliding or creeping (flowing) into a state of natural equilibrium. The pressure varies directly and linearly with the vertical difference in elevation across

Figure 11-1 The basement wall analogy. (a) Basement walls must withstand external soil pressure by reaction at floor and footing levels. (b) Free-standing walls react by cantilever action about the footing.

Figure 11-2 Passive and active earth pressures. (a) Passive soil pressure is the resistance of earth to displacement and can be taken advantage of in retaining wall design. (b) Active soil pressure is assumed to be analogous to fluid pressure. Equivalent fluid pressure depends on soil density, depth, and internal friction.

the retaining wall. The type of soil and the soil moisture (degree of saturation) also affect the magnitude of the active soil pressure.

Passive soil pressure is the reaction of the soil itself to applied lateral forces. This reaction is related to the compressive strength of the soil. Retaining walls can be designed to take advantage of the passive soil pressure reaction by extending deep into the soil. Resistance to sliding is increased by the deeper wall, but usually, the effect should be neglected in the calculation of the overturning moments produced by the active loads. In other words, the footing of the retaining wall must be wide enough and strong enough to resist the tendency to overturn. The footing should be proportional, so as to provide a factor of safety against overturning of 2.0 and against sliding of 1.5 (see Fig. 11-3).

Retaining wall design begins with consideration of the *in situ* soil conditions, the limits of excavation required, and the type of backfill to be used. In many cases, the soils at the site are not satisfactory for backfill and, instead, select granular materials must be acquired for this purpose. It is important that the backfill material be permeable to permit drainage. A drain tile line may be installed to ensure that water is not permitted to build up to saturate the backfill. As an alternative or in addition to the tile drain, weep holes may be installed to penetrate the wall at 4 to 8 ft on centers.

The best retaining walls and footings are constructed of reinforced concrete. For the purpose of design, a segment of the wall 1 ft in length is usually isolated for the analysis of loads, shears, and moments, first on the vertical wall stem and then on the footing segment. For cantilevered wall, obviously, since shear and moment approach zero at the surface, a thicker wall and more steel is required at the top of the footing than at the top of the wall. Tall walls are, therefore, often built with a batter (slope) to the surface of the wall against the backfill (see Fig. 11-4). To increase the reactive capacity of the footing to lateral sliding, the footing for tall walls (8 ft or more) often incorporates a shear key. Low walls (less than 8 ft) are usually of constant thickness, and shear key on the bottom of the footing is usually omitted.

Materials other than poured-in-place reinforced concrete can be used to construct retaining walls that will perform satisfactorily. Brick, concrete masonry units (block), or stone masonry can be used. Treated timber or railroad ties can also be considered. Whatever material system is selected, the structural response must be of the same capacity as the equivalent reinforced concrete retaining wall.

As construction costs escalate, it is not surprising that various alternatives are considered. Sometimes, aesthetic factors dictate the selection of alternative materials. As a general rule, however, it is usually the case that reinforced concrete will be the

Figure 11-3 Loads, reactions and deformations of a retaining wall.

Figure 11-4 Typical reinforced concrete retaining wall. Loads on the wall include its own weight (W1), the weight of the footing (W2), the weight of the backfill on the heel of the footing (W3), and the linearly-varying active soil pressure (P). For stability, the resultant of the reaction must be in the middle third of the footing.

least costly. The inherent material system characteristics of the alternatives, if properly accounted for in the design, will ordinarily result in higher cost.

All forms of masonry retaining walls must be reinforced. Brick and stone masonry must be a minimum of two wythes. All masonry wall stems must be designed to be supported by and to act integrally with an adequate footing. Brick masonry design should be in accordance with BIA Technical Notes 17E and F. Figure 11-5 illustrates the principal considerations relative to stone masonry construction.

Masonry Retaining Walls

(a)   (b)

Figure 11-5 Stone masonry wall construction. (a) Unreinforced, single wythe of stone masonry is obviously *unstable*. An adequate footing is critical to adequate performance. (b) Double wythe of stone masonry, reinforced, and on a properly designed footing, will perform adequately.

Figure 11-6 Concrete block retaining wall.

Concrete block walls (CMUs) can be designed for single-wythe construction if careful detailing is provided. Examples are illustrated in Fig. 11-6. Concrete block is best used as a backup for a stone or brick veneer, as shown. Horizontal joint reinforcement and vertical reinforcement in grouted cores are essential. Buttresses, extending back into the retained soil, will contribute to wall stem stability. A properly designed reinforced concrete footing is required.

Alignment of a wall is also important. Curvature of a masonry wall, if concave outward, can add appreciably to stability. Lateral loads produced by soil induce compression stresses that can readily be accommodated by the masonry materials. However, a curved wall, concave inward, subjects the masonry material to tension and the likelihood of failure is enhanced (Fig. 11-7). Similarly, masonry tree wells are effective, since the wall is placed on compression by the external active pressure. Tree pedestals must be heavily reinforced to resist the tension forces developed (see Fig. 11-8).

Although the need for economy is recognized and appreciated, one cannot help but be dismayed at the apparent boundless optimism of those who install some retaining wall configurations. Examples are seen of reinforced masonry with no footing at all. Stone masonry of single-wythe construction, on roughly constructed footings, are all too common.

In recent years, the quest for economy, supported by ill-considered design, has

Figure 11-7 Curved masonry wall. (a) Concave inward alignment produces internal tensile stress. Reinforcement is required. (b) Arch effect adds stability to masonry wall when concaved outward, since internal stress is compression.

Figure 11-8   Tree pedastal and tree wall. (a) Tension stress will result in failure unless resisted by steel reinforcement. (b) Compressive stress developed contributes to stability.

led to widespread use of salvaged railroad ties as a retaining wall material system. For a rustic effect and for very low applications, this innovation may be justified. In most cases, however, the railroad ties represent the ultimate in inadequacy. Serious failures occur more often than not (Fig. 11-9).

The most common use of railroad ties, as shown by Fig. 11-10, is as a surface treatment for a slope. The wood members are simply stacked against the slope, spiked together, and expected to prevent erosion. There is no structural integrity as far as resisting active lateral loads is concerned. The system is similar in concept to stone riprap,

Figure 11-9   Railroad-tie wall failing.

Railroad Ties
stacked and spiked

Figure 11-10 Treated-timber retaining wall. Actually, this typical configuration is not
a retaining wall at all. It is an attempt to stabilize a slope by surface treatment, analogous
to stone riprap.

and it is relatively ineffective simply because of the relative low density of the wood
material as compared to stone. Lateral sliding or fluid movement is uninhibited. Erosion
behind the retaining wall members also occurs, even in the case of granular stable soils.
Vertical walls formed of railroad ties can be used for very low walls. Even in these
cases, it is difficult to maintain alignment, and loss of soil by erosion can be expected.
Stacking of more than three units in height should be avoided.

High walls of wooden ties are often seen with an occasional tie installed in a
"deadman" orientation. The deadman extends back into the fill material behind the wall.
Apparently, the designer believes that stability can thus be gained. Actually, the deadman (anchor) is almost completely ineffective. The bond stress between the soil and the
surface of the anchor tie (deadman) is very low, and relatively small forces can pull out
the anchor. The shear surface on which the retained soil slides or flows is, more often

Railroad Ties stacked and spiked

Shear failure surface

Railroad tie
Deadman

Figure 11-11 Deadman concept. Stability is expected from the tier installed as "dead-
men," extending back into the fill behind the wall.

Figure 11-12

than not, well beyond the length of the anchor. The configuration shown by Fig. 11-11 is inherently *unstable*.

Retaining walls are a useful device for effecting the desired site surface configuration. Their use can result in good esthetic quality and overall economy. Attempts to economize in the design and construction of the retaining walls themselves, however, are almost sure to degrade quality.

chapter 12

Topography and Surveys

Most of the time your request to a client to acquire a topographical survey at 1- or 2-ft interval will be respected without quarrel. Although an explanation is necessary, more often than not, the client will understand the importance of this document and engage the services of a professional engineer or registered surveyor. However, on those occasions when a site has been altered after a survey or your empirical analysis of the site tells you that something is not "right," you need to know how to execute a small topographical survey on your own. Although it is possible and appropriate under some circumstances to undertake a *limited* topographical check, unless you have the professional qualifications, *do not* engage or contract to do work that involves checking or *describing any property line, easement, or road right-of-way*. The legal implications associated with defining a property line's location, bearing, and distance are significant and in most states the purview of the licensed civil engineer or land surveyor.

In those situations in which an area needs to be checked or the topographical interval is too large to permit detailed grading, instead of interpolating, survey the site. The method is fairly simple and uncomplex. Before going to the site, lay out a square grid on a print of the most current topographical information available. If possible, use one of the longer property lines of the site as a baseline. The baseline can be on the property line or in some other way "fixed" relative to the boundary line survey (Fig. 12-1). This is absolutely crucial to the process, for if the baseline is not correct, the grid and all points on the grid will be incorrectly located. Ultimately, spot elevations at the intersection of each grid line (A/1, B/2, C/9, etc.) provide a matrix of spot elevations (Fig. 12-2). This matrix of spot elevations provides a base of known points that must be related to a bench mark, or reference point, to be of any value. Just as knowing the exact location of the grid baseline is imperative to knowing the location of all subsequent points on the grid, the bench mark is critical to knowing the relative elevation of all points on the grid.

Where the grid interval is such that there are large areas of unknown elevation, intermediate grid lines may be introduced. In Fig. 12-3, horizontal grid line 6 + 85 is

Figure 12-1 Boundary line survey describing baseline.

Figure 12-2 Matrix of spot elevations.

Figure 12-3 Transit and rod.

just such a line. Its nomenclature indicates that it is line 6 plus 85 ft. Other spot elevations not on the survey grid can be located and identified by using a transit, a compass, and a tape.

The equipment necessary to execute the survey properly includes a transit and rod (Fig. 12-3), a steel tape (minimum 100 ft), pins, and a hammer (Fig. 12-4). Solicit instructions relative to setting up the transit before going to the site. Although some of

Figure 12-4 Steel tape, pins, and hammer.

Figure 12-5 Transit set up over known point.

the older instruments must be leveled in two directions, technological advancements in surveyor's equipment have made newer models much less time consuming to set up.

After setting the transit up *over* a known point on the baseline (Fig. 12-5), the grid coordinates are located on the site with the pins. The grid is orthogonal and the surveyor simply needs to make certain that the grid is at 90°. This can be checked with the compass on the instrument. This should be a fairly straightforward process of using the transit to establish a true orthogonal pattern and the tape to establish the proper grid coordinates.

Following the establishment of the grid, the first reading to be made and documented is that of a bench mark. A bench mark is a known, predetermined spot elevation on the site (Fig. 12-6). Some research is necessary to determine the location of a bench mark on the site prior to the survey. The local public works departments can be helpful in establishing these important spot elevations. Determining the location and documenting the elevation of a bench mark is critical, because without some known elevation on the site, all subsequent rod readings will simply be a series of "relative" elevations. As

Figure 12-6 Bench mark close-up.

an example, if the rod reading of a known bench mark of 564.3 ft is 7.22 ft, all subsequent readings and interpolations will be based on that known relationship. When it is necessary to move the transit, it is imperative to take a new rod reading of the bench mark. Failure to do this *every time* the transit is moved will result in major errors in the interpolation process. Although secondary bench marks may be necessary, their evaluations must be read, documented, and interpolated relative to the original bench mark.

It must also be mentioned that a bona fide bench mark may not be on or near the site. Conditions may either be rural, or one cannot be located. Under those circumstances simply use any permanently fixed point. In urban settings curbs or water meters might serve the purpose. In rural conditions a small concrete pile might need to be set. Either of these conditions recognizes that while the survey will not reflect the accurate elevation above sea level, properly executed it will be accurate relative to that particular site and its "bench mark."

Rod readings must be taken at each coordinate point on the grid to identify the elevation of that specific point. Viewing the rod through the transit, the elevation is taken at the center cross hair in the scope of the transit. To permit a detailed fix on any point, the rod has been separated into feet, tenths, and hundreths of a foot. As an example, the reading of the rod in Fig. 12-7 is 4.12 and Fig. 12-8 is 6.97. The space between the black hundredths divisions is sometimes unclear, as the rod is often smaller in the transit scope than shown in the examples.

To identify the exact location of the whole-number contour line between any two spot elevations, the following formula is applied.

$$Y = \frac{B - X}{B - A}(L)$$

where

B = highest elevation (spot grade)
A = lowest elevation (spot grade)
X = whole-number contour sought
L = distance between the two spot elevations
Y = distance from the highest elevation down to the whole-number contour

In those cases where there may be two or more whole-number contours between two spot elevations, treat each contour line in the formula separately, as though there were no other contour lines. This technique is quite accurate and produces consistently good results.

Figure 12-7 Rod reading.

Example:

Figure 12-8 Rod reading.

	Spot Elev.	Spot Elev.
	A	B
	+	+
$B = 94.1$	93.6	94.1
$A = 93.6$		
$L = 50$ ft	$Y = \dfrac{94.1 - 94.0}{94.1 - 93.6}(50)$	
$X = 94$		
	$= \dfrac{0.1}{0.5}(50)$	

Figure 12-9 Grid of spot elevations and contour lines.

$Y = 10$; therefore, the contour line 94 ft crosses 10 ft below 94.1 on a line between 94.1 and 93.6.

As mentioned earlier, the method is rather straightforward and is intended only to provide a check on a site that appears to have been modified, or as an elaboration on *known* topography where interpolation would be inappropriate. The spot elevations taken at the intersections of the grid now permit the identification and location of each contour line on the site. Figure 12-9 is an example of a contour map and base spot grade matrix.

This will, hopefully, reinforce the idea that the grading process is pursued through the establishment of spot grades first. Contour lines are then changed to accommodate the spot grades. The most common mistake in grading is one in which contour lines are changed without due consideration of spot elevations. The results are often radical and unnecessary changes because the site planner failed to remember that the contour line at its *smallest* increment represents a 1-ft change. The spot elevation can become any number and thus more accommodating grading is plausible.

chapter 13

Storm Water Management and Erosion Control

INTRODUCTION

The final segment in the topic of Earthworks deals with the concept of storm water management and erosion control. Storm water management and erosion control are simply a part of grading and drainage. This segment of earthworks will focus on those concepts and techniques that seek to resolve the problem created by large volumes of surface water and precipitation. To begin with, storm water management systems generally have two purposes: (1) the control of water to prevent or minimize damage to property or physical injury, and (2) the control of water to minimize or eliminate an inconvenience in the use of the site during less significant storms.

BASIC CONCEPTS

The basic concepts associated with storm water management are few and, for the most part, follow what most would consider to be good common sense.

First, when plausible, water that falls on a site should be retained on that site to the extent that the rate of discharge is no more than that prior to the development.[1] This is often achievable in suburban sites and in environments in which the impervious surfaces are less than 90%. Where appropriate, storm water systems should be designed to permit aquifer recharge. Conversely, storm water management systems should avoid recharge in those soil conditions where groundwater effects might be harmful. Aside from the environmental advantages, on-site retention often reduces the community's investment in storm sewers, expanded floodplains, or channelization programs. Permanent or temporary ponding is a common method of controlling on-site water but must be considered as a part of the entire development process.

---

[1]*Residential Storm Water Management* [Washington D.C.: Urban Land Institute (ULI), American Society of Civil Engineers (ASCE), and the National Association of Home Builders (NAHB), 1975], p. 11.

Second, the optimum design of any storm water collection and storage system is a balance between capital costs, environmental quality, risk, and operational costs.[2] Each design alternative must be examined through a process that considers all of the foregoing issues, for ignoring any one invites a decision that could result in substantial economic or environmental loss.

Next, emphasis should be placed on natural engineering techniques, that is, those consistent with the natural processes and resources. This obviously begins with recognition that precipitation and storm water are a part of the hydrological cycle. These concepts also require an understanding of the site's natural ecology and the methods by which the existing natural systems dispose of precipitation. An understanding of the character and physiography of the site permits the recognition of valuable opportunities, as well as imminent disaster.

Further, the responsibility for genuine storm water management rests with the municipality and the developer. Do not be misled by polemics that portray the developer as the villain, complete with black hat and muddy boots. The fact of the matter is that no developer can do anything less than that which the local or state governments permit through their ordinances and regulations. The developer is not a nonprofit or philanthropic institution and thus should not be chastised when his or her proposals do not coincide with your perceptions or wants. The author's recommendations to local governments and citizens are to say what you want, be specific about it in terms of quality and quantity, and finally, assume that you will be disappointed. If a local government employs strict regulations and has rigorous controls, the results will more likely reflect environmental quality that has not been left to chance or the developer's CPA's ledger.

Finally, recognize that each site is a different set of circumstances, land use, occupancy, and environment and will require different solutions. The critical aspect of each site planning problem lies in the design criteria established for that particular site. Criteria must be clear and definitive, for without some accepted standard or criterion, every solution is acceptable.

STORM WATER RUNOFF ANALYSIS

Although most architects and landscape architects will relegate the responsibility of quantifying the amount of storm water to an engineer, it is, nonetheless, important to understand the basic concepts and techniques.

Rainfall is a natural phenomenon and no two occurrences are the same. The data used in site analysis are based on historical documentation by the National Weather Service. Their data quantify three primary variables: amount (intensity), duration (for how long a time), and frequency (how often does this event repeat itself?). This information is ultimately translated into descriptions that generalize the real event.

There are various hydrological models for analyzing runoff. The selection of the model depends on a number of variables: the size of the area to be considered, its topography, level of development, the character of natural stream systems, existing storm sewers, aesthetic goals, and the level of detail desired, to name the most important. There are no rules relative to what is the best technique to use under every circumstance, so each site must be evaluated individually.

There are four basic techniques which, with the assistance of a high-speed computer, attempt to simulate rainfall.

1. Hydrological simulation models, which can provide a simulation of quantity (flows) and concentrations.
2. Unit hydrographs, which examine the implications of 1 in. of excess rain in a known drainage area over a limited period.

---

[2]Ibid.

3. Regression models, which utilize statistical correlation to relate a cause such as rainfall in a watershed to an effect such as runoff volume or peak flow.

4. Empirical formulas. Although there are a variety of empirical formulas, the oldest and most commonly used is the rational method. This formula is widely used where a high level of accuracy is not necessary.[3]

The rational method, $Q = CiA$, separates the numerous variables mentioned earlier into four numerical quantities:[4]

> Q = peak runoff of the area in question, in cubic feet per second
> C = runoff coefficient of the land in the drainage area; this factor can often be obtained from the local public works department

Surface Flow Time Curves

Figure 13-1 Graph of water distance flow. (After "Airport Drainage," Federal Aviation Agency, Department of Transportation, Advisory Circular, A/A 150-5320-5B, Washington, D.C., 1970.)

---

[3]Ibid., pp. 27–28.

[4]*Design and Construction of Sanitary and Storm Sewers*, American Society of Civil Engineers (ASCF) Manual of Practice, No. 37, 1970; notes revised by D. Earl Jones, Jr., p. 31.

i = "average intensity of rainfall in inches per hour for a duration equal to the time of concentration, T, for a selected rainfall frequency"

T = "time in minutes after the beginning of rainfall for runoff to peak at the point under consideration"; although T is not a function in the formula, to identify the intensity of the rainfall (i), T must be determined

A = size of the drainage area, in acres

Using Fig. 13-1, begin by measuring the longest distance that the water must flow before discharge. The average slope that the water must traverse must also be determined. Although runoff coefficients can be obtained from local sources, Table 13-1 will be used as the source for this example. If the distance across the site is 720 ft and the slope is 3%, begin by reading from the "overland travel in distance" on the left side of Fig. 13-1 to the point at which the horizontal line intersects the slope line of 3%. Taken as an example, a site that is a 2-acre single-family residential land use, Fig. 13-1 indicates the C coefficient to be 0.30 to 0.50. Reading down on the graph from the intersection of the distance and slope lines to the 0.30 and 0.50 curves, the overland time of travel is from 24 to 31 minutes. Time T can also be calculated with the following formula:

$$T = 1.8(1.1 - C)\frac{D}{S}$$

where

D = distance across the site

S = average slope

T = time, in minutes

TABLE 13-1 Runoff Coefficients

	RUNOFF COEFFICIENTS
DESCRIPTION OF AREA	
Business	
Downtown	0.70–0.95
Neighborhood	0.50–0.70
Residential	
Single family	0.30–0.50
Multiunits, detached	0.40–0.60
Multiunits, attached	0.60–0.75
Residential (suburban)	0.25–0.40
Apartment	0.50–0.70
Industrial	
Light	0.50–0.80
Heavy	0.60–0.90
Parks, cemeteries	0.10–0.25
Railroad yard	0.20–0.35
Unimproved	0.10–0.30
CHARACTER OF SURFACE	
Pavement	
Asphalt or concrete	0.70–0.95
Brick	0.70–0.85
Roofs	0.70–0.95
Lawns, sandy soil	
Flat, 2%	0.05–0.10
Average, 2–7%	0.10–0.15
Steep, 7% or more	0.15–0.20
Lawns, heavy soil	
Flat, 2%	0.13–0.17
Average, 2–7%	0.18–0.22
Steep, 7% or more	0.25–0.35

5-YEAR 30-MINUTE RAINFALL (INCHES)

Figure 13-2 Map of 5 year–30 minute duration rainfall.

The value of T can now be used to identify I in the rational method equation ($Q = CIA$). To do that, either of the following references should be consulted:

1. Rainfall Frequency Atlas of the United States, Technical Paper 40, U.S. Department of Commerce, Weather Bureau
2. Five to Sixty Minute Precipitation Frequency for the Eastern and Central United States, N.O.A.A. Technical Memo N.W.S Hydro-35, Silver Spring, Md, June 1977

These two resources provide the basis for the documentation of the amount of rainfall over a specific duration and with a specific frequency. Using Fig. 13-2, the 5 year–30 minute rainfall map for Ft. Worth, Texas, indicates that the "2-in." curve touches the edge of the county. This provides the remaining information for the formula. Although this process is rather general, the method is used extensively as a preliminary indication of storm runoff potential. The coefficients in these two references are applicable only for storms of 5- to 10-year return frequencies, and were originally developed when many streets were uncurbed and drainage was conveyed in roadside swales. For recurrence intervals longer than 10 years, the indicated runoff coefficients should be increased, assuming that nearly all the rainfall in excess of that expected from the 10-year recurrence interval rainfall will become runoff and should be accommodated by an increased runoff coefficient.

The runoff coefficients indicated for different soil conditions reflect runoff behavior shortly after initial construction. With the passage of time, the runoff behavior of sandy soil areas will tend to approach that of heavy soil areas. If the designer's interest is long term, the reduced response indicated for sandy soil areas should be disregarded.[5]

EROSION: TYPES AND PROCESS

One need only observe the condition of local roads and highways to see the evidence of erosion damage to embankments, graded slopes, and drainage ditches. Although this problem is sometimes the result of poor drainage design, it is often due to inadequate slope stabilization methods. There are factors beyond the control of the site planner which can wreak havoc on recently graded or planted soil. The weather is a perfect example and is all the more reason why care should be taken to ensure proper installation of soil-stabilizing vegetation.

There are two major types of erosion. The first is geological erosion or natural erosion. This is a process of soil formation change through natural processes. Most of our present topographic features in the rural landscape are formed under this long-term erosion process. The second is accelerated erosion. This is deterioration and loss of surface soil as a result of natural or human activities. Accelerated erosion is a brief process and dramatically affects the quality of the environment because the results are often severe in magnitude.

The erosion process involves (1) soil detachment, (2) transportation, and (3) sedimentation. The surface soil is first attacked by an external force such as wind or rain. After the bond is broken that binds the soil particles together, the detached soil particles are then carried by either medium (wind or water) to settle later when the energy source dies away.

There are four types of erosion that threaten slope integrity: sheet erosion, rill erosion, slump erosion, and wind erosion. Sheet erosion is just like it sounds; it is a

[5]Ibid. p. 30.

thorough, somewhat even washing of water down a slope, like a sheet of water. To a point, this is the most controllable type of erosion.[6]

Rill erosion is the creation of rivulets or small channels that collect water and increasingly widen as they make their way down the slope. Some products are quite effective in resisting this type of erosion by providing a consistent deterrent to rivulet formation, thereby eliminating "weak spots" where this may occur. Rill erosion often occurs where fill has been necessary but has not had proper compaction or settlement.[7]

Slump erosion can be the most disastrous of all. It is the result of subsurface failure, where great areas of slope may suddenly sag or give way, necessitating regrading. This usually occurs due to extremely long or heavy rainfalls in which the soil becomes permeated with water, weakening subsurface bonding or compaction. Slump erosion may also be evidence of poor topsoil stabilization and inadequate surface vegetation or material to promote runoff.

Wind erosion most often occurs along ridges, where wind forces are greatest. Wind erosion can cause the loss of valuable nutrient-providing topsoil and mulch, exposing the roots of seedlings until seedlings are blown away, or simply causing poor growth and aiding water erosion.[8] Soil-stabilizing products deter wind erosion by holding mulch and topsoil in place until grass root systems are thoroughly developed.

Erosion control at its first stage should concentrate on the problems resulting from soil detachment. A concern about the loss of prime agricultural soil brought the issue of soil erosion into sharp focus. The effects of erosion on marine life and the associated flood hazard problems have required some site planners to treat erosion as an environmental problem as opposed to an agricultural issue. Studies of erosion control have concluded that surface water creates most of the erosion damage and that surface vegetation is often the most important factor in reducing erosion rates. Surface vegetation can absorb the energy of falling precipitation, reduce the soil detachment effect, and hold soil particles together. Vegetation also absorbs a fraction of the water through transpiration and as a component in the surface of the soil reduces the velocity of the water and the resulting scouring effect of runoff. Although the interception of precipitation by vegetation permits better absorption, impervious surfaces contribute to the volume of runoff and reduce any potential for groundwater or aquifer recharge. When precipitation can be absorbed, the rate of infiltration slows down as the soil soaks up the water. When the rate of the rainfall exceeds the ability of the soil to absorb the water, the residual becomes runoff.

As water runs downhill, the runoff erodes soil as it moves. Excessive runoff will, first, flood the area it covers, and second, carry sediment that clogs flow channels, escalating the flood potential. The volume of runoff depends directly on:

1. The amount and rate of precipitation
2. The ability of the site's soils to absorb the water
3. The topography and intensity of ground cover

In urbanized areas a substantial quantity of land is covered by impervious materials, which are, in most cases, connected to public storm sewer systems. The nature of storm sewer systems is such that they increase the capacity and speed of runoff. The removal of vegetation, soil disturbances, and other construction also increase the rate of

[6]*Handbook on the Principles of Hydrology*, Water Information Center, Inc., Water Research Building, Manhasset Isle, Port Washington, N.Y., p. X1.1.

[7]*Residential Erosion and Sediment Control* [Washington, D.C.: Urban Land Institute (ULI), American Society of Civil Engineers (ASCE), and the National Assoc. of Home Builders (NAHB), 1978], p. 18.

[8]Ibid. p. 22.

runoff and erosion. Changes in the rural watershed due to urbanization and a decrease in the infiltration process result in:

1. An increase in the total volume of runoff
2. An increase in the peak discharge for any given storm, and as a result
3. An increase in the frequency of flood peaks
4. A reduction in the time an area goes from absorption to runoff
5. An increase in the amount and velocity of water in artificial channelization
6. A discernible increase in sediment during the construction process of urban development

Because erosion and runoff problems relating to development extend far beyond the property lines where the development takes place, legal accountability of injury on other properties often becomes quite controversial. A majority of states rely on either the "common enemy" doctrine or the "civil law" doctrine to resolve direct conflicts. The "common enemy" doctrine holds that water is a "common enemy" and permits landowners to improve their properties regardless of resulting injury to other lands. The "civil law" doctrine, on the other hand, burdens the "upper" landowner with the responsibility for any damage created by an increase in downstream discharge.[9] Since following these two concepts to the letter has not been without its problems, state laws have reflected various perspectives when applying these doctrines.

Between the "civil law" and "common enemy" doctrines is the "reasonable use" theory. This is a compromise that permits a comparison of equities of each use in an individual case. In 1948, the Minnesota Supreme Court set down the following guideline for comparison:

> The rule is that in effecting a reasonable use of his land for a legitimate purpose a landowner, acting in good faith, may drain his land of surface water and cast them as a burden upon the land of another, although such drainage carries with it some water which would otherwise have never gone that way but would have remained on the land until they were absorbed by the soil or evaporated in the air if (a) there is a reasonable necessity for such drainage; (b) if reasonable care be taken to avoid unnecessary injury to the land receiving the burden; (c) if the utility or benefit accruing to the land drained reasonably outweighs the gravity of the harm resulting to the land receiving the burden; and (d) if, where practicable, it is accomplished by reasonably improving and aiding the normal and natural system of drainage according to its reasonable carrying capacity, or if, in the absence of a practicable natural drain, a reasonable and feasible artificial drainage system is adopted.[10]

The Soil and Water Conservation Districts Law provided one of the earliest public sector erosion control programs. Because erosion was considered an agricultural problem early on, the Soil and Water Conservation Districts Law focuses on erosion in agriculture. This program was initiated by the federal government and was later adopted by state governments. It provided districts with authority to adopt land use regulations to control activities or practice that would result in soil erosion.

An indirect method to control erosion is through water pollution control ordinances. By regulating the amount of water pollution (among which sediment is the leader) that can be discharged, activities that involve large-scale erosion can be contained. Although the intent of water pollution control was not land use regulation, the relationship between the two is so strong that some regulation of land use practice is recognized as an integral part of water quality control.

---

[9]Ibid. p. 59.

[10]*Ballentine's Law Dictionary* (The Lawyer's Co-operative Publishing Company, Rochester, N.Y.; Bancroft-Whitney Co., San Francisco, 1969), p. 1062.

Instead of controlling erosion problems through the restriction of land uses, erosion and runoff ordinances are more general and focus on performance plans or strategies. Ordinances often require engineering reports and development plans on clearing, grubbing, grading, vegetation preservation, erosion and sedimentation control, drainage improvements, maintenance of the intermediate regional floodplain, or maintenance of retention facilities. Since these plans are methods in which erosion might be abated or limited, they must be prepared, submitted, and approved before building permits are issued. The following is an example of common standards or policies.

1. The smallest amount of land area should be exposed at any time during development.

2. The period of exposure for land under development should be kept to the shortest practical.

3. Temporary vegetation or mulch should be used to stabilize critical areas where staging of development cannot avoid a time lag prior to permanent cover for the land.

4. Reasonable measures should be taken to prevent the carrying away of sediment by runoff water from land undergoing development.

5. Provisions should be made to accommodate the increased runoff caused by a change in surface conditions during and after development.

6. Permanent final vegetation and structures should be installed as soon as practical in the development.

7. Development plans should fit the topography and soils, to minimize erosion potential.

8. Wherever feasible, natural vegetation should be retained and protected.[11]

Again, many of the policies are based on common sense and would be practiced by anyone concerned with the implications of development. The knowledgeable site planner must be conscious of the role and participation of various state and local agencies in the development process. Because of the nature of state laws and the fact that each has an established code that can differ dramatically from its neighbor, each state's regulations must be recognized. Most of the time, these are adopted in local subdivision or development regulations and should state the reason for the regulation, specifics of the policies, and the process for application review and evaluation.

EROSION CONTROL METHODS

There are two conceptual methods of erosion and sediment controls: structural, and natural or vegetative. Natural or vegetative methods are those that employ the use of existing and/or new vegetation and mulches. Since the majority of sites are most vulnerable during construction, good advance planning can reduce the initial damage while facilitating the rejuvenation of permanent cover. When grass or other turf is used to stabilize a graded area, that new material should be planted parallel to the contours to reduce the flow of water. Vegetation used in this form are sometimes called filter strips. In those locales where clover or honeysuckle have a history of hardy growth, they have been used successfully in that capacity. Obviously, no construction or other traffic should be allowed into any area that has been planted as a vegetative buffer or filter strip.

Vegetative cover can be considered in either temporary or permanent terms. The value of temporary planting is that plants, such as annual rye grass, millet, and sudan-

---

[11]*Residential Erosion*, p. 32.

Figure 13-3 Bench terrace.

grass, grow quickly and can successfully stabilize an area for a particular season when protection is critical.

Permanent cover requires some consideration to make certain that the plant material selected is well adapted to the site. Probably the most critical factor in the selection process of permanent cover is maintenance. Although common sense would dictate otherwise, there are examples in every community where turf grasses requiring mowing have been planted on steep or inaccessible slopes. Recognizing the simple fact that plants will mature and that some will require maintenance should influence the decisions that match location, use, and species.[12]

Structural methods of erosion control are those which involve the use of landforms to retard or divert runoff. These techniques involve regrading or shaping the land as a method of slowing the velocity of the runoff or controlling the water's path. A bench terrace, as the term implies, is a flat terrace graded across the slope to slow the flow of runoff. In some cases where the area is large, bench terraces have been substantial enough to be used as building sites[13] (Fig. 13-3). In smaller areas the bench terrace has been used in conjunction with other cut and fill regrading to facilitate the stabilization of vegetation.

Berms are a common landform used in erosion control. Like the bench terrace, the berm can be used to intercept storm water runoff across a slope. The berm is essentially an earth mound and can be used to divert runoff into swales, gutters, or stable conditions below the berm (Fig. 13-4). Berms are used as both permanent and temporary methods of erosion control, but unlike other structural techniques can be modified into a permanent bench terrace form.

Diversion dikes or channels are also used to intercept potentially damaging runoff. A diversion channel is a trough cut in the slope to catch and divert runoff to a controlled outlet (Fig. 13-5). A diversion dike is a temporary ridge built parallel to contours of

Max. Slope 3:1
w/o Stabilization

3ft. - 5 ft.

Natural Slope

1.5 - 2 ft.

Figure 13-4 Filter berm.

[12]Joseph DeChiara and Lee E. Koppelman, *Site Planning Standards* (New York: McGraw-Hill Book Company, 1978), p. 36.

[13]Ibid., p. 34.

Figure 13-5 Diversion dike.

compacted soil. Both methods are used above critical slopes to reduce the potential for serious damage. Since both dike and diversion channels can concentrate significant amounts of surface water, before using either as an erosion control technique, some method must be developed for their integration into the adjacent landscape.

Outlets have been mentioned before as the disposal component of various structural techniques. Special attention needs to be made in the selection of the appropriate grasses to reduce the velocity and scouring effect of the runoff. Although various techniques, both natural and artificial, can be used to protect channels and outlets, every effort should be made toward the maintenance and replenishment of the existing vegetation.

Permanent ponds or lakes are also common man-made erosion control methods. They are popular as amenities and often increase the value of a property while providing an important function in the site planning process. "The Woodlands" near Houston and Reston, Virginia, are examples of sites where permanent ponding has been used to enhance the aesthetic quality of development while functioning to retard erosion and siltation (Fig. 13-6). These two communities have enjoyed a quality of development planning that proved to be a major contributor to their later success. No small part of that planning was based on an extensive environmental analysis which seized those opportunities to create amenities that were extensions of good land management concepts.

"Blue-green" storage areas are another method of storm water management that can often be employed as an amenity. The concept can be used in any situation where the water that naturally drains into a deep swale can be temporarily impounded. If a road needs to cross the swale, the grading to support the road becomes the bank, which retards

Figure 13-6 Permanent pond.

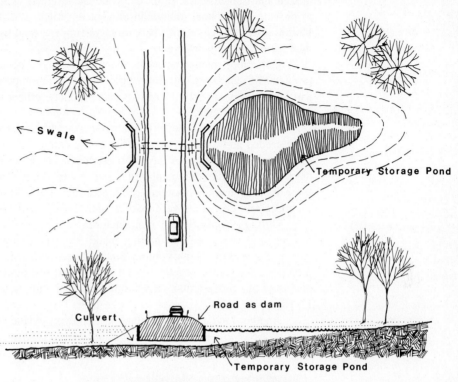

Figure 13-7   A blue-green storage pond.

the flow of water through the swale, changing the dry "green" area to a wet "blue" area until the water has drained through the culvert or pipe at the bottom of the swale (Fig. 13-7). This is a very simple, yet positive mechanism to reduce on-site runoff and to control the volume and rate of water being discharged from a site.[14]

Where possible, parking lots can be designed to hold water. This can be accomplished by designing the lot's slope, surface planes, and curbs to retain surface water and control its release. Some caution must be exercised in the design of the lot, to avoid deep ponding in areas in which people may need to walk. Since the speed of the auto in the parking lot will be slow, hydroplaning should not be a problem. The principal issues are the location of the area to retard the flow of water, the selection of the appropriate drain type, and the type of paving.

SOIL STABILIZATION PRODUCTS

There are numerous products available to assist in establishing proper erosion control on even the steepest grades. Although these products can sometimes be expensive to use, particularly over large areas, their savings in maintenance costs for severely eroded land can be significant.

These temporary soil-stabilizing products vary greatly in material and compositional makeup, but they are all used in a similar manner and toward the same end. Some must be installed after seeding and mulching; some provide their own mulch, and still others can be seeded after installation, thereby providing instant soil support. Most of

---

[14]*Residential Storm Water Management*, p. 35.

the material is available in large rolls and is simply unrolled across the area to be stabilized and stapled to the earth. They are all designed, with varying degrees of success, to provide a beneficial microenvironment to protect and promote seedling growth and inhibit erosion forces until grass root systems are established enough to provide their own natural erosion deterrence.

Over time, many materials and products have been developed to deal with the problems of temporary soil stabilization and vegetation promotion. Although technological innovations are prevalent in various products, others rely principally on traditional materials and methods.

One company has developed a strong, durable, lightweight plastic netting for covering seeded and mulched areas. The netting can also be used to hold sod in place and disintegrates by sunlight as the turf is established (Fig. 13-8). Another manufacturer has developed a product that combines a mat of curled and seasoned wood excelsior with a layer of biodegradable plastic mesh. It is designed to hold soil in place, create conditions for successful grass seed germination, and protect seedlings after sprouting (Fig. 13-9).

Utilizing sophisticated manufacturing techniques, another company produces a flexible soil reinforcement matting made from heavy nylon monofilaments fused together. Since 90% of its volume can be filled with soil or gravel, the mesh of wire provides a matrix for vegetative root growth and soil infiltration. The rigidity and open quality of this product make it a durable material with various erosion control uses (Fig. 13-10).

Another product is a combination of polypropylene yarn interwoven with strips of

Figure 13-8 Plastic netting.

Figure 13-9 Wood excelsior.

Figure 13-10 Nylon monofilaments.

paper. The paper blocks the force of rain and acts as a mulch. When decomposed, the net holds the roots and soil in place as the vegetative mat develops (Fig. 13-11).

A jute mesh of natural fiber is a more traditional product and is ordinarily used to hold soil and seed intact on slopes and other areas of concentrated water flow. The fiber itself acts as a ''built-in mulch'' which will decompose in time and add organic matter to the soil (Fig. 13-12).

There are many factors that must be considered when choosing an erosion control

Figure 13-11 Paper and nylon twine.

Figure 13-12 Jute mesh.

product. Cost, availability, time, and specific applications are all important in making a selection. All products must be compared directly to the use of lay-in sod as a soil stabilizer: While the season, cost, and labor must be part of the considerations in selecting a material, when properly laid, sod is still the only alternative that offers nearly immediate living ground cover.

OPEN PAVING SYSTEMS

A myriad of environmental problems associated with development have forced design professions to reevaluate the real costs of various methods and materials used for years without question. Although the simplicity and low cost of the asphalt or concrete parking lot was widely accepted, their aesthetic qualities left something to be desired. It is only recently, with the problems associated with on-site runoff and groundwater recharge, that the value of alternative systems became real.

At the turn of the century, many roads in American and European towns were paved with brick and cobblestones. At the time, these were simply the only readily available materials dense enough to be considered as a paving surface. Considering the remedial suspension systems for horse-drawn carriages, these pavers were very coarse. Their aesthetic quality, however, was another matter. Their texture, color, and size permitted easy integration into the natural landscape. But with the onset of the automobile and advances in technology, bricks and cobblestones were replaced by more economical and smoother paving methods and materials. The cost of shipping, since kilns and quarries were often remote, and the labor-intensive character of the individual paver, coupled to keep their relative costs high. Compared to construction with monolithic slabs of concrete and asphalt, the construction of a road with individual pavers became exorbitant. Furthermore, the smooth seamless quality of concrete and asphalt was a welcome change from a collection of masonry units.

Since the street was the first parking lot, the natural inclination was to apply the same technology to the parking lot. In a marginally urbanized society, naturally, little consideration was given to the surface runoff from parking lots. Although architects and landscape architects maintained a preference for the smaller masonry unit because of its aesthetic quality, its use has been limited to historical streets and motor courts of expensive hotels or corporate headquarters. More recently, however, problems associated with storm water management and erosion control have resulted in an examination of popular practice and development policies by various state and local governments. Since traditional concrete and asphalt densities accept negligible amounts of moisture, there emerged an obvious need for options to the usual paving standard.

The use of modern open pavers was actually developed in Europe. The Europeans hold their gardens in high esteem and the problem of how to provide access for vehicles to their homes and parks is of major importance. The concept of open paving is as simple as garden flagstones. The open paver is designed to provide a solid surface only for the area necessary to support pedestrian traffic. The area that was unnecessary for support is left as open as possible, permitting plant growth. The green area is filled level to the top with soil to allow for cutting of the planting material when necessary. When in place, the solid surface becomes visually obscured by the grass. The open area accepts the runoff from the impervious surfaces and, ultimately, reduces the amount of runoff into the public sewer systems. Obviously, any reduction on one site can be multiplied by many, with the long-term implications becoming substantial.

Although there are numerous positive aspects associated with open pavers, there are two negatives that must be recognized. It is unlikely that any system will cost less than the traditional poured-in-place concrete or asphalt paving compared as to cost per square foot. If the real economic value of the systems is to be considered at all, it must be considered in a comprehensive way and evaluated as part of the entire drainage system. The other negative has to do with women's fashions. Small, narrow-heeled shoes and open paving systems are not extremely compatible. Some prudence must be used in identifying the placement and pattern of the systems when pedestrians are anticipated users.

Several different manufacturers have created distinct open paving systems which can be separated into four general classifications: (1) individual precast units, (2) precast modular mats, (3) monolithic poured-in-place slabs, and (4) turf reinforcement.

The precast units employ two different conceptual design theories. One has been designed as a solid unit to be laid in place with an open joint between units. The open joint and porous underlayment permit surface water to filter through and recharge the groundwater supply. The second type of individual precast unit has been designed with an open void as an integral part of the unit. The voids are filled either with soil to support turf growth or a mixture of soil and gravel for a stable surface (Fig. 13-13). These open systems are often wire reinforced to accept the static and dynamic loads of vehicles. Although precast modular mats have a variety of configurations, the principles are essentially the same. The mats employ design concepts similar to those of individual open units but have been developed to respond to two principal issues. Designed as an integral interlocking system, the mats can accept higher vehicular loads than can the precast units (Fig. 13-14). Furthermore, because the mats are larger in area than the individual units, they might require less labor and have a lower total cost per square foot.

Figure 13-13 Precast open paving units.

Figure 13-14 Precast open paving systems: mats.

The poured-in-place slab techniques combine the technology of traditional concrete formwork with an open area of approximately 40% of the slab. These slabs have been designed with two-way reinforcing and, because of the nature of the poured-in-place techniques, can be modified to accommodate varying edge conditions and topography (Fig. 13-15).

The last concept is dramatically different from any other system in that it is essentially turf reinforcement. This system is based on the research of John Ritter and the P.E.E.R. Institute, which indicates that grass does not die because of wear on the blades but because of the trauma to its roots when the soil is crushed. A mat of plastic rings is laid prior to the turf. This underlayment acts like a series of pots to provide support to the turf's roots under pressure from the wheels of vehicles (Fig. 13-16).

The uses of open paving systems are as varied as the types. The predominant value

Figure 13-15   Poured-in-place open paving.

Turf/Sod
Netting
Rings
Gravel Base

Figure 13-16   Ritterings.

of open paving systems has been one that resolves the onus of asphalt and concrete parking lots and driveways. Since every system is designed for a specific purpose and has inherent limitations, not every product is made with the capability of supporting firetrucks and heavy equipment. Some municipalities have become involved in the testing of open paving systems for use in fire lanes. Because criteria and standards vary widely from one municipality to another, a check with local building code officials is imperative.

Another prominent use of open paving systems is in erosion control. Open pavers have been used extensively on vulnerable slopes along highways and as stabilizers on stream and lake banks. Systems designed with interlocking characteristics work well across undulating surfaces. The monolithic quality of the poured-in-place systems, even in vertical planes, has effectively resisted the back swelling that commonly pushes out individual pavers along a shoreline.

Compared to concrete or asphalt surfaces, open paving systems can substantially reduce on-site runoff. In some cases, the percolation ability of a site can actually be improved if somewhat impervious soil is replaced by an open paving system with a permeable topsoil and gravel or sand base. When used in drainage swales or culverts, open systems not only permit better groundwater recharge, but the aesthetic quality of the ground cover is much preferred to the glaze of concrete channelization.

chapter 14

Streets and Roads

INTRODUCTION

Roads and parking are two site planning problems which architects and landscape architects approach with cautious optimism. These two aspects of the built environment are sources of intrusion and environmental degradation like nothing else in the client's program of requirements. While concerns and biases are justified, understanding more of the road's function and the precise criteria of parking can provide the basis for a more enlightened approach to the problem. The objective here is to understand the language, vocabulary, and forms of streets and roads as they relate to site planning. Details on parking design criteria are provided in Chapter 15.

The scope of streets and roads must begin with a brief overview of street systems from a conceptual perspective. First, contrary to popular belief, street systems have a design capacity and as such have been designed to support land uses. A street's design capacity has been based on a design speed, a specific cross section, and a designated "level of service." Recognize that these three variables are linked and none can be changed without affecting the remaining two. This is critical to understanding the role of streets and roads as a component of land use planning. Freeways, parkways, expressways, beltways, thoroughfares, major and minor arterials, and neighborhood streets are all terms given to various road systems to serve a collection of land uses. The design of the system is one in which a balance is achieved between (1) public transit, (2) streets or thoroughfares, and (3) a community's land use densities. The common perception is that something is "wrong" with the street system when peak-hour traffic creates congestion on major thoroughfares. It often takes a significant amount of traffic and visibly deteriorating environmental quality for someone to question the zoning or integration between land use and transportation planning. Land use and circulation systems go hand-in-glove and to consider them as separate and independent factors invites a cycle of problems. There is probably at least one example of a road in your community in which the traffic generated by the road created a demand for rezoning (land use) changes, resulting in another demand for the "widening" or improvement of the original road.

The physical configuration of streets and roads at a larger scale has traditionally been separated into various models (Fig. 14-1): radial, orthogonal, linear, and so on. While understanding the nomenclature of a system can prove to be valuable, do not interpret a regions' physiography based solely on the form of its street system. As an example, there are numerous communities in the great plains and southwest where the orthogonal grid was an appropriate system. By contrast, the grid was also used in the early planning of San Francisco, where the topographical relief is extraordinary (Fig. 14-2).

Transportation planning must begin with the identification of land uses that will be served by the system and recognition that each land use will generate a specific number of vehicle trips per day. Obviously, a neighborhood retail shopping center attracts (generates) a significantly larger number of auto/truck trips than does a single-family detached residence. The number and frequency of those trips have been researched extensively by the Institute of Transportation Engineers (ITE). Since national trends con-

Linear

Orthogonal

Radial

Composite

Curvilinear

Figure 14-1 Conceptual diagrams of street systems.

Figure 14-2 Map of San Francisco. (Photo courtesy of City Planning Department city of San Francisco.)

TABLE 14-1 Summary of Rate Tables of Various Types of Dwelling Units

TYPE OF DWELLING UNIT	AVERAGE WEEKDAY VEHICLE TRIP ENDS PER UNIT		
	Average	Maximum	Minimum
Single-family detached unit	10.0	21.9	4.3
Apartment, general	6.1	12.3	0.5
Low-rise apartment	5.4	5.5	4.7
High-rise apartment	4.3	6.4	3.1
Condominium	5.6	5.6	5.6
Mobile home	5.4	6.8	2.8
Retirement community	3.3	4.9	2.8
Planned unit development	7.9	10.0	6.2

Source: Institute of Transportation Engineers, *Trip Generation* (Arlington, Va.: ITE, 1976), Section 200.

tinue to change, the ITE publishes their research periodically. Although some communities have seen the need to conduct their own research on trip-generation factors, many others utilize the ITE's work in the critical step of the transportation planning process. Table 14-1 is an example of their latest report on residential land uses.

Without this base of data, the assignment of any numerical quantity of traffic to a road would be an arbitrary value judgment. Utilizing the data, the transportation planner can convert a land use type and its density into an average number of trips.

Levels of service are also part of the transportation planning process. Since each street's capacity is limited by the number of moving lanes and the planned design speed, the question of "how much is too much?" will always surface. Levels of service from A at the best to F at worst have been assigned for a qualitative evaluation. Since the ability of the system relies, like all systems, on the weakest link in the chain, that link is almost always at the intersections. An explanation of levels of service at an intersection follows:[1]

A: Conditions of free unobstructed flow, no delays, and all signal phases sufficient in duration to clear all approaching vehicles.

B: Conditions of stable flow, very little delay; a few phases are unable to handle all approaching vehicles.

C: Represents stable operation with intermittent loading of the approaches. Drivers may have to wait through more than one red signal, and backups may develop behind turning vehicles. This is the level typically associated with urban design practice.

D: Approaches instability of flow, when delays to approaching vehicles may be substantial during short peaks within the peak period, but enough cycles with lower demand occur to allow periodic clearance of developing queues, thus preventing excessive backups. Level of service D is considered a reasonable operating level for urban intersections.

E: Represents the most vehicles that any intersection approach can accommodate. Long queues of vehicles develop, and delays are excessive (up to several signal cycles).

F: Represents jammed conditions. Backups from locations down-street or on the cross street may restrict or prevent movement of vehicles out of the approach under consideration, hence volumes carried are not predictable.

The selection of a road's cross section is based on supporting land uses, trip-generation factors, acceptable levels of service, and directional and peak-hour assignments. Although everything mentioned here relates principally to auto/truck vehicular systems, public transportation is an important ingredient in every community's transportation plan.

The important concept is to recognize that the automobile, with its insatiable ap-

---

[1]Highway Research Board, *Highway Capacity Manual* (Washington, D.C.: National Academy of Sciences, 1965).

petite for parking and wider paving, can create havoc with any site. Experience reminds us that the pedestrian must be given a priority. Additionally, if every alternative movement is provided for the automobile, little of value will be left for the pedestrian.

As a part of the process, transportation planners continually seek to keep the system balanced and forecast those locations in which segments may be overloaded. As a method to identify what the loads are, checks are made periodically with traffic counters. The counting quantifies the number of vehicles that cross over a line on a street for a given period of time. The counters provide for 24-hour documentation through a sufficient number of weekly cycles that averages can be extrapolated and used in planning. These numbers are referred to as average daily trips (ADTs) and can be obtained from local and state highway departments. ADTs provide accurate identification of the volume, time, and direction of the flow of traffic on freeways and major roads.

THOROUGHFARE CLASSIFICATIONS AND CRITERIA

Just as each community adopts ordinances and laws that reflect its own values and historical precedents, each will also have adopted some general thoroughfare cross sections applicable to that particular municipality. Although there will be some similarities between municipalities, the site planner must begin by documenting the local design criteria.

In the early development of highways and road systems in the United States, the requests for funding of the programs required some method of prioritizing the improvements. Demands by rural legislators for better roads were challenged by their urban counterparts. What emerged was the collective agreement that the roads which received the lightest amount of travel would receive the smallest funding. State governments in the early 1930s also began the development of a classification system based on a road's function. Although the classification system varies from state to state, the National Committee on Urban Transportation recommends four functional classifications: expressway, arterial, collector, and local.[2]

> *Expressway.* This classification includes similar terms, such as "freeways," "beltways," and "parkways." These are limited-access systems that rarely, if ever, have grade crossings. Expressways are designed to accommodate the longer intraregional trip, with the highest legal speed limits. These are multilane divided roads and generally carry over 40,000 trips per day.
>
> *Arterial.* This classification also includes the terms "major" or "primary" road, as it connects major traffic generators within a city. Arterials also bring traffic to expressways and, in some cases, incorporate important rural routes. The system of arterials in a community should reflect a systematic form that integrates the major employment and activity centers with expressways and collectors. These streets will vary in design capacity from 25,000 to 40,000 trips per day.
>
> *Collectors.* The collector is also referred to as a "secondary" road and has two functions. The first is as a connector between the arterial system and local system. The second function is one of access and service to local land uses connecting major intracity functions. The collector is a local street serving an area within an arterial system zone and capable of supporting a traffic volume of 10,000 to 25,000 trips per day.
>
> *Local.* Local systems are known by various terms, including "minor," "tertiary," and "neighborhood." This road classification is the one that generally repre-

---

[2]Frank So, Israel Stollman, Frank Beal, and David S. Arnold, Eds., *The Practice of Local Government Planning* (Washington, D.C.: American Planning Association and the International City Management Association, 1979), p. 216.

TABLE 14-2 Urban Freeway and Thoroughfare Classification System[a]

Classification	Trips per Day	Moving Lanes	Width (ft)	Emergency Lanes (12 ft)	Park Lanes (8 ft)	Access Residential	Access Commercial	Design Speed (mph)	Paving Width (ft)
Freeway	40,000	4–8	12	2	□	□	□	60[c]	112–160
Major arterial	25,000–40,000	4–6	12	2	□	□	□	50	92–116
Arterial	10,000–25,000	4	12	2	□	■	■	40	68
Major collector[e]	over 1500	2	12	□	■[d]	■	■	35	32–40
Major connector[e]	1,500	2	12	□	■	■	■	35	24
Minor collector[e]	1,500	2	10	□	■[f]	■	■	30	28–36
Minor connectors[e]	1,500	2	10	□	□	■	■	30	20
Loop streets[g] (cul-de-sac)	250	1	10					25	26
Parking connectors[g]	250	2	10	□	□	■	■	25	20

[a] □, Inappropriate; □, discouraged; ■, acceptable.
[b] NA, not applicable.
[c] Maximum legal speed 65 mph.
[d] One side or both sides.
[e] Collectors.
[f] One side in residential development.
[g] Locals.

Source: Alan Voorhees, W. G. Hansen, and A. K. Gilbert, "Urban Transportation," in *The Practice of Local Government Planning*, Frank So, Israel Stollman, Frank Beal, and David S. Arnold, eds. (Washington, D.C.: American Planning Association and the International City Management Association, 1979), p. 220.

sents the largest amount of street mileage in any community and the lowest design speed. The local street system is designed to provide access to adjacent land uses. Although local streets in a central business district (CBD) may have traffic counts in the thousands, neighborhood streets generally carry volumes below 1000 trips per day.[3]

Voorhees, Hansen, and Gilbert, in their ''Urban Transportation'' contribution to *The Practice of Local Government Planning,* suggest that in new areas the development of a transportation system might have as many as nine classifications for a street system. The nine-level classification system in Table 14-2 is more definitive concerning the site, function, and performance characteristics of various roads.

(a)

(b)

Figure 14-3 The 90° intersection. (a) conflicts with two-way streets. (b) conflicts with one-way streets.

[3]Ibid.

Every site planning problem presents its own unique set of circumstances relative to land use and circulation systems. Any classification system can only serve as a guide to understanding how the variables of each street fit within the context of other streets. Since each community will have adopted its own standard sections, the site planner must match the municipality's requirements with the road and right-of-way classification most appropriate to the site and circulation problem.

The next level of road design issues of which the site planner should have some working knowledge is the configuration of intersections. The basic model for most communities is the 90° intersection, as it respects the layout of the numerous grid systems throughout the United States. The problem with this configuration is that there are eight points of potential conflict (Fig. 14-3a). If either or both roads are one-way systems, the conflicts are reduced to four and one, respectively (Fig. 14-3b). The T intersection is widely used, as it essentially accomplishes a similar objective (Fig. 14-4). The T intersection works very successfully but should not be used in cases where the T of sets are closer than 120 ft (Fig. 14-5). Local ordinances may be more restrictive than this guideline and should be reviewed before final design decisions are made.

In the older sections of numerous cities and towns, conflicting street geometry often creates dangerous and difficult intersections that should not be duplicated (Fig. 14-6). Junctures of multiple street systems almost always result in at least one five-cornered intersection. It is very perplexing to the driver who arrives at a corner and is faced with four options—one more than normal. With speed, the perplexed driver can become a moving hazard. The "red time" per signal is also longer because of the additional movements that need "green time" in the same cycle. Acute angles should also be carefully considered because the right-of-way that is necessary to accommodate the

Figure 14-4 The T intersection.

Figure 14-5 T-intersection offset.

Figure 14-6 Five-corner intersection.

Figure 14-7 Obtuse-angle intersection.

turning movements at the corner can become substantially larger than that required in the right-angle intersection. Furthermore, the 90° intersection is preferred because it does not favor one particular directional flow. Since the right-of-way is larger for any intersection that is other than 90°, configurations similar to those in Figure 14-7 should be avoided.

chapter 15
Parking

INTRODUCTION

Parking is without question the most difficult and thorny problem to confront the site planner. If all of the time, energy, and financial resources to move vehicles onto a site were not enough, the storage of the devices only adds insult to injury. When submitting projects for consideration by a jury for design awards, many site planners would prefer to avoid *any* photographs or drawings of areas allocated to parking. Parking is, in many cases, addressed as a necessary evil. The reality of the requirements of the machine and the implications of its demand on a site are a source of continual aggravation to the site planner and client.

The user, however, has an entirely different attitude toward parking. Anyone involved in the rental or leasing of residential, retail, or commercial space will testify to the concern any user has for parking. In suburban retail shopping areas, parking is critical to the ability of many merchants to survive economically. That same attitude is paramount to the residential user who prefers a ''bedroom-to-bathroom'' relationship regarding parking and dwelling. The reason is obvious: convenience. What the merchant often undervalues is the quality of the parking/pedestrian linkage. Although an adequate amount of spaces in a visible location is valuable, the aesthetic quality of the path is also important.

The environmental design professional's first encounter with parking is with the local government. Although your community will probably have a transportation plan, it is unlikely that it will have a parking plan. In lieu of definitive plans, most communities rely on ordinances that stipulate minimal off-site parking based on specific land uses. The problem is that many municipalities have waived off-street parking requirements for retail and office activities in central business districts with the rationale that ''the private sector will supply the need.'' That solution has two problems. First, the attitude is based on the notion that streets and highways can be separated from parking. Street systems and parking are rarely considered as integrated components: one as movement, one as storage. The second is the physical and aesthetic character of parking.

Parking is a parasite as a land use. The vehicles contribute nothing positive to the landscape. As a parasite, and left to the whim of the individual developer, parking is found as a primary land use eating away at the fabric of the city. Every community has anguished over the loss of a local historic landmark reduced to a pile of partially recyclable material to make way for a parking garage. If there was ever a reason for zoning, parking is it.

Municipalities throughout the United States have a variety of attitudes toward the involvement of local governments in parking. Some believe "the market will provide," whereas other governments have adopted and implemented local parking authorities. In many cases, parking authorities have the power of eminent domain and are actively engaged in the construction of parking facilities. Most often their principal charge involves the provision of adequate parking in locations to support adjacent land uses at a reasonable price.

The positive aspect of letting an unfettered free market provide parking means that the municipality will not be obligated to commit any of its financial or human resources to providing another "service." That attitude is the manifestation of a philosophy prevalent in many communities which considers any meddling of the public sector in the private sector's traditional domain (development) to be inappropriate.

Parking as a design problem is further compounded because of the inconsistencies associated with simple standards. One would think that with as much research and documentation as city planners, architects, landscape architects, and civil engineers have on the topic, a set of common standards would be easy to develop and adopt. Not so. The industry cannot agree on the size of a standard parking space, much less the curb-to-curb dimensions for a standard 90° parking lot. Although HUD's publication *Barrier Free Site Design* defines the size, dimension, and criteria for various site components, including parking, for the handicapped, it would be inappropriate for the site planner to assume that the specifics of that excellent publication have become part of the design criteria for his or her community. If the concept of a "national standard" for a normal parking space and lot size is still some time away, it is easy to accept the fact that the size and percentage of "small" or "compact" car spaces on a national basis is further behind. The various perceptions of small or compact car parking is as broad as an interpretation of "beauty." Some municipalities require a certain percentage of small car spaces, but the conservative view of others is based on a lack of "local" research and an unknown view of the future.

Because of the inconsistencies between local governments, the site planner must consult his or her local zoning ordinances for specific parking criteria and requirements. It is recommended that some preliminary documentation of those requirements take place to make certain that the number of spaces required is accurate and that minimum sizes are properly recorded.

Always inquire as to the municipality's policy on handicapped spaces and small or compact cars as well. The sizes and arrangements illustrated here will be based on:

1. Normal parking space: 9 ft × 18 ft
2. Handicapped parking space: 12 ft, 6 in × 18 ft
3. Compact/small car space: 8 ft × 16 ft

There are generally four basic forms or configurations of parking.

1. The 90° two-way lot (Fig. 15-1). Because this configuration has the smallest amount of wasted space (in corners and aisles), it is the most efficient. Although some consider it to be the most difficult to negotiate, maneuvering in and out of a 90° parking space is not that difficult in this age of power-assisted steering.
2. The angled one-way lot has three variations: 60°, 45°, and 30° (Figs. 15-2, 15-3, and 15-4), ranging from the most efficient to the least efficient. Since anything less than 90° creates two triangles of wasted area (Fig. 15-5), it is easy to see why the

90° Parking   **Figure 15-1**

efficiency goes down as the angle is increased. Since angled one-way parking can function with a narrower aisle width than any two-way system, it has obvious advantages in those situations where one-way systems are necessary (Fig. 15-6). A parking garage is a good example of the one-way drive.

3. The advantage of two-way angled parking is its easy ingress and egress. Suburban

60° Parking   **Figure 15-2**

45° Parking   **Figure 15-3**

30° Parking   **Figure 15-4**

Figure 15-5 Wasted area in angled parking.

Figure 15-6 Angled parking: one-way.

retail centers often use this form, as it accommodates two-way access down any aisle and has less than a perpendicular angle for those drivers who struggle with the perpendicular double-loaded lot.

4. Parallel parking is the final model. It is the most difficult for people to negotiate and the least efficient of the four models. One basic rule associated with parallel parking is that it should never be mixed with any other form of parking. Figure

Figure 15-7   Mix of parallel and head-in parking.

15-7 illustrates what not to do. The chances for a collision as a driver backs out of a space and into the side of a car parked parallel to the isle are excellent!

PEDESTRIAN TRANSITION AND HANDICAPPED ACCESS

On lots that receive a substantial amount of parking, it is often preferable to orient the parking such that people may walk either on paths between rows of cars or in the access lane (Fig. 15-8). Since the pedestrian is very vulnerable in a parking lot, the possibility

Figure 15-8   Parking organized so that people can walk in access lane.

of an injury can be reduced if the pedestrian is more visible. When parking is organized such that the pedestrian is forced to walk between cars, the possibility of someone stepping out from a line of parked cars into the path of a moving vehicle is ever present.

The ability to separate the pedestrian and the auto successfully is a challenge. Fire lanes and service accesses are also critical aspects of any circulation and parking plan. Since local ordinances will vary relative to a fire lane's paving, width, and structural characteristics, these criteria must be checked.

Single-loaded lots such as that described in Fig. 15-9 are *very* inefficient. Although it is a common form for limited or restricted parking, it is obvious that the ratio of parked cars to paving is very low. Similarly, larger-than-necessary isle widths consume development dollars, increase on-site runoff, and can be very confusing. Since there is little aesthetic value in most parking lots, increasing their size does not increase their contribution to a site plan.

When designing a parking lot that will be bounded on one edge by a building, make certain that one of two things takes place. First, a wheel stop is absolutely critical to keep auto bumpers away from a building wall (Fig. 15-10). Second, sometimes a screen or guard is necessary to protect walls or structures; they may be vulnerable to the motorist who drives "by braille" (Fig. 15-11).

On occasion, small lots present their own variety of problems. One, in particular,

Figure 15-9   Single-loaded head-in lot.

Figure 15-10   Wheel stop in front of building wall.

Figure 15-11   Building protected by bollard.

confronts the site planner forced by limited area to a single-loaded lot parallel to the building. To the inexperienced, there may be a question as to whether the parking should be located next to or away from the building. Under normal circumstances the parking should always go next to the building (Fig. 15-12). On those occasions when either avoiding the intrusion of headlights on a residential building or the noise nuisance created by engines or exhaust is untenable, another response may be appropriate. Since the critical criterion is the user's safety, a question should always be raised where the car has priority over people.

As mentioned earlier, parking is a necessity as well as a nuisance. As such, any consideration given to reducing the level of that nuisance is valuable to any site plan. Screening methods include berms, fencing, walls, vegetation, and in some cases combinations of these basics, as vegetation always adds a softer quality to architectural ele-

Figure 15-12   Single-loaded parking on narrow lot.

ments. The concept of screening parking should also include the development of buffer areas along the edge of the street. The effort to reduce the visual impact of cars and impervious surfaces is always a positive contribution to the streetscape (Fig. 15-13). Numerous local governments have recognized the nuisance potential of parking lots, as many require fencing or screens as a condition of site plan approval.

Handicapped Parking: The criteria associated with handicapped parking need special attention. First, walking distances should be held to a minimum. Second, every effort should be made to locate handicapped parking such that the physically impaired pedestrian can avoid crossing a circulation drive. Most ordinances require a wider (12 ft

Figure 15-13 Parking buffer. (Photo by Patricia McCracken.)

Figure 15-14 Wheelchair access.

Figure 15-15 Handicapped ramp at end of parking lot.

6 in.) space to permit wheelchair access between cars. Signs identifying handicapped parking should be located next to the wheelchair ramps. Common sense suggests that neither wheel stops nor drainage grates should be located in the direct path to the wheelchair ramp (Fig. 15-14). If the handicapped parking area and ramp are at the end of the parking lot, bollards should be used to define the edge of the pedestrian zone (Fig. 15-15). Similar to head-in handicapped parking, parallel parking should also be wider by 3 ft 6 in. Signs and ramps should also be visible and accessible. There is more to accommodating the handicapped on the site than what appears here in these brief paragraphs. See Chapter 16 for a detailed review of dimensional requirements and criteria to support access of the physically impaired on the site.

DROP-OFF ZONES

The interface between the pedestrian and the auto is one of the most difficult problems in the design of the parking lot. Conflicting perceptions as to who enjoys the preferential right-of-way creates a tenuous situation at best. Under some circumstances, zones that provide the auto momentary direct access to the building entrance in a "pedestrian only" environment is a very civilized alternative. Unlike the fire lane, which is based on a public safety issue, the drop-off zone is generally not a requirement and must be promulgated by the site planner. Although ease of access is afforded to all pedestrians, it is of particular value to the elderly and physically handicapped (Fig. 15-8). The drop-off zone should be clearly separated from the main stream of traffic. Although bollards may be used to demark the limits of the zone, no chains or other horizontal obstructions should be used. Drainage grates and other surface irregularities should also be excluded from this zone. When the curb is eliminated from a lengthy segment of the zone, the color of the paving should be in sharp contrast to that of the handicapped ramp.

The drop-off zone is also one of those conditions in which lighting is important.

Figure 15-16   Drop-off zone and shelter.

Where general pedestrian-level fixtures would be a property of the normal lighting plan, supplementary fixtures are necessary to provide a high level of illumination on ramps and curbs of the zone. Finally, some consideration should be given to shelter. To be successful, the structure need only provide shade and obstruction from the elements. The inclusion of a canopy or similar device can, functionally and aesthetically, enhance an important transition between parking and structures (Fig. 15-16).

chapter 16

Pedestrian and Bicycle Circulation

INTRODUCTION

When faced with the problems of building location, stringent zoning, parking, and auto ingress and egress, it is easy to understand how accommodating the pedestrian can become a fourth-level priority. Not only is the pedestrian system often considered as a residual space between buildings, but the design of the pedestrian movement as a kinetic experience demands the most of our creative skills. The challenge to mentally construct the reality of built form is particularly difficult when obligated to assimilate a sequence of diurnal and nocturnal experiences under varying climatic conditions. Issues of movement, direction, and orientation can become complex in an exterior environment where signs do little other than give names to places or streets that we do not know. Each of us has become lost or disoriented in a maze of walls, paths, and plants that left us wondering out loud: "Now where is my car?" This "lost feeling"creates not only a sense of insecurity but one of aggravation, neither of which is necessary or desirable. In *The Image of the City*, Kevin Lynch states that "the environmental image has its original function in permitting purposeful mobility," and "the terror of being lost comes from the necessity that a mobile organism be oriented in its surroundings."[1] Since man's mobility is based on limited assumed images of the environment,[2] it is then the site planner's role to provide reinforcement of those images, at least in terms of orientation.

PEDESTRIAN SYSTEMS

In this chapter the pedestrian system that functions as a link between buildings or activities will be considered separately from the system that is part of a community-wide, comprehensive circulation system. Although both involve pedestrian movement, the

---

[1]Kevin Lynch, *The Image of the City* (Cambridge, Mass.: The MIT Press, 1960), pp. 124 and 125.
[2]Christian Norberg-Schulz, *Existence, Space and Architecture* (New York: Praeger Publishers, 1971), p. 35.

community-scale system has various aspects which are common to those of bikeways and as such are addressed in that section of the chapter.

Pedestrian systems function in at least two general roles: one as a space to walk, another as a place to sit. As a place to walk, the conditions vary according to land uses served and environmental quality. In limited terms many pedestrian linkages, sidewalks, and plazas are part of the public's domain. If the clients and users are the public, the criteria may be more stringent, as the range of alternatives and criteria are more limited than those that could be applied to a private residence.

Pedestrian systems in the public's domain, or those that will be dedicated to the public, need to reflect the design criteria established by the local government. Streets and roads, sidewalks, pedestrian paths, and handicapped requirements will vary from one jurisdiction to another. The experienced site planner checks those requirements together with other development restrictions to make certain that there is complete agreement between the proposed plan and local regulations.

At the smallest scale of site planning, the planning objectives of the system should focus on:

1. The development of a system that functions as a connector while providing an enjoyable experience on its own merit
2. The design of a system sympathetic to the existing environmental context
3. The design of a system appropriate in scale to that of the proposed plan
4. The design of a path and succession of memorable images which create and reinforce the site's sense of place

Although the experienced site planner is cognizant of those objectives, the design of pedestrian systems is often the most primitive and the execution the most hostile. For whatever reasons, we forget that the most indelible impressions of an accommodating site plan begin with the person in the role of pedestrian. As pedestrians, we are more vulnerable and conscious of the quality of the environment. Our contact with light, color, sound, texture, built form, plants, and people is much more pronounced as a pedestrian than as an operator of or passenger in a motor vehicle. Our reliance on the auto for even the most menial trips has served to desensitize us to the genuine quality of the streetscape. To be effective, the design of pedestrian systems must reflect the mobility limits of pedestrians as well as the varying conditions within which the system might be used. As Robert Sommer has put it:

> It is curious that most of the concern with functionalism has been focused upon form rather than function. . . . Design professionals—city planners, landscape designers, architects . . .—would gain by adopting a functionalism based on user behavior.[3]

CONNECTORS AND LINKAGES

In general, pedestrian paths are designed to connect or link activities whose relationships are sufficiently interactive to warrant an articulated space. Paths are potentially significant contributors to creating an identifiable place, as the assembly of images alone can collectively produce an identity for the path itself. Although the functional obligations demand an enlightened response, the ability to design a system that contributes something to a site's sense of place requires an understanding of those objectives. Some are functional, others aesthetic, and others behavioral. In an attempt to analyze the direction that man takes in defining a path, Kurt Lewin employed the term "hodological space"

---

[3]Robert Sommer, *Personal Space: The Behavioral Basis of Design* (Englewood Cliffs, N.J.: Prentice Hall, Inc., 1969), p. 27.

or the "space of possible movement."[4] Lewin maintained that man's paths are not necessarily those of straight lines but are those of preferred paths and represent the results
of continual negotiations between shortest distance, pleasure, minimal effort, safety, and
so on.

Designing a pedestrian system with the potential of creating a sense of place is no
small challenge in a context where quality is often a marginal issue. Although some
communities have adopted strict guidelines to maintain uniformity, site-specific pedestrian paths are often dictated by the road alignment and do little more than provide a
path in the public right-of-way horizontally separated from the street. Unless the developer is willing to spend the time and money to supplement minimal requirements, pedestrian paths in the public domain, through most residential neighborhoods or commercial business districts, are remedial at best. At the smallest scale the path from a
garage to a residence can be designed to accommodate the movement from vehicle to
dwelling while articulating the transition from the quasi-public zone of the street to the
privacy of the dwelling.

Pedestrian movement through a parking lot or in a parking garage traverses some
of the most dangerous and hostile conditions in an urban context. Because of the normal
change in roles from driver to pedestrian, and vice versa, the mix between people and
cars is inevitable. Only in the rarest of circumstances can a pedestrian path through a
parking area successfully transcend the problems associated with bodily injury and
emerge as an enjoyable path. In many cases, the inability to separate people completely
from vehicles creates an unreconcilable conflict. Many parking lots never attempt separation; the design of the facility is based strictly on its efficiency. A prevailing attitude
appears to be: the larger the parking area, the less one needs to be concerned about the
pedestrian. Sports stadiums and college or university parking lots are some of the obvious examples of this type of thinking.

The pedestrian path through a parking lot is particularly difficult because the zone
for the path needs to allow for the overhang of vehicles beyond the front or rear wheels
(Fig. 16-1). The most common solution here is to pave the parking lot up to the line of
the auto overhang and use precast concrete wheel stops to keep the auto bumper clear
of the pedestrian path (Fig. 16-2). Because of the variety of automobile types and manufacturers, overhang distances vary widely and as such create some problems in maintaining clear distances. To reiterate the recommendation made in Chapter 15, when possible, orient the parking 90° to that of the desired pedestrian movement (Fig. 15-9).
This will permit the design of a path network between the cars or at its worst, permit
the pedestrian to walk in the parking lot circulation lanes. Prevailing wisdom is that
there is less likelihood of an accident (auto/pedestrian) when the pedestrian is visible
and walking in the lane with the auto.

Figure 16-1   Vehicle overhang of curb.

[4]K. Lewin, "Der Richtungsbegriff in der Psychologie. Der spezielle und allgemeine hodologische Raum," *Psychologie Forschung*, 1934, p. 19.

Figure 16-2 Paving to curb and wheel stop.

If the pedestrian path is to become a contributor to the site's "sense of place," the system must be considered in a way that permits it to link the significant images of the site. After resolving the parking lot conflicts, the opportunities for successful transitional spaces occur in the pedestrian zones. But a word of caution; be reminded of the user's need to have some sense of orientation or direction. It is all too easy to assume that everyone enjoys the planner's familiarity with the site. In approaching the problem, the following issues may give some order to the considerations necessary in the design of the path.

1. *The location of the path.* Although other aspects of the process contribute to the quality of the path, the location is very important to its success. The expression "the path of least resistance" implies that people will find the most direct route given an open, unencumbered field. Successful pedestrian planning demands that one recognize human nature in a realistic appraisal of pedestrian "desire" lines. People have an enduring way of informing the planner of any error in the assessment of those lines (Fig. 16-3).

2. *The size, dimension, and shape of the path.* The configuration of the system is a group of decisions that are made in concert with the path's location. Since the location of a path is a response to its function and uses served, the physical character of the path will obviously require some adjustment. If a land use acts as a generator of pedestrian activity, the width of the path should reflect the larger demand. In many cases, local governments will stipulate either the size of the path or minimum building setbacks. As is often the case, these setbacks control both

Figure 16-3 Path through turf.

the size and location of the pedestrian path. The most glaring site planning errors exist where large-scale walks and plazas are perceived to be appropriate, where, in fact, there is little along the path's edge to create the demand for a genuine pedestrian function (Fig. 16-4). The interrelationships between the type of pedestrian, speed, and density are described in Fig. 16-5.[5]

3. *The detailed quality of the path.* Every pedestrian corridor is a composition of elements (natural and man-made) that give a path character and vitality. These elements include paving material, texture, and color. The paving material and texture combine as a method not only to tell the pedestrian "this is the path" but also to signal "this is not meant to be walked on." People respond very well to physical barriers, whether they are paving textures, curbs, bollards, or vegetation.

Figure 16-4 Large uninhabited open space. (Photo by Bryan Phillips.)

Speed - density relationships

Figure 16-5 Type of pedestrian, speed, and density.

[5]Boris Pushkarev and Jeffrey M. Zupan, *Urban Space for Pedestrians* (Cambridge, Mass.: The MIT Press, 1975), p. 82.

However, practice suggests that changes in the physical character should not be subtle.

As an example, in *Urban Space for Pedestrians*, Pushkarev and Zupan suggest that "pedestrians totally disregard any color patterns on a walkway."[6] The reasoning is that patterns are often annoying or do not relate to pedestrian flow, and are simply ignored. Although color can effectively differentiate one zone of activity or use from another, the color reinforces the real function. Pushkarev's and Zupan's observations invoke easy agreement, for the pedestrian is first, often one of many using the corridor and may not see the entire graphic, or second, has a purpose for a trip that may not correspond to the color.

As an objective in planning a system, scale seems simple enough at first, but the problem of producing a plan within a scale appropriate to a site is more elusive. Daniel Burnam's pronouncement to "make no little plans . . ." has misled more than one site planner. Some of the most successful plans were really based on simple ideas executed in a modest, sensitive way. Many misinterpreted "little plans" to mean little objects and, as such, equated the size of a system with its potential for success.

To be successful, it is not necessary for open-space systems and pedestrian networks to be either large or grandiose in physical section (Fig. 16-6). Since large pedestrian plazas have a tendency toward monumentality, some consideration should be given to the introduction of elements that maintain a human scale. The ever-popular European plaza in America works no better than Maxim's menu at McDonalds. The experienced site planner approaches the development of pedestrian systems with restraint. Regardless of the scale of the plan, remember that the average pedestrian walks at speeds ranging from 260 to 275 ft/min across flat topography in neutral climatic conditions.

Large paved areas without people are uninviting and are avoided by many who equate people in a public space with security. While we recall examples of those grand and elegant plazas from history, we must also remember the pedestrian quality of the context as well as those supporting land uses adjacent to the plaza (Fig. 16-7).

William Wythe's publication on the "*Social Life of Small Urban Spaces*" is, without question, one of the most enlightening research efforts on people and their use of the exterior environment. Where Wythe's documentation on the use and the activities of

Figure 16-6

[6]Ibid., p. 156.

Figure 16-7   Large uninhabited open space. (Photo by Bryan Phillips.)

people and the characteristics of urban open space may appear obvious, he also presents a lucid set of guidelines on the design and development of the urban space. Summarized, they are as follows:[7]

1. People tend to sit where there are places to sit.
2. Although people are attracted to sunny, wind-protected spaces in the winter, it is important to have a choice between shade and sun.
3. People are attracted to plazas where there are other people.
4. Trees are an important contribution to every site, especially where they are combined with sitting places.
5. Water is an immensely popular element in any public space, particularly where it is accessible.
6. Food service, at even the smallest scale (private vendor), attracts people, who attract more people.
7. The street can contain every quality that makes a successful plaza without a plaza.
8. For indoor plazas, retailing is very important to the pedestrian activity and life of the space.

A review of Wythe's publication is recommended, as his documentation and research for the conclusions mentioned here will provide a good basis for understanding how people use urban public open space.

SCALE

The methods by which a pedestrian system is defined and articulated relative to other open-space elements contributes to its "scale." Vertical or horizontal separation of movement zones from other open-space components helps each to maintain their image and scale. Careful manipulation of grade changes also contributes to the definition of scale (Fig. 16-8). Grade change in the pedestrian path may be broad and gentle or direct and resolute, depending on the desired effect. The grade change has a tactile quality which can contribute to the aesthetic form of the path while giving it scale.

Bridges are always an opportunity for the site planner to reinforce the human scale into a pedestrian system. Whereas the open path is visually part of its edges, the literal

---

[7]William H. Wythe, *Social Life of Small Urban Spaces* (Washington, D.C.: The Conservation Foundation, 1980), pp. 28–94.

Figure 16-8 Grade change at pedestrian scale.

(a)

(b)

Figure 16-9 Photos by Bryan Phillips.

space of the bridge is more definitive. The bridge as a physical departure from two edges tells something of its duality. One is the special quality of the bridge as it absorbs the quality of the creek or street it traverses (Fig. 16-9). The second is the architectural character or linking function of the bridge. The structure as an image on the path reinforces the kinetic experience and the potential for defining ''here'' and ''there.'' There are few components of a path network which have the potential for creating a sense of place compared to that of the bridge. The bridge is not only an event in the memory of the pedestrian but a piece of the network that contributes to the entire image of the pedestrian path.

PEDESTRIAN STREETS

In the early 1970s, the Dutch began a process of reassessing the role and function of traffic, parking, and pedestrian systems in urban neighborhoods. Much of Europe, in the late 1920s, adopted transportation planning concepts developed in the United States. The American methods had good rationale and for that time were simple enough to apply. The component of transportation planning of particular interest here is the interface between pedestrians and vehicles. Based on the vulnerability of people, prevailing wisdom dictated that the pedestrian be horizontally separated from automobiles.

Few, however, forecasted the extent to which the auto would become a problem in urban neighborhoods. The indiscriminate use of the auto, unforeseen storage problems, and pedestrian conflicts created numerous marginally safe conditions. Although the pedestrian was horizontally separated from the auto, on narrow streets, particularly in older historic districts, the safety of pedestrians had become a clear concern.

In Holland, the citizens of Delft petitioned the local government to close and prohibit several streets to auto traffic because of the hazards to pedestrians. Their request, however, was in direct opposition to those of the local public works and police departments. As a compromise, the municipality's planning department developed the concept of a residential street improved to accommodate the pedestrian with reduced automobile access. A plan emerged which designed the street in such a way as to give *no illusion* of separated systems. These *Woonerf streets* were residential streets to be occupied by cars as well as people, and as such were to undergo major changes. In many cases the streets were reduced to one lane, some as narrow as 3 meters (10 ft). In almost every case, alignments were never designed as a straight path. Maximum speed limits were reduced to 15 kph (9.5 mph), which are much more compatible with pedestrians and bicycles.[8] Not only are alignments circuitous and irregular, but design elements such as light standards, bollards, and plants are located so as to interrupt the visual plane of the street and reinforce the disconnected quality of the space (Figs. 16-10 and 16-11).

In some instances additional parking has been introduced, which doubles as play

Figure 16-10   Woonerf street plan.

[8]George Wynne, ed., *Learning from Abroad. Traffic Restraints in Residential Neighborhoods* (New Brunswick, N.J.: Transaction Books, 1980), p. 3.

Figure 16-11 Woonerf street section.

areas when not in use. Although the idea emerged as a compromise (a word with very negative overtones in some design professions), the fact is that it works in various countries and communities in Europe. In France, this concept, known as "rues libres" (free streets), has worked very successfully, particularly where shop owners have had difficulty with the creation of vehicle-free zones. Building on the success of the Dutch Woonerf and German Verkehrsberuhingung programs, the French made minor technical adjustments in the interval and length of free streets to reflect the character of existing urban neighborhoods.[9]

The Belgians and English have also employed the Woonerf concept to varying communities in their respective countries. The English considered the concept to be an alternative to the marginally successful total separation of vehicles and pedestrians at Radburn. Although the "pedestrian only" zones at Radburn worked well, residential access roads also became burdened with quasi-pedestrian and bicycle activity. Application of the Woonerf concept was very successful, as it provided greater vehicular access to housing and commercial districts while giving the priority of use of the space to the pedestrian.[10]

HANDICAPPED

No material on site planning and the pedestrian would be complete without an overview of the guidelines necessary to provide access for the handicapped. Although it is not our intent here to duplicate the efforts of texts that focus solely on the issues of barrier-free design, it is critical to review the most common site-accessibility problems, design criteria, and supporting rationale.

The social consciousness of America in the late 1960s was the force behind numerous changes in our collective attitudes toward people and environment. Among those changes was recognition of the fact that the built environment had, for years, created unnecessary barriers which limited the accessibility of the physically handicapped to public and private facilities. The publication of "Specifications for Making Buildings and Facilities Accessible to and Usable by the Physically Handicapped" in 1961 was based on the realization that the physically handicapped were 1 in 10 of the total American population and that the issues of accessibility were long overdue. Renewed in 1971,

[9]Ibid., p. 21.
[10]Ibid., p. 32.

it became the basis for the American National Standards Institute's publication on accessibility standards for the handicapped, (ANSI A117.1). The criteria set out in the ANSI publication were supported by federal legislation in 1968 and the passage of Public Law 90-480, entitled "An Act to Insure that Certain Buildings, Financed with Federal Funds, Are So Designed and Constructed as to Be Accessible to the Handicapped."

Although the process was slow to start, by 1982 thirty-eight states had adopted legislation based on ANSI standards. In that year the Architectural and Transportation Barriers Compliance Board (ATCB) adopted and published standards for projects using federal financial assistance. Two years later the federal government promulgated its own standards with the release of the Uniform Federal Accessibility Standards (UFAS). It became obvious by the 1980s that although there was no longer a question of the need for accessibility criteria, there were some questions as to how and in what way that need would be met.

The obvious objective in every site plan should be to develop the site, paths, and walkways in such as way as to allow the greatest diversity of people access to buildings and facilities, safely and unhindered. Although the most common issues are those related to topographical change and alignment, others associated with lighting and signs can also harbinger problems for the physically impaired.

Where building codes reflect design criteria associated with handicapped access to buildings, sites and site improvements are sometimes more casual considerations. Paths, walkways, ramps, and signs are not always addressed at the same level of detail as described in building codes.

Although there are obvious omissions and conflicts in the criteria, the vast majority of site planners recognize that without the regulations, access for the handicapped would not exist. Furthermore, the notion that criteria restrict creative solutions to handicapped access problems cannot be sustained by either product manufacturers or designers.[11] Established criteria, functional guidelines, and continued research provide the basis on which real progress toward barrier-free design can be made.

DIMENSIONAL REQUIREMENTS

Where each path should be designed to reflect an anticipated use, there are some minimal standards that must be mentioned. The recommended two-way and one-way path widths to accommodate wheelchair traffic are 6 ft 0 in. and 4 ft 0 in. respectively[12] (Fig. 16-12). Concerning turning radii, it is possible to turn the wheelchair around in its own space, (one wheel moves forward while the second moves in reverse). Comfortable maneuvering distance, however, for the adult chair is 7 ft 0 in. × 8 ft 0 in.; the smaller chair can be turned in a circle of 5 ft 4 in. diameter[13] (Fig. 16-13).

Gradients. If a path has a grade of less than 5%, it is considered a walkway. Those that exceed 5% are considered ramps and have special design requirements. Paths with sustained grades above 4% should have brief 5 ft 0 in. flats interrupting the slope to permit a chairbound occupant to stop and rest. If possible, walks should not exceed a gradual 2% slope.

With the exception of the short ramps that provide access from a parking lot, ramp gradients should not exceed 8.33% slope[14] (Fig. 16-15). Furthermore, if a ramp is designed to this maximum slope, the length should not exceed 30 ft 0 in. without a 5 ft 0

[11] Thomas Fisher, "Technics: Barrier-Free Design," *Progressive Architecture*, July 1985, p. 124.

[12] American Society of Landscape Architects Foundation, *Barrier-Free Site Design* (McLean, Va.: ASLAF, 1977), p. 17.

[13] Ibid., p. 16.

[14] American National Standards Institute, *Specifications for Making Buildings and Facilities Accessible to, and Useable by, the Physically Handicapped*, ANSI A117.1-1961 (R1971) (New York: ANSI, 1971), p. 8.

Figure 16-12 Recommended path widths to accommodate wheelchairs.

Figure 16-13 Wheelchair manuvering distance.

in. landing. Similarly, a 5 ft 0 in. "flat" should interrupt a path exceeding 4% slope. A 6 ft 0 in. clear space should also be provided at each end of the ramp to facilitate wheelchair movement.[15] Because of the incline, the ramp criteria are different from those of the walkway and path. The minimum one-way ramp widths should be no less than 3 ft 0 in., with two way ramps at a 6 ft 0 in. minimum.[16] One aspect of handicapped access must focus on the design criteria for ramps from parking lots and across curbs. Although there are variations, Fig. 16-16 illustrates four basic alternatives.

Stairs are similar to ramps in some respects. Minimum one-way stair widths should be 3 ft 0 in. with two-way widths at 5 ft 0 in. Like the ramp, a topographical change in

---

[15]Ibid.

[16]Ibid.

(a)

(b)

Figure 16-14 Wheelchair dimensions in plan and elevation.

elevation is also a critical component of the design criteria. Where the vertical change is in excess of 6 ft 0 in., an intermediate landing should be provided[17] (Fig. 16-17). Since visual impairments often accompany physical problems, stairs and ramps should be in contrasting colors to those of adjoining walls or paving. Risers in excess of $6\frac{1}{2}$ in. with tread widths of less than 11 in. should also be avoided.

Handrails for ramps and stairs are essential components of both ramps and stairs. The most comfortable height for ramp handrails is 3 ft 0 in. and 2 ft 8 in. for stairs. A second handrail to accommodate children and wheelchairs is often mounted at 2 ft 4 in. In either case, the rail should extend 18 in. beyond the ends of ramps and 6 in. beyond stairways (Figs. 16-15 and 16-17).[18]

The surface is an important safety and aesthetic consideration in the design of paths, ramps, and stairs. Ramps and paths should be all-weather, nonslip, and free of surface irregularities such as large cracks and uneven edges. Although all joints cannot be eliminated in a paved surface they should be minimized, with none larger than $\frac{1}{2}$ in.[19] All exterior surfaces should have a minimum slope of $\frac{1}{8}$ in. per foot to sustain positive drainage. When a ramp or stair is used as a part of a natural environment and its location on the path could become a hazard, a textural signal advising those with visual difficulties of the impending obstacle should be considered both above and below the ramp or stair.

The stability and functional quality of a surface is also dependent on its relative density. Harder surfaces are generally more stable and thus are preferred. Asphalt, brick in concrete, and concrete are considered to be both hard and smooth and to accommodate both pedestrians and wheelchairs very successfully. Rough surfaces, although dense, are generally less desirable unless special attention is given to reducing their inherent irregularities. Paths of flagstone, bricks laid in sand, or exposed aggregate concrete and wood decks could inhibit the mobility of those using crutches, canes, or wheelchairs. Fur-

---

[17]American Society of Landscape Architects Foundation, p. 30.

[18]Ibid., p. 31.

[19]American National Standards Institute, p. 9.

Figure 16-15 Maximum handicapped ramp length, slope, and handrail height.

Inset Ramp with Continuous Curb

Extended Ramp with Flared Sides

3'-0" minimum width for all ramps
Flared sides on extended ramp should not exceed 8%
Maximum grade for all ramps is 17%

Inset Ramp with Flared Sides

Extended Ramp; Corner Location

Minimum 5'-0" x 3'-6" space at bottom of ramp

Figure 16-16 Four basic ramp alternatives.

Exterior Ramps and Stairs
Require a Minimum Average
of 5 Footcandles of Illumination

Extend Handrail
Beyond End of Stair

Handrail Heights
of 3'-0" and 2'-4"

Minimum Stairway Widths
One Way 3'-0"
Two Way 5'-0"

Use Intermediate Landing
When Vertical Height of
Stair Exceeds 6'-0"

Figure 16-17 Stair guidelines and criteria.

thermore, unlike the smoother surfaces, snow and ice removal is much more difficult without inflicting damage to the surface, and when seasonal obstacles are not removed successfully, they can create obvious problems for every pedestrian.

Softer surfaces can create such difficulty for the handicapped that their use as a paving material, except under limited circumstances, is not recommended. The use of crushed rock, tanbark, earth/sand, or river rock should be avoided in the design of paths to accommodate those with mobility handicaps. Because these materials are unstable, they are poorly suited for wheelchairs. In addition to the fact that they drain poorly and create orientation problems for the visually impaired, they are also generally high in maintenance costs. Although their value as a paving surface is limited, discriminate use is appropriate in a natural setting in which their use does not present an access or safety hazard.

LIGHTING AND SIGNS

Lighting on a site commonly functions to provide illumination to avoid obstacles, maintain security, and see adequately to perform certain tasks. Whereas one level and type of illumination may be necessary for general visibility in a parking lot, another is necessary for a residential driveway. As is obvious from the functions mentioned, each not only requires a different type of fixture but a different level of illumination as well.

Probably the first priority in the development of a lighting plan is safety. Although lighting alone does not create a crimeless environment, there is a very obvious cause–effect relationship between personal safety and lighting. Because of its integral role in the development of a safe urban environment, lighting may be the single most important component of pedestrian paths and open space to the elderly. For the physically handicapped, lighting is even more critical. It must be noted that if fixtures are either ill suited for a particular problem or poorly placed, there is little to be gained from increasing the illumination level. As an example, although overhead fixtures above 20 ft can provide an even level of illumination at a relatively low cost, they are often poorly suited for low-level, high-illumination conditions. Low levels of supplemental lighting often need to be provided for stairs, ramps, intersections, or other areas that would be hazardous if inadequately lit. This applies to pedestrian paths and parking lots as well as rest areas. In those conditions where low lighting is used, it should be below eye level. For the standing adult, eye level is below 5 ft 10 in.; for the wheelchair occupant, eye level is 3 ft 8 in.[20]

Developing a lighting plan that matches the scale of the problem with an appropriately scaled fixture has more than the obvious benefits. A functional approach requires that the site planner recognize that lighting energy cannot only be wasted unnecessarily but that careful articulation of light levels and direction is necessary to keep lighting from becoming a nuisance to adjacent land uses. Furthermore, the range of illumination levels often required for a good lighting plan provides the opportunity for good nocturnal visual variety. There are five general types of site fixtures, three that have a pedestrian-related scale and two that support automobile functions. The first is the smallest in scale and provides illumination for a path, outdoor stair, driveway, or other specific function. Depending on the circumstances, this low level of lighting may be either a free-standing fixture or mounted to a wall. The fixture may be either incandescent or fluorescent and should be mounted within 24 in. of the ground plane.

The next fixture up in scale is that which provides lighting for public sidewalks or other major pedestrian spaces. This fixture should be 10 to 15 ft in height and may be incandescent, fluorescent, or mercury vapor. There are numerous types of fixtures at this level which provide broad down-lighting, focused down-lighting, or general area lighting.

The third level in scale provides illumination for a special purpose. These include small-scale recreational uses (tennis, volleyball, etc.) and industrial, residential, or commercial activities (town square or amphitheater). The height of the fixture will vary between 20 and 30 ft above the site to achieve the desired level of illumination.

The last two types of fixtures support the operation and parking of automobiles. Lighting to accommodate parking lots and roads is between 30 and 50 ft in height. These fixtures are either mercury vapor or high-pressure sodium, as these lamp types provide high levels of illumination very cost-effectively. The "high mast" type is the largest in the scale of illumination and provides lighting for freeways, interchanges, and large

---

[20]American Society of Landscape Architects Foundation, p. 43.

Figure 16-18 Regulating or controlling sign.

Figure 16-19 Directional sign.

parking lots. Similar to the fixture used for smaller-scale roads and parking lots this fixture utilizes a mercury vapor or high-pressure sodium lamp. A note concerning these large-scale lighting types: They lack scale in lighting patterns. Additionally, the taller the fixture is from the ground plane, the more likelihood there is for the light to become a nuisance to adjacent land uses.

Unlike lighting, site signs are not necessarily an issue on every site. While a visible and readable address is sufficient for a residential site, a school or shopping center is another type of problem. The four principal functions of signs are:[21]

1. *To regulate or control:* "STOP," "Emergency Entrance," "No Swimming," "No Parking." These are the most common types, as they often involve health and safety issues (Fig. 16-18).

2. *To give directions:* "IN," "OUT," "To Interstate 20," "To Parking." These are often accompanied by directional graphics, as ambiguity or interpretation defeats the purpose of the sign (Fig. 16-19).

3. *To provide information:* "You are here"—the large-scale maps of parks and shopping centers, which identify the context of a campus or the alignment of a nature trail (Fig. 16-20).

4. *To give identification:* "Fine Arts Building," "Student Parking," "Ranger Head-

---

[21]Ibid., p. 47.

Figure 16-20 Informational sign.

quarters.'' This is the last level of information in the hierarchy of signs: communication.

Similar to other site components, the objective of signs should be to facilitate the use and accessibility of the site. Although signs are a valuable contribution to those without handicaps, to those with visual impairments, orientation is essential to an individual's sense of well-being.

BICYCLES AND BIKEWAYS

The other general level of quasi-pedestrian activity is the bikeway. The cyclist in the United States is often relegated to paths that are either a hazard to their own safety or a hazard to others. Unfortunately, it appears that acceptance of the bicycle as a legitimate transportation system is some years away. The few bikeways that exist are predominantly limited to those conditions where the distance between housing and employment are relatively short, land costs and housing densities are high, and social pressures for two cars per household are minimal. University campuses are excellent examples of these criteria.

Close proximity between housing and employment is particularly important if a system is to enjoy broad use. Although numerous cities have very high density commercial or industrial employment centers, without adjacent residential land use, interest in the use of bicycles as an alternative to the automobile fails to materialize. The development of freeway systems has stretched the distances between employment and housing such that the relationships are often at marginally acceptable riding distances. When housing is relegated to strictly suburban locations, the impact of time and distance are often so high that only cycling enthusiasts are willing to brave the conflicts with motor vehicles and weather on a day-to-day basis.

In some of the more urban communities in the United States, bicycles are emerging as an acceptable alternative transport system. The concept of *alternative* is important to stress because cycling is not for everyone, nor could it be. It is important to remember that the cyclist depends on a system of paths or lanes just as users of other vehicles require paving and rights-of-way. Like vehicular circulation systems, bicycle paths are not complete with the construction or marking of a lane. Where appropriate, parking, locking devices, and lockers are necessary, just as there are provisions for parking cars. The inclusion of all components is necessary to encourage people to utilize bicycles instead of motor vehicles. Exploiting the renewed attention in cycling is in the best interest of both cyclists and communities, as the cost of the supporting infrastructure is minute compared to that for other vehicles.

From the time when the bicycle was little more than a frame and two wheels propelled by the rider's feet, the bicycle has been an attraction. After 1866, when a patent was granted for a pedal drive, the use and success of the bicycle became dramatic. The "velocipede" enjoyed broad popularity in Europe and the United States during the heyday of the industrial revolution. The machine's economy, size, and speed provided the basis for a transport system that rivaled that of trains. Its broad social acceptability contributed to its use, and by 1899 the Cyclist Touring Club in Britain had 60,000 members, its largest ever.[22]

Times and the transportation system have changed. Although the value of the bicycle as an alternative system had been demonstrated in country after country, following World War II, the bicycle became increasingly of interest only to the young and a few unusual adults.

By 1970, the growth of the automobile industry, which had caused the demise of the bicycle, was seized by a fuel crisis. Lightweight-bicycle sales soared from 1.4 million units in 1970 to 10.6 million in 1974 and represented 75% of the total bicycle market. Although sales have not sustained that significant growth, the resurgence in the use of bicycles in the early 1970s produced a real change in the way Americans view and use bicycles.[23] Figure 16-21 portrays total bicycle sales in the United States compared to sales in England.[24]

Figure 16-21 Graph of bicycle sales in England and United States.

---

[22]Mike Hudson et al., *Bicycle Planning: Policy and Practice* (London: Architectural Press Ltd., 1982), p. 1.

[23]Charles F. Floyd, "Whither Goest the Bikeway Boom?" *Planning, Design and Implementation of Bicycle and Pedestrian Facilities* (New York: American Society of Civil Engineers, 1975), p. 475.

[24]Hudson et al., p. 27.

In both the 1973 Federal Highway Act and the Surface Transportation Act of 1978, Congress supported the use of bicycles as an alternative transportation system, with additional federal financial assistance to be administered by the states. But in spite of that commitment, a 1980 report, "Bicycle Transportation for Energy Conservation," indicated that by-and-large, state governments had not allowed the funding support to local governments for bicycle programs at anything close to the levels authorized by Congress.[25] Recalcitrant highway departments failed to provide funding for anything to compete with highways and stifled the development of bicycle networks, and concomitantly, their use. Some of the interest in bicycles in the early 1970s was a response to the energy crisis of that decade and receded with the flow of oil. There were others, however, who believed that the bicycle had long been overlooked as a legitimate transportation alternative.

In *Bicycle Planning*, Mike Hudson et al. suggest the following reasons for the continued interest in cycling:

1. From the public's viewpoint, it is a very cost-effective means of transport. The capital costs are modest relative to the potential use and has been expressed as "freeways at the cost of footpaths."

2. The size of the lanes and storage facilities is much smaller than those required for automobiles. This is particularly important in urban areas, where space is at a premium.

3. Walking and cycling are the two most energy-efficient forms of transportation. In a world of expanding population and finite limits of fossil fuels, every effort to conserve fuel should be made.

4. The public's cost of cycling is similar in scale to the private sector's costs. The machine is simple and maintenance costs are minimal.

5. Cycling is a reliable and quick form of transport. Breakdowns are minimal and door-to-door times for urban journeys between 2.5 and 4 miles (4 to 6.5 km) can be quicker on a bicycle than by any other means. Research in Tempe, Denver, Los Angeles, and Minneapolis/St. Paul indicates that the length of most bicycle trips is 5 miles or less.[26] In urban areas, walking or cycling can assist in improving the level of service on roads and thoroughfares.

6. Cycling is a "benign means of transport" for practically everyone. The machine is noiseless, pollution free, and can provide mobility for all age groups.

7. In the process of accomplishing all of the aforementioned objectives, cycling and walking are the only two systems that are healthy in the process of getting there.[27]

PLANNING CRITERIA

Bicycle and pedestrian systems have similar issues that must be addressed in their planning process. Although each aspect will have some variation, their commonalities suggest concurrent consideration.

Safety is the first priority for both systems. The fundamental concern is with the vulnerability of the cyclist or pedestrian relative to autos and trucks, but care must also be taken to avoid conflicts between cyclists and pedestrians. Horizontal separation has been the predominant method of developing a safe system for both cyclists and pedestrians. Figures 16-22, 16-23, and 16-24 illustrate the three classes of bicycle paths and the value of independent systems.[28]

---

[25]Ibid., p. 8.

[26]Nina Dougherty Rowe, "The Energy Crisis/Bicycles/Federal Government," *Planning, Design and Implementation of Bicycle and Pedestrian Facilities* (New York: American Society of Civil Engineers, 1975), p. 20.

[27]Hudson et al., p. 2.

[28]Carmen W. Daecher, "A Guide for Municipalities for Bicycle Planning," *Planning, Design and Implementation of Bicycle and Pedestrian Facilities* (New York: American Society of Civil Engineers, 1975), p. 118.

Figure 16-22

Figure 16-23

In some cases vertical separation has proved to be a legitimate method of reducing conflicts between pedestrian, cyclists, and vehicles. Horizontal separation is appropriate only in those conditions where the number of people and cars would create congestion and/or create serious safety problems (Fig. 16-25).

Pedestrian and cycle security is also high on the list of priorities. If either system is to be utilized at all hours and to the level of intensity expected, paths and storage facilities should be well lit. Visual obstructions of public spaces and conditions that provide concealment should be minimized. Closed-circuit television has become an in-

CLASS III : No Separation. Shared Right-Of-Way on the Same Surface

Figure 16-24

Figure 16-25 Pedestrian overpass.

creasingly common method of providing surveillance of building lobbies, transit terminals, and so on, where security is difficult because of the flow of people.

For pedestrian and cycle systems to function properly, they must be convenient and direct. Systems need to be designed to accommodate changes in modes (from auto to pedestrian) as well as the walk at lunch. Minimizing the impact of mailboxes, light standards, newsstands, and other street furniture also facilitates the movement of people. Often, the most direct route is the path that encourages walking or cycling. Routes through midblock or connecting lobbies can often create important linkages for what would otherwise be a circuitous route (Fig. 16-26). If either a bicycle or a pedestrian system does not maintain continuity throughout, the network will probably not be used. Convenience to the cyclist necessitates that locking and storage facilities exist at points

Figure 16-26 Midblock pedestrian connection.

Figure 16-27 Pedestrian underpass at Lake Anne. (Photo by Patricia McCracken.)

of modal transfer. Shelter and seating also enhance and expand the use of both cycle and pedestrian networks.

On occasions, grade-separated linkages may be necessary to maintain the continuity of a network. Since the construction costs of underground systems are extremely high, these should be designed and built in conjunction with bridges or other structures. The underpass shown in Fig. 16-27 is a very crucial link in the pedestrian system of Lake Anne Village at Reston, Virginia. But unless there are no alternatives, pedestrians are reluctant to walk up stairs to use elevated bridges. The safety hazard must be a genuinely perilous condition, as studies indicate that people would rather risk confrontation with vehicles than walk up stairs.

Clarity is essential, as every user must be able to understand the entire network. This is particularly crucial for the cyclist at intersections, where the simultaneous movement of vehicles is always potentially hazardous. Good signs and directions are essential to provide the user with a sense of security and understanding as to a path's location, adjacent land uses, landmarks, and public facilities. In turn, understanding generates a higher use of the system and enhances its total cost-effectiveness.

chapter 17

The Building and Energy

by George Truett James

INTRODUCTION

Any change in the natural environment to accommodate a habitable structure should involve an analysis of the site with a focus on comfort and energy conservation. Historically, man accepted the proposition that his welfare and nature were inextricably linked. His survival often depended on his ability to adapt to climatic circumstances. The development of sophisticated, energy-intensive environmental control systems has freed us from the programmatic concerns of comfort and climate, and permitted the construction of habitable structures anywhere. However, recent energy supply disruptions and escalating utility costs have fostered an awareness of the finite nature of our resources and the importance of energy conservation in the built environment. Although our perception of the immediacy of our energy problems changes, our fundamental understanding of those problems should not (see Table 17-1). Because our resources are not limitless, design professionals must provide the leadership required to suppress the waste of conventional energy resources in our built environment.

The United States, with 5% of the world's population, uses 35% of the world's energy resources (see Table 17-2). Between 36 and 40% of U.S. energy consumption is used to heat, air-condition, light, and provide hot water for our buildings.[1] Our nation's buildings are therefore responsible for approximately one-eighth of annual world energy consumption. If these figures are not startling enough, consider that if our buildings and sites had been designed to reduce energy consumption, a conservative estimate of possible savings might be in the neighborhood of 20%.[2] This is simply a reduction of energy waste that has no effect on the standard of living. That wasted energy would be equivalent to the energy used for all purposes by the combined countries of Canada, Australia, New Zealand, and temperate Latin America. It is therefore important for the design

---

[1] R. Stobaugh and D. Yergin, *Energy Future* (New York: Ballantine Books, Inc., 1979), p. 207.

[2] Ibid, p. 167; Yergin states that a 30 to 40% reduction of national energy use is possible with no effect on the standard of living.

TABLE 17-1   World Recoverable Energy Reserves, 1974

	COAL	OIL	NATURAL GAS
Estimate of life (years) based on 1974 consumption			
Highest estimate	1600	123	238
Average estimate	677	65	87
Lowest estimate	43	28	24
Estimate of life (years) based on a 5% growth in rate of usage			
Highest estimate	88	40	53
Average estimate	72	26	32
Lowest estimate	25	18	15

Source: P. W. O'Callaghan, *Building for Energy Conservation* (Oxford: Pergamon Press Ltd, 1978), p. 2.

TABLE 17-2   Comparison of World Energy Consumption by Country

WORLD AREA	1973 POPULATION [MILLIONS (% OF TOTAL)]	1973 ANNUAL ENERGY USE PER CAPITA (MILLION BTU)	TOTAL ANNUAL ENERGY USE [MILLION BILLION BTU (% OF TOTAL)]
United States	210 (5.5)	357	75 (35)
Japan	108 (3)	87	9.4 (5)
Europe	472 (12)	107	50.5 (23)
USSR	250 (6.5)	129	32.2 (15)
Canada, Australia, New Zealand, temperate			
Latin America	80 (2)	82	6.4 (3)
Underdeveloped countries	2740 (71)	15	41.5 (19)

Source: A. Davis and R. Schubert, *Alternate Natural Energy Sources in Building Design* (New York: Van Nostrand Reinhold Company, Inc., 1974).

professional to understand the implications of planning and design decisions on building energy use in order to reduce building energy waste. Site planning can profoundly influence the total energy demand of a building. An energy-conscious site planning effort is simply one that directs the design decisions toward the concept of energy conservation and appropriate utilization of the site's natural energy resources. It has been estimated that proper site planning for a building can provide 30% energy savings without increasing development costs.[3] The site planner should therefore develop an understanding of the ways in which buildings use energy and the nature of the climatic forces acting on them. In response to these concerns, in this chapter we focus briefly on building energy use and how predesign analytic techniques can inform the site planning process.

BUILDING METABOLISM

Buildings and their environmental control systems are affected by external thermal loads imposed by the climatic elements discussed in Chapter 8. Buildings are also affected by the thermal loads produced when heat is generated inside the building by people, lights, and equipment. This internal heat generation can be thought of as the building's metab-

---

[3]E. G. McPherson, ed., *Energy Conserving Site Design* (Washington, D.C.: American Society of Landscape Architects, 1984), p. 298 citing R. M. Byrne and L. Howland, *Background Information Summary* (Washington, D.C.: The Urban Land Institute, 1980).

olism. A building's metabolic rate, the rate at which internal thermal loads are generated, is dependent on and varies with building type, building function, and the way in which the building is used.

Without heating or air conditioning, the temperature of the air inside buildings with low metabolic rates, such as a house or warehouse, is primarily dependent on the external thermal loads produced by climate on the building's envelope or "skin." The rate of internal heat generation is insignificant compared to the rate of heat flow generated by climatic conditions. This type of building is referred to as a skin-load-dominated (SLD) building. Without the assistance of an interior climate control system (heater or air conditioner), inside air temperature is primarily a function of exterior climatic conditions. When it is cloudy and cold outside, it will be cold inside. When it is sunny and hot outside, it will be hot inside.

By contrast, in buildings with high metabolic rates, so much heat can be generated internally that the influences of climate on the building become insignificant by comparison (such as in a steel smelter). This type of building is referred to as an internal-load-dominated (ILD) building. When it is cloudy and cold outside, it may be perfectly comfortable inside without supplementary mechanical heating. It is not uncommon for buildings with high metabolic rates to require air conditioning to maintain occupant comfort even during cold winter weather. There are instances of buildings where heating systems are rarely, if ever, activated because of their high internal heat generation rates.

When internal thermal loads are balanced by the rate of heat loss from the building, a thermal balance or equilibrium is achieved. This is a set of circumstances where neither mechanical heating nor cooling is required to maintain the inside temperature prescribed by the mechanical system's thermostat (the thermostat set point).

Disregarding the effects of solar radiation (cloudy conditions or nighttime), thermal balance is usually achieved in skin-load-dominated buildings when the outside temperature is only a few degrees Fahrenheit below the thermostat set point. For example, the internal heat generated in a single-family detached residence might produce a temperature of 72°F inside when the outside temperature is 65°F, a difference of 7°F. In other words, if the thermostat is set at 72°F, thermal balance will exist when it is 65°F outside. In order to maintain the 72°F prescribed by the thermostat setting, supplementary heating will be required when the outside temperature falls below 65°F, and supplementary cooling will be required above 65°F. Still disregarding solar radiation, the outside temperature at which the internal loads are balanced by the building's heat loss rate (65°F in this example) is referred to as the balance point temperature.

With a high rate of internal heat production, an internal-load-dominated building will have a balance point temperature significantly lower than the earlier residential example. ILD buildings with very low balance point temperatures can, in a sense, eliminate winter heating loads, because internally produced heat can be sufficient to keep the inside temperature in the comfort zone during a cold winter day. Conversely, when summer climatic loads, including solar radiation, are added to these large internal loads, air-conditioning requirements can be quite substantial. Consequently, ILD buildings often require a great deal more auxiliary cooling energy than auxiliary heating energy.

The balance point temperature of a building can be estimated if enough programmatic information is available. As identified by Charles Benton and James Akridge in "Balance Point Exercise,"[4] balance point temperature is described by the following equation:

$$T_{bp} = T_{th} - \frac{Q_i}{UA + \text{infil}}$$

---

[4]C. Benton and J. Akridge, "Balance Point Exercise," *Laboratory Exercises* (prepared for the U.S. Department of Energy Passive Solar Curriculum Project, *Teaching Passive Design in Architecture*, June 1981).

where

T_{bp} = balance point temperature

T_{th} = thermostat set point

Q_i = average hourly internal loads (over a 24-hour period) (sum the number of Btu generated daily by people, lights, and equipment, and divide by 24 hours; the result is the average internal gain in Btu per hour)

UA = building's heat loss rate in Btu per hour per °F (Btu/hr-°F) calculated using standard steady-state heat transfer calculation procedures; this includes heat transfer due to conduction through the walls, windows, roofs, and floors

infil = infiltration rate in Btu per hour per °F

Following is an example of the calculation procedure for a small, residential structure with the thermostat set at 72°F.

House plan: 1000 ft² (25 ft × 40 ft), 8-ft walls, volume = 8000 ft³

Floor area: 1000 ft², avg. U-value = 0.1, UA = 100 Btu/hr-°F

Ceiling area: 1000 ft², avg. U-value = 0.05, UA = 50 Btu/hr-°F

Wall/window area: 1040 ft², avg. U-value = 0.077, UA = 80 Btu/hr-°F

Total UA = 230 Btu/hr-°F

Infiltration = air changes (cubic feet) per hour/60 minutes per hour = ft³/min

Estimating one-half air change per hour:

[(8000 ft³ × ½ air change per hour)/60 minutes per hour] × 1.08

(1.08 is the conversion factor for ft³/min to Btu/hr-°F)

Infiltration = approximately 70 Btu per hour per °F (Btu/hr-°F)

$$UA + \text{infil} = 230 + 70 = 300 \text{ Btu/hr-°F}$$

Internal loads:

4 people at 250 Btu (sensible heat) per hour	1000 Btu/hr
Lights	300 Btu/hr
Equipment	800 Btu/hr
Total	2100 Btu/hr

$$T_{bp} = T_{th} - \frac{Q_i}{UA + \text{infil}}$$

$$= 72 - \frac{2100}{230 + 70}$$

$$= 72 - 7$$

$$= 65°F$$

The balance point temperature will decrease if the thermostat set point is lowered, insulation levels are increased (lower U-values), or internal heat generation increases.[5]

When used in conjunction with a matrix describing daily temperature profiles for each month of the year, balance point temperature can provide a preliminary indication of shading requirements for a building. This can be useful to the site planner for preliminary building orientation, siting, and design decisions. Shading calendars are developed

---

[5]There are other approaches that can be used to calculate balance point temperature; see G. Z. Brown, *Sun, Wind and Light* (New York: John Wiley & Sons, Inc., 1985), pp. 56–62 and D. Watson and R. Glover, *Solar Control Workbook* (prepared for the U.S. Department of Energy Passive Solar Curriculum Project, *Teaching Passive Design in Architecture*, November 1981), pp. 60–63 and Appendix E.

time	factor	J	F	M	A	M	J	J	A	S	O	N	D
12M	.222												
2am	.139												
4am	.056												
6am	0												
8am	.111												
10am	.583												
12 N	.861												
2 pm	1.0												
4 pm	.917												
6 pm	.694												
8 pm	.444												
10pm	.306												

Figure 17-1 Shading calendar.

using the balance point temperature and normal temperature data contained in *Local Climatological Data*, *Comparative Climatic Data*, or the *Airport Climatological Summary* (see ''Information Sources and Interpretation,'' Chapter 8). Bruce Novell of the Alabama Solar Energy Center describes a series of adjustment factors that can be used to develop the daily temperature profiles from normal daily maximum and minimum

time	factor	J	F	M	A	M	J	J	A	S	O	N	D	
12M	.222	39	43	48	59	67	75	79	79	73	61	49	42	
2am	.139	37	41	46	57	65	73	77	77	72	59	47	40	
4am	.056	35	39	44	55	63	71	75	75	70	57	45	38	
6am	0	34	38	43	54	62	70	74	74	69	56	44	37	sunrise
8am	.111	42	49	51	63	69	78	78	82	74	62	51	42	
10am	.583	47	51	57	67	74	82	87	87	81	69	58	50	
12 N	.861	53	57	64	73	80	88	93	93	86	76	65	56	
2 pm	1.0	56	60	67	76	83	91	96	96	89	79	68	59	
4 pm	.917	54	58	65	74	81	89	94	94	87	77	66	57	sunset
6 pm	.694	49	53	60	69	77	85	89	89	83	72	61	52	
8 pm	.444	44	48	54	64	71	79	84	84	78	66	55	47	
10pm	.306	41	45	50	61	68	76	81	81	75	63	51	44	

Figure 17-2 Shading calendar. Balance point temperature—65°F.

time	factor	J	F	M	A	M	J	J	A	S	O	N	D
12 M	.222	39	43	48	59	67	78	79	79	73	61	49	42
2 am	.139	37	41	46	57	65	73	77	77	72	59	47	40
4 am	.056	35	38	44	55	63	71	75	75	70	57	45	38
6 am	0	34	38	43	54	62	70	74	74	69	56	44	37
8 am	.111	42	49	51	63	69	78	78	82	74	62	51	42
10 am	.583	47	51	57	67	74	82	87	87	81	69	58	50
12 N	.861	53	57	64	73	80	88	93	93	86	76	85	58
2 pm	1.0	56	60	67	76	83	91	96	96	89	79	68	59
4 pm	.917	54	58	65	74	81	89	94	94	87	77	66	57
6 pm	.694	48	53	60	69	77	85	89	89	88	72	61	52
8 pm	.444	44	48	54	64	71	79	84	84	78	66	55	47
10 pm	.306	41	45	50	61	68	76	81	81	75	63	51	44

Figure 17-3 Shading calendar. Balance point temperature—55°F.

temperature data.[6] These factors are shown along the left-hand side of the calendar, next to the hours of the day (Fig. 17-1). Intermediate temperatures during the course of the day are calculated by

$$T_{\text{intermediate}} = \left[(T_{\max} - T_{\min}) \times \text{factor} \right] + T_{\min}$$

The balance point temperature (65°F for the residential example) is plotted as shown in Fig. 17-2. The shading calendar indicates that afternoon shading is necessary from March through November for the example house. Complete shading is desirable from June through September. Afternoon solar gain is desirable in December, January, and February, and morning solar gain will be beneficial from October through April.

The shading calendar for a commercial building, which has higher internal loads and a balance point temperature of 55°F, is illustrated in Fig. 17-3. Here afternoon shading is suggested year-round, and early morning solar gain is useful for only a few months—November through March. This type of information can be valuable when making preliminary siting, massing, and orientation decisions.

PREDESIGN THERMAL LOAD AND BUILDING ENERGY ANALYSIS

With only limited, preliminary program information, there are methods available to the site planner to anticipate more precisely the nature of the thermal loading problems a building will experience when located on a site. Based on programmatic information similar to that used to calculate balance point temperature, a hypothetical base-case building can be subjected to analysis to identify thermal loading problems before the building is designed or even located on the site. This type of analysis will be discussed briefly.

---

[6]B. J. Novell, "Passive Cooling Strategies," *ASHRAE Journal*, Vol. 25, No. 12, 1983, pp. 23–28.

One simple and extremely useful method for this type of analysis, described by G. Z. Brown in *Sun, Wind and Light*, is based on balance point temperature calculations.[7] The calculations can quickly be performed by hand, and the graphic depiction of results simplifies interpretation by the designer.

A hypothetical base-case building approach is used in the procedures presented in *Energy Graphics* by Booz, Allen & Hamilton, Inc.[8] Similar to Brown's method, the calculation procedures are designed to be performed by hand. However, the calculations are tedious and time consuming, which may inhibit the designer's investigation of alternatives. These calculation procedures are ideally suited for solution by computers, and many thermal load and energy analysis programs exist which can be used for the predesign analysis of a hypothetical base-case building.

A base-case building used in this type of analysis is hypothesized in the program information shown in Table 17-3. For this example the building is square (112 ft × 112 ft × 48 ft). The percentage of unshaded glass area for all four elevations is estimated to be 30%. In an effort to simplify the base analysis, all exterior walls will be considered as vertical planes, as opposed to being stepped or battered. Occupancy, lighting, and equipment schedules are developed from the building program, and the base-case building is "subjected" through analysis to these internal loads, as well as the external loads imposed by temperature, solar radiation, and humidity. The results of a computer analysis (using a microcomputer program called MPEG 1.0 developed by the author and based on *Energy Graphics* procedures) are illustrated in Fig. 17-4. Component loads (internal, solar, envelope, and ventilation loads) are graphed individually to facilitate comparative evaluations. "Total heat gain or loss" is obtained by summing the component loads. Loads below the "0" line on the "total heat gain or loss" graph indicate heating loads that will require auxiliary heating to maintain prescribed inside temperatures. Loads above the "0" line, but below the dashed "allowable heat gain" line, indicate heat gain which will not raise the inside temperature above the allowable limit. Loads above the dashed line will require mechanical cooling to mitigate their effect on interior temperature.

TABLE 17-3 Preliminary Building Program

1	Name of project analysis				Four-story bank/office building		
2	Floor area: volume				50,000		500,000
3	Roof area: roof *R*-value				12,500		10.0
4	South wall: area; % glass; shading coefficient				5,376	0.3	0.83
5	West wall: area; % glass; shading coefficient				5,376	0.3	0.83
6	North wall: area; % glass; shading coefficient				5,376	0.3	0.83
7	East wall: area; % glass; shading coefficient				5,376	0.3	0.83
8	*R*-value of walls; *U*-value of glass				7.00		0.58
9	Mechanical ventilation required; infiltration rate				10.00		1.0
10	Heat generated by occupants (Btu/hr/person) sensible; latent				250		200

		12M	4 am	8 am	12N	4 pm	8 pm	12M
11	Indoor temperature: upper limit	80	80	75	75	75	75	80
12	Indoor temperature: lower limit	60	60	65	65	65	65	60
13	Occupancy schedule	4	2	500	500	500	50	4
14	Internal heat from equipment	0.16	0.16	8.00	8.00	8.00	2.40	0.16
15	Internal heat from lighting	0.84	0.84	10.80	9.60	10.80	3.60	0.84

16	Heating equipment; cooling equipment efficiencies		0.70	2.00
17	Heating energy cost; cooling energy cost ($/MMBtu)		5.00	14.65
18	No changes to data			

[7]Brown, *Sun, Wind and Light*, pp. 56–62.

[8]G. K. Hart, J. M. Kurtz, and W. I. Whiddon, *Energy Graphics* (Washington, D.C.: Booz, Allen & Hamilton, Inc., 1981).

Figure 17-4   Four-story office/bank building heat gain/loss analysis.

The base-case building that is being analyzed is a four-story building with a bank on the ground floor and three stories of office space above. The "total heat gain or loss" graph (Fig. 17-4) indicates that on a normal January day in Dallas under clear skies, this building will experience excess heat gain and will require auxiliary cooling. This condition is exacerbated during warmer months. It is evident that "internal heat gain" from people, lights, and equipment is the dominant factor contributing to excess heat gain. "Solar heat gain" is also problematic, as well as "ventilation heat gain" in the summer, due primarily to latent heat gain. "Envelope heat gain or loss" is comparatively insignificant. With this type of thermal load profile, *Energy Graphics* recommends the following generalized "design directives":[9]

1. Decrease internal loads.
2. Decrease solar heat gain.
3. Increase ventilation/infiltration heat loss (when outside air temperature and humidity are suitable).
4. Increase envelope heat loss.

The base building has a balance point temperature of 36°F, and the shading calendar, illustrated in Fig. 17-5, indicates that shading for windows is desirable for the entire year. This, along with the "directives," would suggest to the site planner that building massing and orientation should be designed to reduce solar heat gain and take advantage of natural ventilation when it is appropriate. Artificial lighting is responsible for a significant portion of internal loads. This is primarily an architectural design problem—the utilization of daylighting to reduce artificial lighting requirements—but the site planner can respond by locating the building so as not to reduce access to daylight. The design directives suggest the following general architectural strategies:

1. Reduce electric lighting requirements through the use of daylighting.
2. Carefully shade all windows to reduce solar heat gain.
3. Utilize stack or natural ventilation if possible. Employ an economizer cycle in the air-conditioning system.

The office/bank building assumed in the base-case model is modified and re-evaluated as a structure that has a 4:1 length-to-width ratio. It is oriented along the east–west axis to facilitate daylighting and to simplify the shading of glass. Since east and west glass is difficult to shade, the glazing area of these two walls is reduced to 10% of

time	factor	J	F	M	A	M	J	J	A	S	O	N	D	
12 M	.222	39	43	48	59	67	75	79	79	73	61	49	42	
2 am	.139	37	41	46	57	65	73	77	77	72	59	47	40	
4 am	.056	35	39	44	55	63	71	75	75	70	57	45	38	
6 am	0	34	38	43	54	62	70	74	74	69	58	44	37	sunrise
8 am	.111	42	49	51	63	69	78	78	82	74	62	51	42	
10 am	.583	47	51	57	67	74	82	87	87	81	69	56	50	
12 N	.861	53	57	64	73	80	88	93	93	86	76	65	56	
2 pm	1.0	56	60	67	76	83	91	96	96	89	79	68	59	
4 pm	.917	54	58	65	74	81	89	94	94	87	77	66	57	sunset
6 pm	.694	49	53	60	69	77	85	89	89	83	72	61	52	
8 pm	.444	44	48	54	64	71	79	84	84	78	66	55	47	
10 pm	.306	41	45	50	61	68	76	81	81	75	63	51	44	

Figure 17-5 Shading calendar. Balance point temperature—36°F.

[9]Ibid, pp. 56–59.

the wall area. It is assumed that the narrower building with its emphasis on daylighting will permit a reduction in electric lighting by 50% during daylight hours. The effects of reorienting the building, carefully shading glass, and reducing electric lighting are shown in Fig. 17-6. The balance point temperature has been elevated to 45°F, and the effects on shading requirements are illustrated in Fig. 17-7. With the exception of early mornings in December and January, shading is still required for the entire year. The estimated annual load reduction produced by these simple strategies is 24%. The estimated $82,000

Figure 17-6 Modified four-story office/bank building heat gain/loss analysis.

time	factor	J	F	M	A	M	J	J	A	S	O	N	D
12 M	.222	39	43	48	59	67	75	78	78	73	61	49	42
2 am	.139	37	41	46	57	65	73	77	77	72	59	47	40
4 am	.056	35	39	44	55	63	71	75	75	70	57	45	38
6 am	0	34	38	43	54	62	70	74	74	69	56	44	37
8 am	.111	42	49	51	63	69	78	78	82	74	62	51	42
10 am	.583	47	51	57	67	74	82	87	87	81	69	58	50
12 N	.861	53	57	64	73	80	88	93	93	86	76	65	56
2 pm	1.0	56	60	67	76	83	91	96	96	89	79	68	59
4 pm	.917	54	58	65	74	81	89	94	94	87	77	66	57
6 pm	.694	49	53	60	69	77	85	89	89	83	72	61	52
8 pm	.444	44	48	54	64	71	79	84	84	78	66	55	47
10 pm	.306	41	45	50	61	68	76	81	81	75	63	51	44

Figure 17-7 Shading calendar. Balance point temperature—45°F.

annual cost of air-conditioning and electric lighting has been reduced to $57,000, a savings of 30% or $25,000 per year.

Again, this type of analysis can suggest strategies for preliminary site planning decisions concerning buildings. Once building location and massing have been determined, the site microclimates should be remapped, using the mapping procedures outlined in Chapter 8 in the section "Site-Microclimate Mapping." The analysis of climate, site-microclimates, and the thermal loads on proposed buildings can inform the site planning process, increase the opportunities for thermal comfort in exterior spaces, and reduce thermal loads on buildings and requisite energy use in buildings.

chapter 18

Land Use Controls

INTRODUCTION

The last but least visible force affecting a site is the law. There are numerous public agencies whose regulations may affect the development of a site. Although the purview and jurisdictions of the various state and local authorities widely vary, the site planning checklist in Chapter 4 will provide a start.

The most common condition where legal constraints materially influence site planning is through zoning. Zoning exists at the city, town, county, and at least in one case, at the state level. Although state zoning is unusual, it has permitted the state of Hawaii to control the encroachment of urban land uses into prime agricultural resources and areas of scenic beauty. The island's landform may have induced Hawaii to adopt a concept of land use controls that has not been imitated by any mainland state since its adoption more than two decades ago.

But Hawaii is the exception. Zoning is basically a local governmental issue. What is done in a neighboring county, city, or other political jurisdiction does not necessarily mean that there are always commonalities. Like other conditions in site planning, never assume anything relative to zoning and land use controls. Aside from a state's enabling legislation, which is common to all municipalities within a state, each will have adopted its own laws controlling land use controls.

What is most common from state to state and city to county is the process and the players. These will vary to some degree because one state may have given the power to zone only to its cities, another to its counties. Depending on the state, the nomenclature of local governments will vary: a city council, county council, county board of supervisors, county commissioners, and so on. Do not confuse your elected officials, who in most communities make the decisons concerning zoning, with those they appoint. These relationships and the process will be discussed later in this chapter. For an understanding of zoning and its influences, it helps to have some understanding of the evolution of the concept.

Misconceptions associated with individual rights abound. The popular belief is that each American has an inalienable right to do as he or she wishes with his or her land and that governmental control borders on an illegitimate exericise of police power. As Bosselman, Callies, and Banta observed in *The Taking Issue*, "there is an opinion by many that foreign concepts like environmental protection and zoning were sneaked through by the Warren Court."[1]

The image that most people have of the colonist in the wilderness with absolute freedom from land use controls is far from the fact. A certain lack of regulation was not only acceptable but appropriate in the struggle to survive during the decades of the seventeenth and eighteenth centuries. What is not widely understood is that the colonists brought with them a set of legal concepts that were 400 years in the making.

HISTORY AND BACKGROUND

As a monarch, the King of England exercised broad power over the country's people, land, and treasury in the thirteenth century. He controlled the kingdom through noblemen on estates and levied taxes as he saw fit. John's abuses of his authority were so extensive that his noblemen collectively demanded that their rights be defined. This confrontation between noblemen and their king culminated in the development of the Magna Carta in 1215. John's reluctant acceptance of the Magna Carta is considered to be the keystone of individual rights in England and her colonies. Chapter 39 is of particular importance since it required the crown to respect "the law of the land," and consider the "judgment of peers" in the acquisition of a freeman's property.

> No freeman shall be arrested, or detained in prison, or deprived of his freehold, or in any way molested; and we will not set forth against him, unless by the lawful judgment of his peers and by the law of the land.[2]

Although there is some doubt as to whether subsequent monarchs respected the intent of the law, many continued to employ the crown's authority to regulate without pause. Elizabeth I, as an example, issued several proclamations associated with land use, density control, and building height and design in an effort to reduce the squalor of urban London.[3] Following the Great Fire of London in 1666, Parliament invoked and enforced strict building codes which regulated roof lines, materials, and construction techniques.[4] It was from a tradition that respected the rights of the individual while acknowledging the important concept that property could be regulated for the public good that colonists set sail for the New World.

The New World immigrant had lived with land use controls, and as urban centers emerged, recognized the value of building codes and ordinances that restricted nuisances. Boston, New Amsterdam, and Philadelphia all had ordinances that sought to reduce the potential of fire or delineated specific design criteria for the landscaping of public streets and individual properties.[5]

The acceptance of the concept of the public good, or health, safety, and welfare, was also critical to the establishment of a German concept of land use regulation zoning. The notion that there was an appropriate arrangement or relationship between various

---

[1] Fred Bosselman, David Callies, and John Banta, *The Taking Issue* (Washington, D.C.: U.S. Government Printing Office, 1973), p. 1.

[2] Translated from an original Latin text by Edward Coke (Milite), *The Second Part of the Institutes of the Laws of England* (London: printed for E. and R. Brouke, Bell Yard, New Temple Bar, and William S. McKechnie, 1797), p. 45.

[3] 31 Elizabeth I C.7 (Statutes at Large, Vol. 6 at 409, *et seq*).

[4] 19 Ch. II C.3 (8 Stat. large), pp. 233–251.

[5] 2 Pennsylvania St. 66, Chap. 53.

land uses was based primarily on nuisance laws. It was not unreasonable to accept the premise that gunpowder factories, slaughterhouses, and stockyards should not be located adjacent to residential land uses. But although the concept of separating ''incompatible'' uses was reasonable, in the absence of the concept of zoning, the only recourse that one property owner had against a nuisance (another property owner) was a civil lawsuit. As the noted attorney Richard Babcock observed: ''There is little evidence in the history of land development in the U.S. [in which] the private decision maker, left to his own devices, can be trusted to act in the public interest.''[6]

Although land use regulation was broadly accepted, when the colonists sat down to draft the new law of the land, a fundamental difference relative to government and private property emerged. Where there was little disagreement as to the authority of the colonial legislature to take land for a public service, the concept of ''just compensation'' became a recurring text in various state constitutions. The principle appeared first in Vermont's first constitution in 1777,[7] to be followed by Massachusetts three years later. Madison's initial draft of the Bill of Rights included the following text:

> No person shall be subject, except in cases of impeachment, to more than one punishment or one trial for the same offense; nor shall be compelled to be a witness against himself; nor be deprived of life, liberty, or property without due process of law; *nor be obliged to relinquish his property, where it may be necessary for public use, without a just compensation* [emphasis added].[8]

The reasons for the ''taking clause'' text of the Bill of Rights have been debated by numerous legal scholars.[9] Among those considered are two plausible rationales for the distinct departure from the English tradition. The first was the simple fairness of a condition in which a property could be taken without compensation. Although this was an acceptable situation with a monarch, the government in the colonies was the people and, as such, was seen more as an extension of the authority of individuals than one ordained by birth or church. Second, the revolutionary army was apparently arbitrary and oppressive in the acquisition of supplies from the colonial farming community. Compensation was never discussed as the army consumed precious livestock and foodstuffs in their struggle against the British.[10] The propertied class was also somewhat apprehensive that those of lower ''status'' might one day administer the country and, as such, favored the ''just compensation'' clause.[11] Madison and his colleagues supported the principles of eminent domain inherited from the English, but they believed that the concept could lead to abuse without some controlling mechanism that maintained the rights of the individual property owner.

Land use controls in the United States conceptually separated into two areas: one as eminent domain, in which just compensation is mandatory; the second as police power or restrictions on land use, wherein no compensation is involved as long as the government (local, state, or federal) is acting in the interest of its citizenry. One of the earliest cases documenting the land use controls and police power in the United States is the *Brick Presbyterian Church* v. *The City of New York*; 1826.[12] The church had a history of permitting the bodies of deceased parishioners to be interred in the churchyard. The municipality had a real concern that the natural processes of decay would contaminate the municipality's groundwater supply and filed suit. The court held for the municipality,

---

[6]Richard F. Babcock, *The Zoning Game* (Madison, Wis.: The University of Wisconsin Press, 1966), p. 185.

[7]J. B. Wilbur, *Ira Allen: Founder of Vermont* (Boston, Mass.: Houghton-Mifflin Co., 1928), p. 96.

[8]*Annals of Congress*, pp. 451–452; Schwartz, p. 1057; William B. Stoebuck, p. 595; Edmund Dumbauld, p. 207.

[9]Bosselman, Callies, and Banta, pp. 99–104.

[10]St. George Tucker, *Blackstone's Commentaries with Notes of Reference to the Constitution and Laws of the Federal Government of Virginia and Commonwealth of Virginia*, Book 1, Part 1, 1803, pp. 305–306.

[11]Oscar Handlin and Mary Handlin, eds., *The Popular Sources of Political Authority* (Cambridge, Mass.: Harvard University Press, 1966), p. 336.

[12]The Brick Presbyterian Church v. City of New York, 5 Cow (New York, 1826), p. 538.

maintaining that the rationale for its decision to sustain the city's right to restrict land use was the health, safety, and welfare of the community.[13] The *Brick Presbyterian Church* case is an early model example of how a municipality's exercise of police power can control a property without "taking" the property.

One of the next critical issues that would need to be heard and tested would deal with the acceptable limits of the municipality's control. The inevitable argument would examine the case where the municipality's efforts to control a property's use result in a reduction in the property's value. In 1915 the California Supreme Court provided some clues as to the limits of property reduction when sustaining a Los Angeles ordinance that prohibited the operation of a brick kiln in a residential area. In spite of the fact that the manufacturing function had been in place for some time and that its value would be reduced from $800,000 to $60,000, the court ruled that the ordinance was a reasonable restriction protecting the health and welfare of the community.[14] The guideline that delineates the difference between police power and eminent domain is that the state controls, through police power, the use of property for the public good, without compensation for diminution in value, when its use otherwise is harmful, whereas through eminent domain the state takes property, with compensation, when it is useful to the public.[15]

Although other cases provide insights into the changes in the court's attitude toward land use controls, few provide the conceptual examples presented in *Pennsylvania Coal* v. *Mahon* in 1921. At the turn of the century, northern Pennsylvania had extensive deposits of anthracite coal. Pennsylvania Coal, together with numerous other mining operations, had acquired the mineral rights to thousands of acres of land throughout the state and was actively involved in the extraction of the resource. In the exuberance of the industry to mine coal, many shafts and tunnels were excavated without proper shoring. The results were often surface collapse or subsidence. Since numerous tunnels and shafts transversed towns and communities throughout the state, many cities found the hazard of collapse to be a common occurrence.[16] Broken water mains, fires from broken gas lines, and the collapse of structures plagued numerous cities. The situation became so serious that the state adopted legislation (the Kohler Act) which prohibited subsurface mining that would cause subsidence and collapse of streets, buildings, and property damage.[17]

John and Mary Mahon owned and resided in Pittston, Pennsylvania, where, 20 years earlier, Pennsylvania Coal owned land and mineral rights. Upon sale of the property, Pennsylvania Coal retained the mineral rights to its property as well as a waiver of any claim (against Pennsylvania Coal) for subsidence.[18] The Mahons were given written notice in September 1921 that Pennsylvania Coal was mining in their community and that the operation might create subsidence. If they were concerned about the safety of themselves or their household, they should evacuate the premises. Pennsylvania Coal reminded the Mahons that the mineral rights were theirs and that Pennsylvania Coal was not liable for any personal or property damage resulting from its mining.[19]

The Mahons relied solely on the Kohler Act for protection and filed an injunction to prohibit Pennsylvania Coal from mining. Litigation ensued, and following disagreements between lower and appeals courts, the case was ultimately heard by the U.S. Supreme Court. The Court's decision, penned by Justice Oliver Wendell Holmes, held for Pennsylvania Coal and ruled the Kohler Act unconstitutional. In spite of the obvious

---

[13]7 Cow (New York, 1826), p. 595.

[14]Hadacheck v. Sebastian, 239 U.S. 394 (1915).

[15]*Words and Phrases*, Vol. 32A (St. Paul, Minn.: West Publishing Co., 1956), p. 404.

[16]Bosselman, Callies, and Banta, pp. 126–127.

[17]Public Law 1192.

[18]Brief on Behalf of the City of Scranton, Intervenor in the Supreme Court of the United States, October 1922, p. 1.

[19]Transcript of Record (29,099) filed August 17, 1922 in the Supreme Court of the United States, October 1922, p. 10.

health, safety, and welfare issues involved in the case, Chief Justice Holmes considered that "the right to the coal consists in the right to mine it."[20] The Court maintained that in the interest of the public's health, safety, and welfare, some rights may be taken with police power. But when the state attempted, through the Kohler Act and its police power, to take the rights to mine *any* of the coal, the state essentially attempted to acquire the property rights, which more appropriately should have been accomplished through eminent domain, where just compensation is required.[21] The implication was that although the state had appropriately tried to address an issue of "health, safety and welfare" through police power, where no obligation for just compensation was necessary, the results of the controlling legislation took *all of the rights* to the mineral (property). Although the Court maintained that taking all the rights was unconstitutional, they did not, nor have subsequent Supreme Court decisions, render any judgments that have given any guidelines as to "how many is too much."

The court's decision in *Pennsylvania Coal* v. *Mahon* established a clear line between the concepts of eminent domain and police power. As the nation grew, governments, at all levels, used the power of eminent domain to acquire property for a variety of uses—but always with compensation. The question as to the amount of just compensation is normally measured by the fair market value of the property at the time of the taking. Compensation also means

> full indemnity or remuneration for the loss or damage of property taken or injured for public use; and just compensation means the full and perfect equivalent in money of the property taken, whereby the owner is put in as good a position pecuniarily as he would have occupied if his property had not been taken.[22]

Although there may be conditions in which "just" may be argumentative, there is no question as to the importance of this legal mechanism in the operation of government. The police power segment of government's authority is equally important. This power to regulate and control the use of private property has been defined as

> the inherent right of a government to restrict individual conduct or use of property to protect the public health, safety and welfare; it must follow due process of the law but, unlike eminent domain, does not carry the requirement of compensation for any alleged losses.[23]

For years the concept of nuisance law worked to keep a needed separation between incompatible uses. In a time when land was cheap and life was simple, common sense prevailed and people kept some distance between the town's powder magazine and their homes. Although pigsties and rendering plants were also unwelcome in a residential atmosphere, in many cases the argument as to whether a use was, in fact, a nuisance was left to the civil courts to decide. The notion that there might be a variety of nuisance land uses that should be separated from residential activities emerged as a logical strategy through which local government might protect the public's interest.

In 1916, the City of New York became the first municipality to adopt a comprehensive zoning ordinance.[24] Although numerous communities throughout the United States later adopted and employed zoning ordinances, they were all challenged in the courts. State and district judges had failed to render any decision (one way or the other) with any argument of such profound logic that might mandate others to follow. The

---

[20]Commonwealth v. Clearview Coal Company, 256 Pennsylvania St. 328, 331.

[21]Pennsylvania Coal Co. v. Mahon, 260 U.S. 393 (1922).

[22]Corpus Juris Secundum, Sec. 96, p. 390.

[23]Diane Maddex, ed., *The Brown Book: A Directory of Preservation Information* (Washington, D.C.: Preservation Press, 1983), p. 52.

[24]Frank So, Israel Stollman, Frank Beal, and David S. Arnold, eds., *The Practice of Local Government Planning* (Washington, D.C.: American Planning Association and the International City Management Association, 1979), p. 416.

nature of the situation in the mid-1920s was quite unsettled. The dilemma was that although one might accept the concept that an industrial land use would be a nuisance to a residential neighborhood, questions concerning whether a grocery might be a nuisance to a sheet metal shop left the question open to debate. The basic legal haze that clouded the issue of control over private land now focused on the 14th Amendment. The salient section of the amendment provided that "no person be deprived of his property without due process of law." The question came to this: Even when state enabling legislation permitted zoning, was zoning a scheme of municipal regulation, structured to prohibit land uses that had never been considered a nuisance?

So it was not an unusual set of circumstances for the Village of Euclid, Ohio, to become engaged in litigation upon the denial of a request for the rezoning of a residential property to a commercial property. Ambler Realty, the plaintiff, maintained that the zoning ordinance was an unconstitutional taking of property rights and further, that the imposition of the zoning diminished the potential value of the property. After an unusual rehearing of the case, the high court overturned a federal trial court and sustained the concept that zoning was a legitimate function of police power.[25] The landmark decision favoring the Village of Euclid was one of the most significant in American land use law and established precedents that are still referenced by the courts. Although this was a very tumultuous time in the development of land use regulations in the United States, *Village of Euclid* v. *Ambler Realty Co.* became the cornerstone on which the system rests today.

Since zoning is a power passed from state to local governments, there are broad variations from state to state and from city to city. For further reading on the topic, the reader is referred to *American Land Planning* by Norman Williams, a five-volume text that examines the multiplicity of state laws in detail. Although efforts in 1922 and 1928 to develop a standard state enabling legislation was widely received, each municipality has interpreted and implemented laws to reflect local values and conditions. Although the court's ruling in 1926 closed one door, it opened many, as communities across the land struggled with the site-specific decisions associated with land use planning and zoning.

Some municipalities misread the Supreme Court's *Euclid* decision and found themselves before state supreme courts for unreasonable and/or capricious application of their ordinances. The courts maintained, among other things, that a reasonable use of the property was an essential consideration in the administration of an ordinance.

Maher v. *The City of New Orleans* in 1975 provides some clues and an interpretation of the term "reasonable." The Vieux Carre is a nationally famous historic district and was one of the first in the United States to adopt a historic district ordinance. The ordinance was *very* restrictive, and when Mr. Maher's request for a demolition permit was denied, litigation ensued. The municipality maintained that the one-story apartment building was a reasonable use, providing the owner with a reasonable income as it existed. Although the city recognized that the structure was not of historic merit on its own, the property was part of the "tout ensemble" of the entire French Quarter. That is, the Historic District was not a landmark alone but a collection of structures. Change to any one part inflicted damage on the entire collection. Mr. Maher, however, considered the municipality's Historic District zoning an economic burden. He contended that the modest structure was not historically significant, and that the obligation to maintain a structure for the public benefit "combined with the rising costs of a more profitable development caused him 'irreparable harm' and amounted to a regulatory taking."[26]

The case ultimately came before the U.S. Supreme Court, and their decision held for the City of New Orleans. Basically on the grounds presented by the city of New

---

[25]City of Euclid v. Ambler Realty Co., 272 U.S. 365, 384 (1926).

[26]Complaint, Morris Maher v. The City of New Orleans, Civil Action No. 71-119, U.S. District Court, Eastern District of Louisiana, filed January 13, 1971.

Orleans, the high court maintained the existing use to be a *reasonable* use of the property.[27] The decision not only reinforced the city's historic zoning ordinance but on a national scale provided another example where the reduction in a property's value would not be an overriding issue in land use controls. No decision to date has resolved the question of "how much" (control) is considered "too much" and "taking" without compensation. What has been observed is that the courts maintain that a segregation of incompatible land uses, prevention of congestion, and an ordinance based on a plan are all components of sound ordinances. The problems that have developed since 1926 are built around several *assumptions* associated with zoning:

1. That segregated land uses would result in a high-quality environment
2. That a zoning map, once prepared, would exist for all time
3. That local and state government would not change the rules
4. That nonconforming uses would, under pressure of redevelopment, go away
5. That zoning could be used as a method to cure problems that were *not* restricted to physical land use[28]

The problem is that none of the points listed above were correct assumptions. This is not an attack on the concept of zoning, but one must acknowledge that there were perceptions (of success) associated with zoning that left many with second thoughts. Euclidean zoning was an appropriate start; it just could not resolve all problems. Second, the concept has not been skillfully administered in every community. Any tool, poorly applied, will produce questionable results. This is an enduring misunderstanding by many communities as to the function of zoning. Zoning is a tool used to develop a community plan. Without a plan, the community and its local government have little guidance. Without a well-conceived and specific set of implementation strategies, including zoning, any plan is little more than a wish.

EUCLIDEAN ZONING: THE BASIC ORDINANCE

As the variety of local governments in the United States is extensive, the effort here will not cover every known set of circumstances but will outline in general terms the components and their influence on the development of a site plan. Some variations will be explored, but strict application cannot be made in all cases without some interpretation for local laws, process, and nomenclature. Since the Euclidean zone is the foundation of land use controls in the United States, the language of the zoning text and its meaning warrant closer inspection.

Apparently, the term "Euclidean zoning" has two origins. Some are of the opinion that "Euclidean" refers to the geometric patterns of zones. Others suggest that the nomenclature refers to the origin of the landmark zoning case: Euclid, Ohio. But regardless of opinions as to the term's origin, there appears to be no disagreement relative to the meaning of the term "Euclidean zoning." It is that traditional prescriptive zoning which, in very specific terms, identifies land use and density, with a rubric of performance standards. Euclidean zones have been the backbone of all zoning ordinances. The performance standards, or design controls, are both loved and hated by the developer, the community, and citizens. Since there is no variation in the standards, everyone knows, within certain limits, what the building mass and location on a site will be. The performance standards establish front, rear and side-yard set backs, building height limits, and in some cases, building coverage. These performance standards also include parking

[27]Maher v. City of New Orleans, 256 La. 131, 235 So. 2d 402 (1970).

[28]Ira M. Heyman, "Legal Assaults—On Municipal Regulation," *Management and Control of Growth* (Washington, D.C.: Urban Land Institute, 1975), pp. 187–188.

requirements. All too often the site planner applies the requirements established in the zoning ordinance and finds little flexibility in the alternative location for building and parking. The problem is that Euclidean zones are structured so that they can be applied to any site without deviation, regardless of context or topographical relief.

Euclidean zones treat every site as though there is no encumbrance to development in the form of slopes, vegetation, hydrology, geology, and so on. The notion that "one size fits all" (tube socks) or one set of standards can be applied to any site has some rueful consequences. Although the administration of Euclidean zones is simple, "what you see is what you get," there are obviously circumstances in which all agree that the building envelope and its location on a site need adjustment.

Many ordinances begin with a "purpose and intent" paragraph which spells out the reason for that particular section of the ordinance. This opening section in many cases capsulizes the uses and general densities specified in the text. The section of the ordinance that prescribes permitted uses has three characteristics. One is normally a laundry list of "uses permitted by right." This is an alphabetical catalog of land uses for which a property may be developed. In a review of the range of permitted uses in a residential zoning classification, the difference between land use and zoning will become obvious.

CUMULATIVE ZONING

The second characteristic of "uses permitted" is the reference to other zoning categories in the ordinance. This is a method utilized by some communities to avoid duplication within the text of the ordinance. Although it does reduce the volume of text, uses can get lost in the translation. It is very important to keep an accurate record of the references so that the real development potential of a zone can be clearly identified and understood.

The most potentially negative aspect of this form of referencing is the inclusion of uses within a zoning category that are incompatible with other uses in the zone. This concept is called cumulative zoning. Some zoning ordinances are structured so as to restrict residential land uses to residential zones as it should. In a cumulative zoning structure residential uses are not limited to residential zones, and that is where the conflict occurs. Cumulative zoning is organized to keep commercial and industrial activities out of residential zones but does not prohibit residential *land uses* in a commercial or industrial zoning category (Fig. 18-1).

Because of the variety of land uses permitted by right in the ordinance that is cumulative, the development community is known to have provided broad support for the concept. But imagine the problems created by a situation in which a developer builds a housing project in a commercial zone, then, clearly within his or her rights, builds a shopping center adjacent to the housing. Anyone can understand the anger and frustration of a person who has purchased a home assuming this to be a property zoned as residential but finds that the land use does not imply zoning, and worse yet, a shopping

Figure 18-1 Cumulative zoning.

center as a neighbor is within the law. Although many communities have structured their Euclidean zones to reduce potential conflicts by limiting residential uses to residential zones, the experienced site planner reads the fine print.

SPECIAL EXCEPTIONS AND SPECIAL USES

The third characteristic of the permitted uses section references those uses permitted by special exception or special use permit. This is another category of uses that are permitted *but* only under certain circumstances. The inclusion of this section in an ordinance is a recognition by the municipality that there are circumstances in which a particular segment of uses may be compatible with uses permitted by right in this zoning category. Because of the range of variables involved (access, topography, adjacent land uses, existing zoning, public facilities, etc.) these uses must be evaluated on a case-by-case basis. Obviously, the municipality wants to monitor and control carefully the location of uses listed under "special exception."

PERFORMANCE STANDARDS

This section provides the development guidelines for the uses prescribed in the preceding section. In most ordinances this section will, as a minimum, establish:

1. Minimal front-, rear-, and side-yard setbacks
2. Maximum height limits (Fig. 18-2)
3. Off-street parking requirements

These minimums and maximums provide the basis for the maximum building envelope on a site. Sometimes, these two requirements are coupled together in more restrictive language. As an example, the ordinance might state "the minimum front yard dimension will be 10 ft for the first 12 ft in vertical height of the building. After that point, the setback will be 1 ft back for each 2 ft in building height to a maximum building height of 48 ft 0 in." (Fig. 18-3). This language evidences strong control over the shape and location of any building that exceeds the dimensions established in the minimum setback. These statements need to be separated and graphically analyzed for their site-specific implications. This section may also embody restrictions on building forms which

Figure 18-2 Euclidean zoning setbacks.

Figure 18-3 Setbacks and height limits.

vary from one zoning category to the next. For example, the setback of a building in a residential category may, logically, be more restrictive than a setback in an industrial zone.

Building coverage is another restriction common to Euclidean zones. The word "coverage" has different interpretations in different communities. Some ordinances consider "coverage" only as it refers to the building; in other ordinances, the term includes building and parking. In the first case the concept of coverage is a response to the method used to control a building's mass. In the interpretation that includes parking areas, the method employed is designed to keep runoff and man-made surfaces to a minimum. In either case, the effect on the site plan can be significant.

Whereas all of the performance standards noted above can be the subject of a request for a variance, density normally is not. Recall that density, like land use, is a decision that is normally made by the local legislative authority.

Density requirements take on two general formats. The first is the expression of density in the form of a floor area ratio (FAR). This is a term that is given to the numerical relationship between a building's floor area and the area of the site. FAR is a term the zoning ordinance will use to quantify and limit the amount of square footage of building area as a function of the building site. With both building and site areas in square feet, the quotient of the building area divided by the site area is the floor area ratio. Expressed as a formula,

$$\frac{\text{building area } (\text{ft}^2)}{\text{site area } (\text{ft}^2)} = \text{floor area ratio (FAR)}$$

It must be emphasized that the floor area ratio has absolutely nothing to do with *any* other performance standard in the sense that it does not specify height limit, setback, or coverage. To the contrary, a 1.0 FAR can be achieved by building a two-story building over half of the site area or a four-story building over one-fourth of the site area (Fig. 18-4). FAR is strictly a method to control or limit the amount of building floor area that can be built on a site. It is also important to mention that some ordinances use percentage in lieu of the decimal equivalent. For example, 100% would equal 1.0 FAR. In any case, a check with the zoning administrator is imperative.

By and large, the concept of FAR as a density control mechanism is used predom-

One Storey Building
over 100% of Site
F.A.R.=1
Property Line
Property Line
Street

(a)

F.A.R.=1
Two Storey Building
on 50% of Site Area
Property Line
Property Line
Street

(b)

F.A.R.=1
Four Storey Building
on 25% of Site Area
Property Line
Property Line
Street

(c)

Figure 18-4 Three alternatives for an FAR of 1.

inantly to restrict commercial retail, office, and industrial land uses. It is easy to see how the concept works when a building's use and economic potential are functions of the building's gross floor area and parking requirements.

For residential land uses, FAR is not a popular density control device. In many zoning ordinances, the maximum density permitted is expressed simply in terms of a number of dwelling units per acre. For example, a maximum density of four dwelling units per acre will commonly result in single-family detached housing. The lot size will probably range from 8000 to 9000 square feet, depending on the amount of public right-of-way or open space required by the subdivision process. Other performance standards influence control over a building's location and form on an individual lot.

In residential zones of higher densities, the number of dwelling units per acre becomes more critical. Density control permits the client and the site planner to design a project that reflects a specific number of dwelling units per acre. Normally, each dwelling unit type in a housing project will require a different amount of square footage. As an example, in a residential zoning category where the maximum density permitted is 20 units per acre (a nominal density for a 2–3 story walk-up apartment) one might expect a one-bedroom unit to range in size from 700 to 800 ft^2. In the same project, a three-bedroom unit might range from 1200 to 1400 ft^2. It is easy to understand why in residential zones density control in terms of dwelling units per acre is more effective and equitable than FAR.

Some ordinances express density in terms of land area. As an example, the ordinance might read: "the maximum permitted density in the R.20 zone is one dwelling unit for each 2000 ft.^{2} of net land area assigned to residential development." The net results from the mathematics that follows might range from 19 to 21 units per acre, depending on the way "net land area assigned to residential development" is defined in the zoning ordinance. Many communities have found that there is a certain beauty in the simplicity of a zoning ordinance which states: "The maximum density permitted in the R.20 zone is 20 dwelling units per acre." It is hard to misunderstand that type of directive. Obviously, the community knows the density and can calculate the number of trips that will be generated by a residential zone of 20 units per acre. Similarly, the developer knows how density can affect and dictate an economic pro forma and dwelling unit mix. The site planner, then, interprets the program and resolves any emerging conflicts between the permitted density, performance standards, parking requirements, and the site's ecology.

Another method of density control involves tying residential density to an open-space or recreational area requirement. This concept is a variation on the "bonus" or "incentive" theme of zoning strategies. Essentially, it holds that residential densities should be a function of passive and active recreational facilities. This method is largely mathematical and is not limited to residential land uses. Similar "density for open-space areas" are, in many urban areas, linked to office and retail activities.

In 1926 no one imagined the future proliferation of density control mechanisms or stratification of zoning categories. The three ordinary zoning categories—residential, commercial, and industrial—have multiplied like junk mail. In urban areas, the array of Euclidean zones is phenomenal, as each community struggles to delineate finer lines between highway commercial zones, regional retail centers, and mixed-use commercial-office zones. Regardless of the community, the practice of developing the right zoning text has become a high art.

THE PARKING SCHEDULE

The final aspect of the zoning ordinance, which has a major impact on site planning, is the municipality's parking schedule. The parking schedule provides the site planner with an index of parking requirements for each land use. Just as there is no uniform national agreement on the size of the parking space, there is no agreement on parking demands for any specific land use. There is so little commonality on the way the schedules function that it is not worth discussing.

What is important is that, in some cases, the parking requirement can become a surrogate density control mechanism. There is a basic rule in the development community which suggests that as long as the price of structured parking (per square foot) exceeds the cost of additional land (per square foot), the parking requirement will be met with parking "at grade." A theorem of real estate development is that the cost of structured parking, either above or below grade, must be paid for by the rents generated from the principal land use. Only under unusual circumstances, where a corporation's goals include the development of an image that is incongruous with the "least cost" method, does the site planner find that an alternative is plausible. Often in the case of office, commercial, and retail land uses, the process to define the holding capacity of a site is simple. For example, assume the following:

1. A 100 ft $\times$ 200 ft site
2. A zoning ordinance that permits:
   a. An FAR of 1.5
   b. A maximum building height of 60 ft or six stories
   c. Parking: 1 space for every 350 ft^2 of gross floor area of office buildings

Assuming that the cost of the land is significantly below the cost per square foot of structured parking, the following would provide an outline of the site's development potential.

$$100 \text{ ft} \times 200 \text{ ft} \times 1.5 \text{ (FAR)} = 30,000 \text{ ft}^2 \text{ maximum building floor area}$$

$$\text{permitted by zoning}$$

As a method for preliminary identification of the area of the site that will be occupied by the building, assume that the total building area permitted in zoning is achievable.

$$30,000 \text{ ft}^2 \text{ divided by six stories} = 5,000 \text{ ft}^2 \text{ per floor}$$

Then:

$$
\begin{array}{ll}
20,000 \text{ ft}^2 & \text{site} \\
- \ 5,000 \text{ ft}^2 & \text{building area} \\
- \ 1,000 \text{ ft}^2 & \text{building/parking transition} \\
\hline
14,000 \text{ ft}^2 & \text{gross site area remaining for parking}
\end{array}
$$

Assume that for normal and compact car spaces the average area (parking and circulation) required for each space will be 300 ft^2:

$$14,000 \text{ ft}^2 \text{ divided by } 300 \text{ ft}^2 = 46 \text{ parking spaces}$$

Recall from the example zoning requirements that one parking space will be required for every 350 ft^2 of gross building area. The amount of gross building area that could be achieved on the site is the product of the number of parking spaces conceptually possible (46) and the maximum building area permitted for each parking space (350 ft^2):

$$46 \text{ spaces} \times 350 \text{ ft}^2 = 16,100 \text{ ft}^2 \text{ building area}$$

It is interesting to note that just over 53% of the 30,000 ft^2 permitted "by right" can actually be realized, given:

1. Surface parking only.
2. A requirement of one parking space for every 350 ft^2 of building area.
3. The total land area for parking is not to exceed 14,000 ft^2 and 300 ft^2 per car.

Since the height limit is six stories, an alternative is to raise the building and minimize the amount of the site that must be allocated to the building's access. Although this modification will provide for some additional building square footage, it is obvious that the 30,000 ft^2 of building floor area permitted by the zoning can be achieved on this site only with some form of structured parking. This is an example of a condition wherein the ordinance implies that the development potential is almost twice that which can realistically be achieved given the realities of the marketplace. The experienced site planner is cognizant of these quirks in the ordinances and takes the time to evaluate the implications before a property is purchased.

THE DECISION MAKERS

Sometimes, understanding the difference between who makes a recommendation and who makes the decisions can be the difference between success and starting over. Because of the process and the distinct obligations of each, the responsibilities for a review of requests have generally been divided among three entities: the local legislative authority, the planning and zoning commission, and the board of appeals or adjustment. Although the nomenclature will vary, each will be more identifiable given its role in the process.

THE LOCAL LEGISLATIVE AUTHORITY

With a few exceptions, the local legislative authority makes the final decision concerning zoning in a community.[29] These are the people elected to serve as the principal governmental authority at the local level. Depending on whether the local government is a city or county, the elected officials will have various titles. These include, but are not limited to, city councils, county councils, county board of supervisors, and county commissioners. To emphasize the importance of the elected officials in the process, in most communities they *appoint* the members to serve on both the planning commission and the board of zoning appeals (Fig. 18-5).

PLANNING AND ZONING COMMISSIONS

Although the name for this agency does not vary widely, the organization and its authority might. Common variations are (1) a separate, but appointed, planning commission and zoning commission; and (2) an elected planning and zoning commission. This separation between planning and zoning may appear to be paradoxical, as it institutionalizes a division between the planning and implementation functions. Although it can create some friction between the appointed bodies, they appear to work together more effectively in circumstances in which a member of each group serves as an ex-officio member on the other commission.

There are some municipalities whose enabling legislation has given the power to make zoning decisions to elected planning commissions. Although this structure is unusual, a review of the authority of each entity in the process should readily clarify the

---

[29]So, Stollman, Beal, and Arnold, p. 434.

Figure 18-5 Diagram of rezoning participants and process.

functions of each. In most cases, the operative word for the planning and zoning commission is "recommendation," as they *recommend* changes to the legislative authority. Under some circumstances, the planning commission may have final approval of the site plan in a two-stage performance zone (PUD). Recall, however, that the initial decision concerning land use and density was made by the local legislature. This is critical to understanding the process. It is highly recommended that prior to making a decision to rezone a property, one attend at least one public hearing of both the legislative authority (city council, county council, etc.) and the planning commission. The public hearing permits an examination and evaluation of a council's and commission's values, biases, and sophistication.

THE BOARD OF ZONING APPEALS OR ADJUSTMENT

If the performance standards thwart the achievement of the existing zoning or create a hardship, one should consider a request for a waiver from the board of zoning appeals (or local equivalent). In most cases, this process is extremely short and does not require an extensive amount of preparation or exposure, and rightfully so. Communities have adopted various terms for this function in local government, the most common two being the board of zoning appeals or adjustment (BZA) and the zoning board of adjustment or appeals (ZBA). One of the functions of this board is to review cases or appeals in which the performance standards of the ordinance, when applied to a site, create a unique condition and unusual (economic) burden or hardship. The text from Robert M. Anderson's *American Law of Zoning* sets down two generally recognized rules. "Where an applicant for a variance can demonstrate that owing to the size and shape of his land, he cannot make any reasonable use of it unless the literal application of the zoning regulation is varied, he is entitled to a variance" and "in most jurisdictions, an applicant whose problems in the use of his land are caused by his own conduct, rather than by circumstances which are peculiarly related to the land, is not entitled to a variance."[30]

---

[30]Robert M. Anderson, *American Law of Zoning* (Rochester, N.Y.: The Lawyer's Cooperative Publishing Co., 1968).

In most communities, the BZA can only consider waivers of performance standards, not land use or density. Land use and density are generally the purview of the legislative authority of the community (city council, county council, board of supervisors, county commissioner, etc.). These authorities appoint their respective BZAs and in most communities the BZA's decision is *final*. If an applicant makes a request for a variance and is refused, an appeal to that decision must be heard before the local courts. Depending on the way the BZA/ZBA has been charged, in many communities they also hear special exceptions or special use permits. The point here is that the BZA has an extraordinary amount of control, and the effectiveness of the zoning ordinance in many ways rests with the way the BZA interprets "unique and unusual economic burden or hardship." Many BZAs are very strict and any request for variation will be scrutinized extensively. Others are somewhat more liberal and interpret their role in a different way.

As an example, the board of adjustment (BDA) for the city of Dallas, Texas, reviewed a case for eight variances at the junction of two major freeways in the city. The applicant's request for variances was not recommended by the planning staff but was approved by the BDA. The site plan and schedule of variances for the proposed development are as follows.

Schedule of Variances for Dallas Galleria

1. Setback variance of 228 ft for building 10 (shopping mall)
2. Setback variance of 664 ft for building 11 (hotel)
3. Setback variance of 10 ft 6 in. for buildings 2, 3, 5, and 6 (office)
4. Setback variance of 10 ft 0 in. for building 1 and 7 (parking)
5. Height variance of 128 ft for buildings 5 and 6
6. Variance to reduce the width of a parking space from the required 9 ft 0 in. to 8 ft. 6 in.
7. Variance to reduce the parking required by 3637 total spaces (14,959 required; 11,322 approved reduction)[31] (Fig. 18-6)

If variances of this magnitude were commonplace, they could create a degree of cynicism within a community relative to its government and zoning. Since performance standards may be the single aspect of zoning important to many citizens, variances should

Figure 18-6 Dallas Galleria plan.

---

[31]City of Dallas, BDA Request 80-152/5161.

be scrupulously evaluated. What must be recognized is that the application of "unique hardship or burden" prescribed by Anderson is obviously not universally accepted.

As a contrasting example, the Montgomery County Maryland Zoning Board of Adjustments received a request from a friendly government in 1975 to convert an existing parochial school to a school for the children of embassy personnel. The physical changes to the site and facility were none: no new roads, parking, or buildings, and no environmental degradation. But since there was a proposed "use" change, the ordinance required a review by the zoning board of adjustment. The ZBA took their responsibility for thorough review very seriously. A public hearing on the request permitted proponents and opposition alike to express their opinions. Lengthy testimony by various witnesses and thorough examination as to the implications of the "new" school became part of the extensive record on which the ZBA's final approval was based. Two different municipalities in two different regions reflect dramatically different views of the role of the board of zoning adjustments.

As a footnote on variances, in some communities the authority for minor waivers is invested in the zoning administrator's office.[32] Since neither the office nor the power to give a variance is common to every community, the rule is to call and inquire. It could be a much less time consuming process than the BZA hearing.

THE HEARING EXAMINER

The employment of a hearing examiner is one of the variations in the traditional process that is growing in use throughout the United States. This format involves a review of the rezoning application prior to consideration of the request by the local legislative authority (Fig. 18-7). This review is executed by a person referred to as a hearing examiner. In many cases this individual is an attorney who has been hired by the local government to review, analyze, and conduct his or her own hearing on a rezoning request. Often the hearing examiner is empowered to call and cross-examine witnesses and take testimony. This quasi-judicial forum provides the basis on which the hearing examiner develops a case record. This record will include testimony from the planning and zoning commission, professional planning staff, and those on both sides of the re-

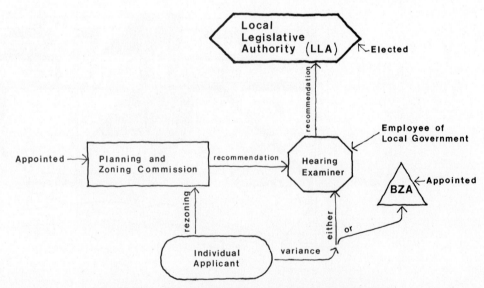

Figure 18-7 Diagram of rezoning process with hearing examiner.

---

[32]So, Stollman, Beal, and Arnold, p. 434.

zoning request. The intent of this process is to develop an objective opinion, insulated from political pressure and influence, based solely on the facts presented in the record.

The hearing examiner's opinion is then forwarded to the local legislative authority and becomes, together with the planning commission's recommendations, part of the case record. Although the recommendations of the hearing examiner are not binding, they do provide an additional layer of testimony and documentation that is very important for a fair and equitable evaluation in a process that is often emotionally charged.

In some communities the function of the hearing examiner is also less formal. Depending on the obligations of the position, the hearing examiner may also consider variances. Although the additional layer of review and evaluation may not be appropriate for every municipality, the number that find the process beneficial has been steadily increasing.

NEIGHBORHOOD ZONING

The increase in public participation over the past few years has emerged to become a significant force in the zoning process. Almost every community has watched the success of a few politically savvy citizens' organizations affect the decision-making process of the planning commission and local legislative authorities. Some have mustered enough votes to change local ordinances and establish neighborhood zoning authority. As with the zoning process, the influence and working relationship with the local legislature will vary. In some cases the role of citizens is sought and valued. In others, citizens are tolerated as an obligatory segment of public hearings. Whereas many design professionals avoid discussing a rezoning request with neighborhood groups, others consider it an opportunity to present the case for a proposal before stepping into an intemperate public hearing. Since there seems to be little reason for the demise of the neighborhood zoning authority, taking the time to understand the concerns of citizens can provide a basis for reasonable and successful compromise.

THE REZONING PROCESS

The rezoning process begins when a person decides that the existing zoning on a property will not permit the desired development program. This decision may be necessary because (1) the land use or densities desired are not permitted in the existing zoning, or (2) the performance standards within the existing zoning will not permit the development program to be achieved. Recognizing that there will be local variations, a rezoning request for a Euclidean zone will follow a fairly common format. The rezoning request is filed with those responsible for the administration of the zoning ordinance. In most communities, this will be a function of the planning staff, zoning administrator's office, or the city/county manager's office and will be accompanied by their recommendation. The planning and zoning commission will review the rezoning request at a public hearing. Depending on local and state laws, the planning and zoning commission may be required to examine specific aspects of each rezoning request. In some communities a rezoning request is required to meet certain proofs if it is to be approved. These proofs might necessitate that an applicant prove that the existing zoning was a mistake or that there had been a change in the neighborhood that would support rezoning.[33] Compliance with the adopted municipal land use plan may also be a requirement. Obviously, some rationale or justification for the rezoning is necessary or every request could be based on new criteria and attract a charge of arbitrary and capricious decision making.

In some communities an applicant may discuss a rezoning request with the planning and zoning commission or members of the legislative authority. Although this is

---

[33]Ibid.

often the custom, in other municipalities discussion of a zoning request with an elected or appointed official is absolutely prohibited. This is referred to as an "ex parte communication" and is based on the concept that the rezoning should be based on the record of the public hearing, and as such, *no* communication with any elected or appointed official outside that hearing is appropriate. The opposing opinion holds that there is no harm in a person-to-person discussion of the rezoning request. Whatever the case, know and respect the local practice and ethics codes, as a moderate infraction could jeopardize the success of an application.

Following the planning commission's public hearing and recommendation, in most communities the request is forwarded to the local legislative authority for its decision. Assuming that the request is a Euclidean zone, the local legislative authority will consider the request at one of its meetings. This is an important phase of the process, as the meetings are public hearings and permit the local legislative authority and citizens to discuss the application and its implications. This phase of the process is one of the very rare, ongoing examples of local government interacting with its constituency. Of all the obscure and fragmented examples of government of, by, and for the people, a public hearing on a controversial rezoning request gives a new meaning to the word "democracy." There will always be circumstances in which a good proposal is dismembered by citizens while one of obscure socially redeeming value goes unchallenged. The process does not ensure against regrettable decisions but does permit changing the leadership if stupidity seems to be the continual "bill of fare." The local legislative authority's decision will be based on a number of elements. These cannot be listed in order of importance, because there is no way of knowing what is important to every local government, but the list should include the following:

1. The compatibility of the rezoning request with the existing neighborhood
2. The land use and zoning recommended in the municipality's adopted land use plan[34]
3. The recommendations of the planning and zoning commission
4. The recommendations of the municipality's zoning administrator or professional planning staff
5. The responses (opposition or support) of citizens' organizations in the neighborhood
6. The impact of the request on the health, safety, morals, and welfare of the community
7. The relative success of the applicant's presentation, which would be based on:
   (a) A rationale for the request
   (b) The request's ability to accomplish a public good (school site dedication, etc.)
   (c) A respect for the neighborhoods's concerns reflected in the rezoning request prior to filing the application
   (d) A respect for the municipality's adopted plan or the intent of the plan
8. The record of the hearing

In the event of a denial, the range of alternatives open to the applicant depends on the municipality. Each community will have some restriction limiting the resubmittal. As a last resort, the courts are always available to redress a grievance.

---

[34]Do not confuse the zoning map with the adopted land use plan. The land use plan is just that—it identifies land uses, densities, and defines zones only. If you check one of the residential zones you will probably find a number of permitted uses that are *not* residential. The land use map and zoning map are *not* the same.

REZONING ALTERNATIVES

The first, and most traditional request, is one to change the Euclidean zone classification. This is the simplest request and probably accounts for 95% of rezoning cases in the United States. The second, a variation on the first, is a request for a change in Euclidean zones with "conditions." This strategy is somewhat more unusual and in some states and local governments is absolutely prohibited. Conditional zoning can take on other variations. One of the more prevalent involves the application for a Euclidean zone, but with certain restricting conditions attached. For example, restricting conditions may take the form of a height limit or increased setback, but whatever the case, can be an acceptable strategy to "tailor" the zone to fit a set of unusual contextual conditions. It is imperative that a check be made with local government and its attorney to make certain that conditional zoning is legally acceptable. This needs to be discussed with the municipality's attorney on a case-by-case basis. Land use laws are constantly changing and the directions of state supreme courts today may differ greatly with those of 10 years ago.

PERFORMANCE ZONES

The third alternative is a request for a performance zone. These zoning forms are site specific; that is, the zoning category usually requires a site plan that delineates precisely what the applicant plans to build. Even with the latitude available in variances, the site planner presented with a moderately large site (20 to 100 acres) often has a problem compounded by its size. Until the late 1960s, there were no alternatives to the Euclidean zone. Large acreages throughout the United States were subdivided into small tracts following the specifications outlined in the ordinance. The results of the 1949 Housing Act and Euclidean zoning sponsored the mindless conversion of millions of acres of land into low-density subdivisions of $\frac{1}{4}$-acre lots. The notion of separating incompatible uses in some communities meant that each housing type needed to be separated from the others. That is, detached houses should be segregated from attached homes (townhouses), which should be separated from multifamily housing.

Although the concept of segregating housing types is prevalent in many communities today, to some it thwarted the potential of developing communities that could offer a variety of housing types for a variety of life-styles. As long as the zoning ordinance dictated the physical outcome of any site of any size, the results were going to be stolid and unimaginative. Furthermore, any possibility to save any unique ecology or open space was jeopardized by the necessity to make certain that the density permitted by the zoning was achieved. The concept of planned unit development (PUD) emerged as a direct response to the prescriptive qualities of Euclidean zoning. The PUD is different in various ways, but most important, it was the first form of *performance zoning*. Simply stated, performance zoning is based on the site plan prepared by the applicant. This site plan must not be confused with the site plan that many developers commission their architects or landscape architects to prepare for a hearing on a Euclidean rezoning. In most communities the illustrative site plans prepared for a Euclidean rezoning have no legal status and are prepared to beguile the citizens or neophyte planning commission member.

The planned unit development text can be found in various forms and descriptions in zoning ordinances throughout the United States. The nomenclature may be planned development (PD), residential or planned residential development (PRD), planned unit development (PUD), or other. The variations are limited only by the ability of planning commissions and their staffs to find another name for a rose. But regardless of title, the concept is generally the same.

Performance zones traditionally require a site-specific plan as a part of the rezoning request. These characteristics are not nationally uniform, but there are some generally common qualities. Most PUDs have very liberal setback and height-limit controls. The idea is that the site planner needs the flexibility to do good design work and as such needs some release from the arbitrary dictum of Euclidean zones. In many cases a maximum density might be established with setbacks respecting adjacent properties. The prevailing policy is flexibility, with an emphasis on the quality of the plan. Often, the PUD plan requirements are very detailed and require the location of all buildings, parking lots, pedestrian circulation systems, open space, and recreational facilities. Although this may appear to be a burden, it is also not uncommon for a municipality to grant higher densities as an incentive to a developer to plan development comprehensively and utilize a PUD ordinance.

Unlike the Euclidean zone, the PUD often permits a mix of housing types. Some municipalities go so far as to provide for a mix of uses, that is, residential and commercial. This is again an important departure from traditional zoning, but it must be emphasized that this varies across the United States. The mix of housing types, for example, is easy to accept, but the mix in land use types might appear to fly in the face of the rationale for zoning in the first place. This departure from the traditional zoning concepts puts the rationale for the zoning squarely on the quality of the plan, which is where it always should have been. To reiterate, the applicant prepares and submits the PUD plan for approval to the same authority as one would for a Euclidean zone. A word of caution: In most communities, when a PUD plan is approved, the site must be built just as the plan describes. Since the PUD plan is considered the zoning, it is recorded as the basis on which building permits will be reviewed. Although the PUD has some very definite advantages, in many communities the PUD plan is a definitive commitment of the developer's intent.

Why, with the flexibility of the PUD, is the zoning concept not used more extensively? There are at least three reasons. The first two can be attributed to the developer. The PUD requires the development of a plan, and that means some front-end costs for consultants that most entrepreneurs would like to avoid. Furthermore, the plan must be followed regardless of the owner. An undeveloped property locked into a specific PUD plan can certainly restrict its speculative value.

The third issue that has retarded wide acceptance or implementation of performance zones has its origin in the strict interpretation of zoning and the role of the local legislative authority. This more conservative perspective suggests that performance zones are a form of ''conditional'' zoning and in some states are simply illegal. The same philosophical viewpoint contends that in the evaluation of a performance zone, the local legislative authority is often forced to rely on the advice of its professional staff. Under normal conditions that would appear to be appropriate and an intelligent way to utilize a community's professional planners. But the conservative position contends that if the PUD is not successful, local governmental officials would attempt to shift the responsibility for failure to their professional advisors.

Similarly, some planning commissions and councils do not permit their professional planning staffs to make any recommendation on a zoning case. That position maintains that the planning commission and council should not be influenced by any recommendation that might cloud their objectivity. So regardless of political philosophy, there are some encumbrances to what is unquestionably a proven feasible alternative to Euclidean zoning. There is at least one variation on the theme of PUDs that is prevalent enough to mention and remember. There are some local governments that have adopted two-stage PUD ordinances. The first stage obligates the applicant to develop a plan that identifies land uses, density, and major circulation systems. If the first stage of the applicant's plan is approved by the local legislative body, the applicant is then permitted to develop a plan of the more specific elements: buildings, parking lots, recreational facilities, and so on. More often than not, the second stage is only a phase of an entire development plan.

As with most innovations, this PUD variation has both positive and negative effects. The two-stage process has some benefits for both developer and the municipality. Identifying the land use, density, and primary circulation plan permits the developer and the municipality to focus on those issues alone. At the public hearing there is no discourse in this first stage on the location of a building or the orientation of a parking lot. Additionally, the limited focus of this conceptual planning in the first stage is simply easier to deal with at all levels. If the first-stage plan is approved, the applicant has at least some assurance that if the property must be sold, it will have some basis for economic value without the adoption of the second, more restrictive phase. If sold, the new owner could develop the second-stage plan to reflect his or her own preferences in the context of the adopted first stage. The problem is that unless the municipality has drafted some very specific policy statements relevant to open space, recreational facilities, storm water management, and so on, it could have adopted a plan of dubious conclusion. But since the zoning does not provide the developer with a building permit, the process still provides the community with an opportunity to negotiate an acceptable site-specific plan.

Although the variations on the PUD are extensive, the commonalities are flexibility, land use mix, and the opportunity for creativity. Check your local ordinance for the alternatives and the process for application and review.

This section on performance zones would not be complete without mention of another variety of "performance zones." The term "performance zoning" has been used here in the generic sense. Another form of performance zoning emerged in the mid-1970s as "Performance zoning," with a capital "P." This classification refers to a zoning method that defines performance standards and establishes guidelines associated with on-site runoff, trip generation, open space, recreational facilities, and water and sanitary sewer requirements. Although these requirements would obviously vary from project to project, the concept was based on the hypothesis that each land use generates certain demands on a community's public facilities. Since those demands can be documented, they could, in turn, become the rationale on which land use decisions (zoning) could be made. This concept, also termed "Fiscal zoning" or "impact zoning," was an important step toward a structure or format that attempted to qualify the rationale for land use decisions at the local level. The problem is that this method is not simple to administer and in most cases requires a substantial amount of review time on the part of the community. Also, the preparation of the documentation is no simple task, and many developers would simply prefer to take their chances with simpler mechanisms.

This is by no means the last word on performance zoning. There are numerous other variations as municipalities continue to explore alternatives to the straitjacket restrictions of Euclidean zoning.

Bonus and incentive zoning have enjoyed general popularity in the past, with some ordinances more successful then others. This was a form of PUD in which the developer could achieve certain bonuses, normally an increase in density, if certain public amenities were incorporated in the plan. The value here again is in the flexibility and the process to develop a plan that respects a specific context. Transfer of development rights (TDR) is also a variation on land use controls. Similar to zoning, TDR is a mechanism adopted by a municipality, on its own volition, to control the density of development. Transfer of development rights is based on the concept that since the municipality gives development rights (land use and density) away in the form of zoning, it also has the power to facilitate the transfer of those rights from one area of the community to another. TDR has been particularly effective in circumstances in which public facilities are strained beyond capacities or preservation and conservation are valued community objectives.

Planning and zoning have been an effort to balance the health, safety, and welfare of citizens with the growth objectives of the development community, yet minimizing the bureaucratic review processes—not an easy task.

The final alternative to a request for an existing Euclidean zone or performance zone is to consider the development of a text for a new Euclidean zone designed to respond to a specific set of conditions. Zoning laws change, as they must, to reflect changes in technology and society. Ordinances written 20 years ago may not reflect the densities and performance standards appropriate for the varying types of development today. As an example, historic landmark ordinances were uncommon components of zoning ordinances as recently as 1970. That situation has changed dramatically over the past decade as communities, citizens, and developers have worked to conserve these special resources.

A zoning ordinance can be amended and under some circumstances may be the only remaining feasible alternative. This option should be pursued as a last resort, as it is probably the most time consuming and expensive. The need for an additional zoning classification must obviously go beyond the immediate needs of your client or otherwise will appear to be totally self-serving. It goes without saying that a new zoning classification must have the support of the local zoning administrator and professional planning staff. Without visible evidence of the staff's favor, a request to expand an ordinance will probably be met with suspicion and recalcitrance by local elected officials.

DOWN-ZONING AND BACK-ZONING

When a local legislative authority believes that the densities allocated by a previous action to a specific property are incongruous with the community's health, safety, and welfare, the action of changing a zoning classification to one of a lower, permissible, or more restrictive performance standard is commonly called down-zoning or back-zoning. The reduction of a permitted residential density from 20 dwelling units per acre to 10 dwelling units per acre would be an example of down-zoning. Contrary to popular belief, it is unusual for a property owner to enjoy any vested rights to a zoning classification on a vacant parcel unless some on-site construction has taken place.[35] Although the application for a building permit is also a common companion to establishing a vested right, state laws vary widely, and legal counsel on this matter is imperative. Although it is not a common procedure, it does occur often enough to warrant understanding the process. The courts have generally sustained the concept that the local legislative authority that has the power to rezone property to a higher use has the power to rezone to a lower density as well. Because the legal authority exists does not necessarily mean that the municipality does not have certain obligations with respect to process and criteria in down-zoning. Although legislative action to down-zone a property must not be arbitrary, capricious, unreasonable, or discriminatory, the property owner should be reminded that the burden of proof rests with those challenging the decision of the municipal legislative authority. Since the vast majority of those whose property is to be down-zoned seek private legal counsel, the process can be very excruciating to both the public and private sectors. Chapter 15, written by Richard Babcock, of So and colleagues' *The Practice of Local Government Planning* is a good general resource that sets out in greater detail some of the interrelationships between the comprehensive community planning and the administration of the zoning ordinance.

---

[35]So, Stollman, Beal, and Arnold, p. 429.

Streetscape and Site Improvements

chapter 19
The Site Planning Process

INTRODUCTION

Paramount to understanding site planning is understanding that it is a process. By definition a process is a sequence of interrelated events or decisions that result in a product or conclusion. This characteristic of site planning must be fully comprehended, as attempts to short circuit the process can produce unnecessary and unfortunate consequences. There is always a cadre of those who believe that process planning subverts the creative, esoteric aspect of the art. Nothing could be further from the truth. If you believe that anything can be done on any site, that the only constraint is the financial and political will of those involved, read no further; the process discussed here will definitely be an encumbrance. If, however, you are of the persuasion that various factors influence the development of a site plan, read on. As will become evident, there are various stages in the process that require creative thinking other than that required to locate a building on the site.

It is of principal importance for the site planner to grasp the difference between the objective and subjective issues of the process. Clear objectivity is imperative for various stages of the procedure and anything less than an unbiased evaluation of critical issues could jeopardize a successful resolution of the problem. There is a place in the process for the integration of subjective issues. These ''softer'' issues can often be identified as functions of design preference, style, or taste. These vary widely and will depend directly on the preferences of those participating in the process. This is where the collection of ''I want . . .'' or I believe . . .'' appear. Although these components are strictly a matter of personal preference, they are essential to transforming a collection of facts or data into built form. It must also be understood that the building and the site must be considered as an integral design problem. Neither should be developed without the other, as the success of the ultimate union is then risky, at best.

Recognizing that site planning is a procedure directed toward problem solving also accepts the participation of others in the process. Just as every creative designer abhors a situation in which the client takes over the role as designer, the same holds true for the designer who usurps the role of client/user. Recall that each design problem has a collection of identities to be recognized. If developed properly, the process permits these identities to materialize.

For the most part, site planning in the United States is practiced in a reactionary way; the architect develops a site plan as a response to design criteria based on short-term economic parameters, the zoning ordinance, and current architectural form vocabulary. Although the practice of site planning is not the purview of one profession, the notion that it may be interdisciplinary in scope is not broadly accepted. Historically, it was the obligation of the architect. The process today, however, often becomes a perfunctory exercise for the civil engineer, the architect, and the landscape architect, as each alternates in the role of site planner. Too frequently, we forget that coalescing the focus of these disciplines into one set of design decisions can occur only when there is a complete understanding of the process and the range of issues to be considered.

Site planning begins by assuming that we are ignorant of the site. This is not to say that one is oblivious to the process or components, but that, in accepting lack of knowledge of a site, the planner proceeds with objectivity and without preconceived notions as to the conclusions. Initially, these early stages of research, data collection, documentation, and synthesis are an analytical procedure and provide the foundation of information and data for future design decisions.

To facilitate an understanding of that process, two hypothetical sites with separate development objectives are used as examples. Site R is a residential land use; site C is a commercial/retail use. Each site is used to explore the application of various site planning issues discussed in previous chapters.

GOALS AND OBJECTIVES

The initial stage of the site planning process begins with a qualified acceptance of the client's development program. The emphasis is on "qualified" because subsequent research and analysis may not generate complete support for the client's program on the site. The professional seeks to develop a working relationship in which a candid dialogue of both good news and bad news can be held. What is important here is to recognize that accepting a given site and given program, without caveat, is hazardous at best. If the site planner and client approach matching a program to a site with specific goals, the test of the match can be made through research and analysis.

At this stage it is very important that the planner glean from the client any expression of other goals or images that he or she wishes to objectify in the project. Drawing out the client's preferences at this stage will greatly encourage participation in the process, while forcing any latent or obscure objectives to surface.

Site R (Fig. 19-1) is a wooded 1-acre lot in a residential subdivision at the edge of a small creek. The client wants to consider subdividing the acreage into four lots, permitted by the existing zoning. Because of the topographical relief and the floodplain created by the creek, it is unknown whether the four $\frac{1}{4}$-acre lots could be developed within the minimum areas and dimensions prescribed in the zoning ordinance. Whatever the circumstances, the client's principal objective is to build four single-family detached dwellings on the site, selling three and retaining one for personal use.

Site C (Fig. 19-2) is a 5.07-acre parcel zoned for commercial office and retail land uses. It is adjacent to a residential PUD on the west and a suburban shopping center on the east. Richardson Blvd. exists on the north and a new road (Sullivan) is under construction to the south. A local developer has acquired the site and with it a promise from a local bank to occupy 12,500 ft^2 of ground floor space. The developer would like to supplement the bank's function as a generator with 10,000 ft^2 of retail (commercial) space. The remaining floor area allowed by the ordinance would be "built out" as spec-

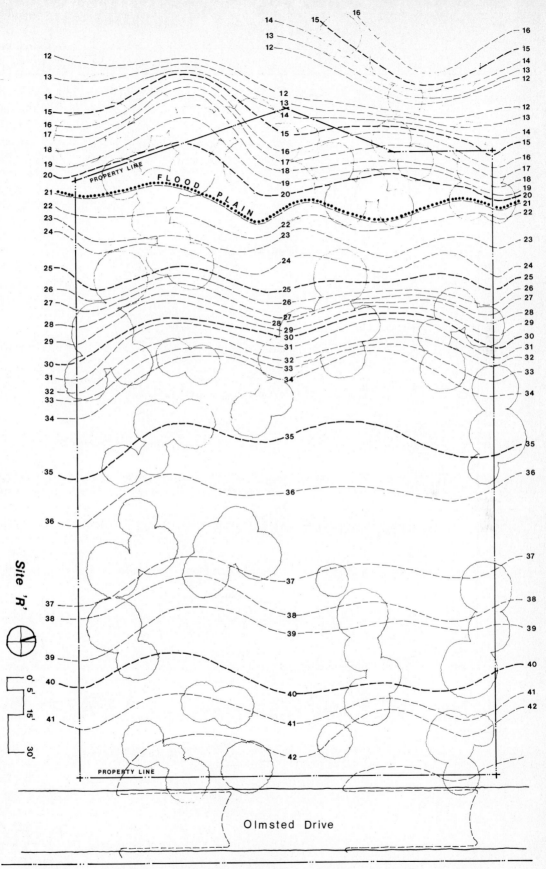

Figure 19-1 Plan of site R.

Richardson Road

Centerline Public R.O.W.

S e n e c a C r e e k

Pipeline Easement

Sullivan Street

Centerline Public R.O.W.

0 10' 25' 50'

Figure 19-2 Plan of site C.

ulative office space. The new owner wants to achieve the 0.7 floor area ratio currently permitted under the municipality's zoning ordinance.

RESEARCH AND DATA COLLECTION

Good site planning begins with good research. There is no substitute for getting the right information properly documented the first time. Even when the private sector is the client, the public sector is always a participant in the site planning process. Although the client may provide the site planner with a program and development criteria, various public entities will have jurisdictional control over the development of a site.

It is more than appropriate to check the local zoning ordinance at this time to make certain that the client's proposed use for the property is permitted by the current zoning. If rezoning is anticipated, it is important to recognize that requirement as a part of the process.

Following an environmental analysis the site needs to be evaluated for alternative locations of the building and parking. Since each land use has its own criteria, there are likely to be specific areas of the site uniquely suited for each use. What is important is to make certain that the site is appropriate for each use in the client's program. For example, surface parking should not be located on any slope exceeding 7%; buildings are generally more adaptive to sloping topography. Structured parking can be developed on slopes in excess of 7%, but the cost of surface parking must also be considered in a total evaluation. Environmental maladies such as floodplains, swales, easements, and other dubious areas obviously should be avoided.

The zoning ordinance needs to be consulted again to identify two variables associated with the development of the site. One is the "zoning envelope" or buildable volume created by the performance standards of the zoning. This volume is described by the density, height limits, setbacks, and area coverage in the text of most Euclidean ordinances. Although ordinances will vary widely, delineating the correct profile of the zoning restrictions is imperative. The other controlling element in the zoning ordinance is the parking requirement. The owner's development objectives must now be interpreted in the form of general floor areas and parking requirements. It is important at this point to know the limits of development prescribed in the zoning ordinance. No knowledgeable site planner pursues the design process further without having researched the ordinance. Make no assumptions concerning the ordinance; any questions should be answered by the zoning administrator and preliminaries confirmed.

INVENTORY

An inventory of the site and its resource requires the collection and documentation of various site components. The first level of data collection requires documentation of the legal description of the site and would include, but not be limited to:

1. Plat or boundary-line survey and description
2. Acreage
3. Restrictive covenants or deed restrictions
4. Easements or other encumbrance
5. Topography at 1- or 2-ft intervals, depending on the amount of slope and irregularity.

This research would also document the public's control, which would include:

1. Zoning (existing and proposed) (if rezoning is contemplated)
2. Public right-of-way (existing and proposed)
3. Street standards and design criteria
4. Utilities (existing and proposed)
5. All special permits or inspections required by local, state, or federal agencies

Data collection requires documentation of the site's existing natural and man-made conditions as well as its off-site contextual qualities. In addition to the checklist in Chapter 4, the following characteristics should be noted in the site reconnaissance phase.

- Views and vistas
- Rock outcroppings
- Context (built and natural)
- Vegetation (species, variety, and maturity)
- Abandoned roads or cemeteries
- Streams or water courses
- Recent construction
- Oil and gas transmission lines, electrical and telephone lines

While the data collection and mapping process continue, the experienced site planner makes a visit to the site. There is no substitute for a personal walking reconnaissance. No amount of slides or photographs can communicate the experience of being there. Look for things that might not necessarily be on the maps, and note any discrepancies between the information that is documented and that which actually exists on a site.

This inventory process is essential, as it provides the site planner and client with an unqualified understanding of the site. The combination of photographs and field notes provides the site planner with physical documentation of the site's character. This personal inspection provides the opportunity to assess the quantifiable elements of the research and evaluate their contribution to the entire context. This documentation is also an important reference during the process. Although 35mm slides are often desirable for a large group, color prints are preferable since they can be used as reference without the need for a projector and darkroom (Fig. 19-3). When accompanied with a written text, this research can describe the general character and specific circumstances, which are always valuable as part of a permanent record.

A visit to site R has revealed waterborne debris on the site at a level which appears higher than that indicated by the most recent floodplain maps. The higher floodplain level may be the result of additional development above the site since the documentation of the 100-year floodplain. Further research indicates that there is also a rock outcropping in the area of the site. Since the rock outcropping can be the precursor of expensive excavation and foundation work, a soil testing lab is contacted immediately. Test borings always clarify the geology of the site and provide the site planner with a more accurate "picture" of the site's physiographic past (Fig. 19-4).

The initial visit to site C produces no visual surprises. Trees are confined to the creek's edge and are scattered sparsely throughout the remainder of the site. Although signs identifying a pipeline easement confirm the indication of that encumbrance, there is something puzzling about the alignment of the easement (Fig. 19-5). The drawing describes one thing; reconnaissance implies something else. Under these circumstances, a request is made of the owner to engage the services of a registered engineer to clarify the question.

A review of the Soil Conservation Service's research for site C suggests that the

(a)

(b)

Figure 19-3 Photos on board with notes.

← Reddish brown clay
with roots

← Reddish brown clay
with limestone pebbles

← Tan weathered limestone
with tan clay seams

← Blue limestone

← Bottom of core at 20'

Figure 19-4   Test boring.

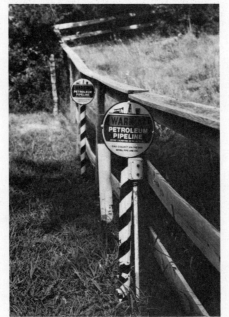

Figure 19-5

permeability of the dominant soil type north of Seneca Creek is moderate at best. This comes as no surprise, since soils close to creeks and streams are often borderline sites. A topographical depression on the south side of the site is predominantly sandy loam and might be considered as an on-site detention pond if necessary.

Climatological analysis might be considered as the next stage in the inventory. Of the various methods presented in the Chapter 8, it appears that microclimate mapping for these sites would have genuine applicability. Microclimate mapping will delineate those zones of both the R and C sites which are either sunny and windy, sunny and calm, shaded and windy, or shaded and calm in both summer and winter. This information is particularly valuable for residential land uses, as it identifies those areas of an open site that are inherently suited for outdoor activities as well as those locations where a structure might enjoy maximum solar exposure. Remember that a residential use is a "skin"-loaded structure whose heating can be supplemented by various passive solar methods.

Site C, with its commercial and retail activities, is somewhat different. These are structures which are "internally" loaded. That is, the thermal loads for the HVAC systems are created by the heat generated from the occupants and lights inside the structure. It is very unlikely that supplementary heat will be required and more than likely that cooling will be necessary even in the winter. In this circumstance, where the interior is already a heat load, any additional solar heat gain only aggravates the problem.

Whereas the intent is to limit the amount of solar gain at all times to the C site, the residential sites should be scrutinized carefully to identify those areas where there is maximum solar exposure in the winter and maximum shading in the summer. Again, this preferential location is not unique to a particular region but has general applicability.

Following the format described for microclimate mapping, Fig. 19-6 illustrates the character of site R. The addition of structures to the open site will obviously require modifying the microclimate map. Since structures create a man-made shelter from the wind, knowing those zones where an outdoor seating area is most accommodating would influence the location of a terrace for either a residence or a restaurant.

For site R the total acreage must first be subdivided into four lots, each with the minimum area, distances, and frontage prescribed in the ordinance. The parking schedule in the ordinance reflects the current ''marketplace'' demand and requires two parking spaces for each dwelling.

For lot C the parking component of the zoning ordinance is somewhat more complex. The bank and retail uses are permitted without caveat, but the setback and height limits are somewhat more confining. It seems that the zoning ordinance has a very restrictive setback for any retail use that adjoins a multifamily residential category. Figure 19-7 illustrates various physical conditions of the site as well as the basic controlling performance standards of the zoning ordinance. Additional development controls include a 10% open-space requirement. It must be noted that the zoning ordinance's definition of ''open space'' excludes slopes in excess of 25% and water courses.

The parking requirement will also require interpretation at this point. A realistic appraisal of the impact of parking must be delineated since miscalculations can have a deleterious effect on the site plan. ''Realistic'' needs to be emphasized since many people have a bias toward structured parking. Recall that the simplest way to conceptualize the feasibility of structured parking in open-market conditions is to compare the price of unimproved property with that of the cost of unimproved property plus a parking structure. In most cases clients will favor the alternative that provides the parking required by ordinance at the lowest cost per square foot. This analysis is very straightforward, but it must recognize that there can be circumstances in which a decision will not be made on economic issues alone.

Careful attention has also been given to the parking requirement, particularly since there are three uses: retail commercial, banking, and office space. The 10,000 ft^2 of retail space has a parking requirement of one car for every 300 ft^2 of retail space. The banking function has a requirement of one space for every 250 ft^2 of gross building area. The remaining allowable building area, planned office activities, has a requirement of one space for every 350 ft^2 of gross building area. The ordinance further stipulates that every parking lot for office, retail, or banking activity will have at least two handicapped spaces for lots up to 50 cars. Above that size, handicapped spaces are required at a ratio of one for every 30 cars. Figure 19-8 describes the numerical extension of the parking requirements in addition to the spatial allocations of site functions.

A review of the client's development objectives reveals he anticipated more density than the site can accommodate. The 0.7 FAR permitted by the ordinance would require 380 parking spaces! Since committing that much area to parking alone has some serious implications relative to the developer's objectives, the client is contacted for a preliminary review. First, an extension of the parking spaces in terms of site area indicates that most of the site must be committed to parking if the permitted FAR could even be approached. This might be ameliorated if the use considered for the site was speculative office space alone. But given the fact that one potential user is retail com-

Figure 19-6 Microclimate mapping.

Site 'R'

20 ft. x 20 ft. Cells

Open unprotected areas classified as

Winter Northers

Ventilating Winds

	Wind	Calm
Sun	a	b
Shade	c	d

Winter x / y Summer

0' 5' 15' 30'

Figure 19-7 Physical conditions and zoning restrictions at site C.

Site C

1. North parcel   1.63 acres × 43,560 ft² =   71,002.8 ft²
2. South parcel   2.37 acres × 43,560 ft² = <u>103,237.2 ft²</u>
3. Creek   <u>1.06 acres</u>
4.   Total   5.06 acres   174,424.4 ft² (total buildable area)

5. 174,424 ft² × 0.7   floor area ratio (FAR) = 121,968.0 ft²
                     of building area permitted by zoning ordinance

6.   121,968.0 ft²   total building area
7. − 10,000.0 ft²   of retail activity
8. − <u>12,500.0 ft²</u>   of bank
9.   99,468.0 ft²   potential area for speculative office space

Parking Requirements

10. 10,000.0 ft²   of retail requires 1 space / 300 ft² of gross
                       floor area = 34 parking spaces
11. 12,500.0 ft²   of banking use requires 1 space / 250 ft² of gross
                       floor area = 50 parking spaces
12. 99,468.0 ft²   of office space requires 1 space / 350 ft² of gross
                       floor area = 284 parking spaces

13. Total parking required: 368 parking spaces

14. 368 × 350 ft²/space = 128,800 ft² of site area
      368 × 400 ft²/space = 147,200 ft² of site area

Allocation of Site Functions

15.   174,240.0 ft²   of site area
16. − 15,000.0 ft²   marginally developable area in south parcel
                       between Seneca Creek and property line
17. − 17,424.0 ft²   10% of site area for open space
18. − 10,000.0 ft²   of retail space on ground floor
19. − 12,500.0 ft²   of banking activity on ground floor
20. − 2,250.0 ft²   (10% of lines 18 and 19) for pedestrian
                       circulation)

21.   117,066.0 ft²   of site area remaining for parking and auto
                       circulation

Summary: Since area required for parking based on 0.7 FAR ranges from 128,800 to 147,200 ft² (line 14),
some downward adjustment on the realistic development potential must take place.

Figure 19-8

mercial and the second a bank, eliminating the entire ground floor of a functional use would create major problems with the project's economic pro forma. The developer concedes that the commitment from the bank and retail activities have more priority, and instructions are to continue development of the site plan by reducing the floor area of speculative office space.

ANALYSIS

The overlays for site R provide two illuminating facts. One is the site has a zone of steeper slopes than first appeared in the site visit (Fig. 19-9). This is a reminder of how deceptive land forms can be. The second revealing aspect of the analysis is that the floodplain is, in fact, higher than the older drawings indicated. The height of water in Rock Creek has increased due to the amount of development in the watershed, and contact with the Corps of Engineers confirms that their latest hydrograph establishes a new 100-year floodplain at the (5)21 foot contour. Other than the isolated rock outcrop-

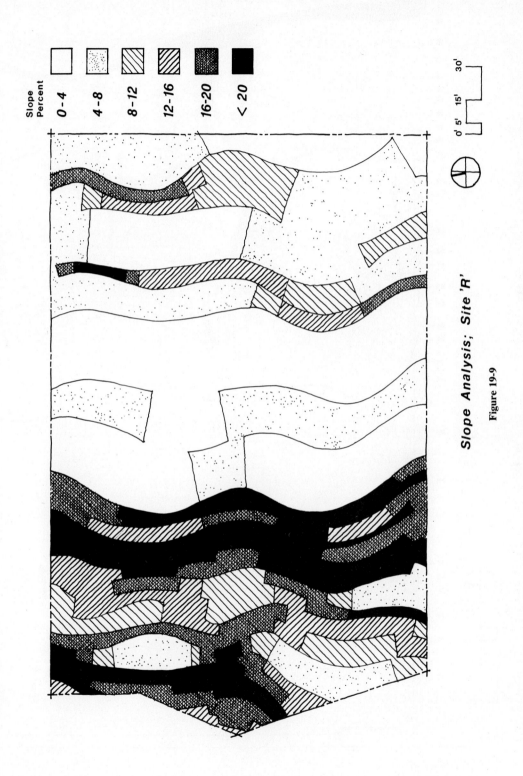

Slope Percent
0 - 4
4 - 8
8 - 12
12 - 16
16 - 20
< 20

0' 5' 15' 30'

Slope Analysis; Site 'R'

Figure 19-9

Figure 19-10 Drainage analysis, site R.

ping, the soils and subsurface geology for site R indicate that there are no major problems associated with the soils.

On site C, a review of the utilities and their alignments confirms their common location parallel to the roads. The petroleum pipeline easement was a discrepancy and has been corrected on the final base map.

Documentation of the drainage patterns for both R and C provide another level of information to be considered in analysis. Site R has a major swale that almost bisects the property from east to west. The existing natural growth disguised the swale, which will influence the development of any parcel in the center of the 1-acre site (Fig. 19-10).

Site C appears to be simple. The north and south portions both drain into Seneca Creek. There is one area to the southeast that is a depression and appears to drain away from the creek.

Design criteria form a critical aspect of the design process and should be delineated in written as well as visual form. Both public and private sectors will have criteria, both specific and implied. The criteria should be articulated, as they can become a development constraint that will have to be resolved before legitimate design alternatives can be considered. On occasions, the site planner may be confronted with the necessity to change the criteria. On others, however, exceeding recommended standards would be inappropriate and invite serious consequences. As an example, topographical fill that exceeds 4 : 1 slope without stabilization considerations could result in serious erosion or even slumping.

Some criteria have already been established. Zoning is a form of criteria that will ultimately dictate parking and general building locations on both sites.

As to site C, the community has also been faced with major property damage resulting from flooding. Since Seneca Creek is dry most of the time, it has not yet created a problem. But the city council has adopted a new development policy which stipulates that any new construction must demonstrate a reduction in on-site runoff by 30% to that of comparable land uses. Earlier considerations associated with on-site detention and/or open paving systems must now become an integral part of the program.

PROBLEM STATEMENT

Although it is not the condition with the example sites C and R, it is not uncommon to find that the client has chosen the wrong site for a use that may be a legitimate contribution to a specific area of the community. Although clients often engage the counsel of others with regard to market analysis and economic feasibility, the site selection effort is often a decision based primarily on land cost, without benefit of the site planner's critique.

Site planners are commonly provided with programs and sites much like mail-order brides or husbands. Under this set of circumstances, it is most important to determine, in precise terms, where the conflicts exist, the methods to resolve their incongruities, and the implications of that resolution. This stage in the process permits the client to review the circumstances and make the next, more crucial set of decisions. Remember, a valuable service has been rendered when a client says, "I am glad to know that now before we entered the building process." Comments like, "Why didn't you tell me that before we started all this?" often carry the seeds for a long, bitter relationship that all parties wish to avoid.

PROBLEM STATEMENT: SITE R

For site R the total acreage must be evaluated relative to the subdivision of the property for four lots. Traditionally, the property would be subdivided so that each lot has equal

Figure 19-11   Site R: four lots.

frontage on the street (Fig. 19-11). Following that method would create four lots of approximately 42 ft × 260 ft. Although that formula has some advantages, it has some fairly obvious disadvantages.

First, Olmsted Drive is a fairly busy arterial. While turning into a driveway off of the street is simple enough, exiting from any of the lots forces the driver to back into an often heavy flow of traffic. Second, between the side-yard setbacks (minimum 6 ft 0 in. for the first 8 ft 0 in. thereafter 1 ft back for every 3 ft in vertical height) and the existing vegetation, the shape of the structure and location of private outdoor open space are very restrictive (Fig. 19-12). Third, although the lots could be oriented with their long sides almost due north–south, the design flexibility necessary to keep one structure from obscuring the southern winter sun from another is marginal at best (Fig. 19-13). Fourth, the drainage swale that traverses the property will also affect the development of either lot 2 or lot 3 and possibly both. Finally, the opportunity to create a sense of place for four dwellings along the edge of a thoroughfare is extremely limited. The object building model restricts the site to a condition in which each building has little opportunity to contribute something to the adjoining structure. As with the traditional residential subdivision, the identity of each residence becomes relegated to an address and zip code.

ALTERNATIVES: SITE R

Following the earlier review of site R's size, topography, drainage patterns, zoning, and floodplain, the developable limits of the property are now clear. One conceptual alternative to the four parallel lots is subdivision of the property with two lots about 100 ft deep fronting on Olmsted. This would permit the design of a road to reinforce the natural drainage of the existing swale as well as the development of the site with four less radically shaped lots (Fig. 19-14). Although this appears, at first glance, to be a reasonable method of subdivision, the city's minimum right-of-way for a public street is 40 ft 0 in., with an accompanying 60 ft 0 in.-diameter cul-de-sac. Although the impact of these criteria on the site is substantial, it would provide access to the rear lots. An

Figure 19-12   Site R: four lots with setbacks.

alternative would be to serve the two rear lots (2 and 3) with a private road built in an easement across lots 1 and 4 (Fig. 19-15). The easement could be granted in perpetuity and "run" with the deeds of all four lots.

The problem with the second alternative is that the municipality has a rule which prohibits the subdivision of any property that does not have access to a public street. The third alternative is a variation on the second. If lots 2 and 3 have a 10 ft 0 in. strip of land that connects the "body" of the lot to Olmsted (public street) (Fig. 19-16), the two 10-ft strips are sufficiently wide enough to build a *private two-way* road complete with cul-de-sac. The configurations of lots 2 and 3 are unconventional and are sometimes referred to as "pipe stem" or "flag" lots. The design flexibility now possible with all four lots is significantly better than the traditional format. The configuration of the four lots not only provides a broader range of site planning and architectural solutions, but the ingress/egress problems are substantially better, as all four lots can now use the private drive.

The private drive can also be designed with a concave section and open paving. This will imitate the natural drainage characteristics of the site as well as reduce the amount of runoff that would normally occur following development. Another benefit of the private drive is that it permits the orientation and design of the four dwellings into an identifiable residential cluster, as opposed to the parallel lots facing the street. The potential for the development of four independent, yet cohesive units becomes more plausible when the scale of the street is broken and a hierarchy becomes a visible and functional part of the site plan.

The architectural solutions to lots 1 and 4 will be significantly different from those of 2 and 3. The two westerly lots should have units that have been designed to accommodate the steeper slopes. Since the slopes on part of the site considered for residential development are in excess of 20%, a review of the surface soil conditions and test borings is in order. Since the sewer line that will be built in the private drive to serve all

Figure 19-13 Site R: four lots with buildings.

Rock Creek

Flood Plain

4 3 2 1

Line of major topographical change

Olmsted Drive

0' 5' 15' 30'

Figure 19-14 Site R: alternative plan.

Figure 19-15 Site R: alternative plan with easement.

Figure 19-16 Site R: with ''pipe stem'' lots.

four units will be at elevations ranging between 31 and 39 ft, any uses in the dwellings on lots 2 and 3 below elevation 31.0 ft which require a sanitary sewer connection will also require a sump pump to lift the waste to the gravity flow sewer. This is not an uncommon occurrence, but it emphasizes the need to consider each site and building as an integral design problem. Although overlooking the need for a sump pump is not itself an insurmountable problem, it is *always* an embarrassment.

Structures for all four lots can now be oriented as need be with considerable flexibility. The small private street can also be designed as a pedestrian street. Like the Dutch Woonerf streets, the residents are conscious of its multifunctional role. Because of the lot configurations, private road and smaller front/rear yards, the use of a performance zone (PUD) should be requested. While this is an additional "cost," recognize too that the scale of the small neighborhood cluster would have been extremely difficult to achieve without it (Fig. 19-17).

PROBLEM STATEMENT: SITE C

Early resolution of the differences between the perceived and realistic development potential diffuses a problem that makes all others pale by comparison. Figure 19-18 describes the revised development program and the areas necessary to be allocated to parking. When this area is distributed in equitable percentages to both north and south sectors, the residual land area becomes apparent. Although nothing prohibits locating all the uses in one structure on one side of the creek, it makes little sense considering the implications of walking distances alone. Since the site is bordered on the north and south by major roads, providing access to both zones divided by the creek is largely a matter of building location and the configuration of parking and circulation. Although a vehicular bridge connecting both north and south zones has been considered and discounted as unnecessary, it appears that a pedestrian connection of some type is required.

The soils, slopes, and drainage patterns present few problems. The site's topography, parking lots, and paving systems will be evaluated collectively as methods to resolve the municipality's runoff policies. Although the creek is a problem in the sense that it has divided the site, it should also be considered an asset, as it contains and supports most of the larger trees on the site.

Since the office, retail, and bank uses create an "internally" loaded building, reducing the additional heat load of the summer sun is a primary objective in the siting and orientation of the buildings. Furthermore, the use of any reflective material on both buildings will be carefully evaluated. Glare and reflected heat can damage surrounding vegetation as well as create additional heat loads to adjacent structures. This poses an issue that must become part of the architectural problem statement. A strategy must be developed which permits exploitation of views of the creek without increasing the direct solar gain.

ALTERNATIVE: SITE C

Since the revised development objectives are more compatible with the zoning, proposed land uses, and parking requirements, the question now evolves to the distribution of uses, allocation of parking, and the method by which the site can be developed as a cohesive whole. The cost of connecting the northern and southern segments with a road and bridge would be extremely expensive and provide marginal utility. Thus it appears that at least one alternative should examine the development of the site with two buildings connected by a pedestrian bridge. As two separate buildings, both bank and retail uses could enjoy individual identities, while the pedestrian bridge facilitates a good integration of uses. Where the bridge helps to tie two commercial uses together, it is also easy to see how important it would be to a residential and commercial mix.

Olmsted Drive

0' 10' 30'

Figure 19-17 Site plan, site R.

North Parcel

Retail area	10,000 ft²	requires:	34 parking spaces
Office space	17,500 ft²	requires:	50 parking spaces
		Total:	84 parking spaces

First floor	Retail:	10,000 ft²
Second floor	Office:	10,000 ft²
Third floor	Office:	7,500 ft²

South Parcel

Bank area	12,500 ft²	requires:	50 parking spaces
Office space	37,500 ft²	requires:	107 parking spaces
		Total:	157 parking spaces

First floor   Bank: 12,500 ft²
Second, third, and fourth floors   Office: 12,500 ft² each

SUMMARY:

Total north parcel:	27,500 ft²
Total south parcel:	50,000 ft²
Site total:	77,500 ft² of building area

Approximately 0.45 FAR reflected in site C development plan, shown in Fig. 19-19.

Figure 19-18   Revised development program for site C.

The pedestrian bridge and path also contribute to the development of an identifiable place. Without the bridge the plan is dependent on the design of two object buildings. The bridge also presents an exceptional opportunity to bring human scale into an auto-dominated environment. Where pedestrian systems are so often minimal components of the site plan, this site and its uses require a well-articulated system.

Where the north–south linkage is imperative for site C, it appears that there may be some value in extending a path to the western edge of the property. A path that parallels the creek and provides direct access from the adjacent residential land uses could provide a valued exposure for both bank and retail commercial uses. Although the functional issues must be scrutinized before a final decision can be made, an additional east–west path would clearly be a welcomed amenity for residents, employees, and retail customers alike.

Following the decision to locate the bank to the south of Seneca Creek and the retail activity to the north, the next task was to achieve some balance as to the site's area and required parking. To some degree this phase is "trial and error," as estimates must be adjusted until an acceptable relationship between building, parking, and open space can be found. Just as the example portrayed in Chapter 18 on the parking schedule, the parking requirement had a direct relationship to the ultimate achievable office and/ or retail area.

The next phase is to locate the buildings and support parking so as to provide a visible and efficient auto and pedestrian system that integrates and exploits the residual open space. The development of a pedestrian bridge between the north and south sections of the site terminating at each building resolves both functional and aesthetic issues. The bridge can become a physical unifying element while creating its own set of views and images. The geometry of the man-made path, buildings, and parking also evolve to contrast sharply with the natural sinew of the creek (Fig. 19-19).

RECONCILING CONFLICTS

Structures on site R have been located in those areas that provide maximum solar exposure with minimal environmental degradation. The long sides (north and south) have

Richardson Road

Centerline Public R.O.W.

Seneca Creek

1st.fl. Retail
2nd. and
3rd.fl. Office

1st.fl. Bank
2nd., 3rd. and
4th. fl. Office

Sullivan Street

0' 10' 25' 50'

Centerline Public R.O.W.

Figure 19-19 Site C development plan.

Figure 19-20 Site R with preliminary finish floor spot elevations.

been oriented so to enjoy maximum solar exposure and direct gain for winter heating. The narrower elevations have been oriented toward the east and west, minimizing the potential heat gain during the summer months. Since the topography on site R generally slopes from east to west, structures on all four lots will probably run perpendicular to the contours (Fig. 19-20). Since the topographical change across the length of the slab is rather substantial, "breaking" or separating the slab into two elevations would be an appropriate consideration. This articulated response permits locating the eastern portion of the slab sufficiently high to provide the vertical distance adequate for the design of a swale. An additional advantage is that the length of the swale along the east side of each building can be modest because the length of the building parallel to the contours is relatively short. Figure 19-21 illustrates some of the primary spot elevations necessary to accommodate structures on lots 1 and 4.

Although the western-most lots have substantially steeper slopes, the principles applied to the two east end lots (1 and 4) still apply. Obviously, the floor levels should

Figure 19-21   Site R: partial preliminary grading plan.

Partial section through Lot 2

Figure 19-22   Site R: section through buildings.

reflect that of the topography, and in this case the structure can become two stories (Fig. 19-22). Were it not for a very stable soil condition, this would be a questionable solution. Furthermore, the potential for more floor levels makes the view of the creek available to more of the house. Fortunately, the grove of deciduous trees alongside the creek is sufficiently dense as to screen out much of the intense heat from the summer sun.

Similar to lots 1 and 4, the water that flows from east to west must be carried around the building. The problem is accentuated on lots 2 and 3, as the amount of runoff increases with the increase in the parking area. Care needs to be taken here to make certain that any additional water is either directed away from the building with grading or with a closed drainage system or a combination of both. Any time a parking area is topographically higher than a structure, the potential exists for a drainage problem.

The grading plan for site C is fairly uncomplicated. Although the north side of the creek drains toward the creek and the building, coordinating the relationships between the finish floor elevations, peripheral walks, and drives will permit the design of a positive surface drainage plan. Recall the process of establishing spot elevations first to determine the necessary topographical changes. As before, some of the issues on the north side of the creek also exist on the south. Although a large area of the parking in the south will drain naturally toward the creek, another area drains toward the topographical depression near Sullivan Street. Retaining the trees in this area and directing some of the runoff into this zone will enhance the aesthetic as well as the functional qualities of the plan.

Ingress to and egress from the site are reasonably straightforward. The parking lots are oriented such that the pedestrian might use the drive as the path. A drop-off zone has been integrated into the fire lane, which is accessible to the three sides of the building. Handicapped parking has been located on two sides of the building in an effort to keep walking distances to a minimum.

Entrance drives have been located so as to communicate a clear understanding of the circulation and parking system on both sides of the creek. Two-way drives and head-in 90° parking have been used to keep the area of impervious surfaces to a minimum. Since storm water runoff is also a specific problem with site C, the use of an open paving system has a high priority.

CONCLUSIONS

The final resolution of the site plan is a concomitant part of the architecture. The range of alternatives and their evaluation relative to the client's goals cannot be completely assessed without the structure. Site planning in its earliest phases simply expresses a process through which decisions relative to the union of building and site might be made. The building must begin to evolve in function and form through the development of alternatives; otherwise, the alternatives are abstract and the notion of an integrated site and structure are lost.

While the examples advanced here in sites R and C may never approach the complexity or simplicity of other sites, the process is the same. Although issues will vary, good site planning judgment is based on a knowledge of the facts and an understanding of the interrelationships between the natural and man-made components. The subjective qualities of preferential forms and design vocabulary will be expressed and articulated by the biases of the site planner throughout the process. The methodology simply serves to separate the "objective" from the "subjective" and to create a firm and cogent target for the designer's creative leap from problem statement to alternative solutions. With the exception of the general references to trees or vegetation, recall that there has been little mention of beauty. Since the mention of beauty creates broad interpretations and responses, the thought was to approach the achievement of that quality from other quarters. It is not that aesthetics is a minor issue but more that the concepts and process suggested in previous chapters delineate the fundamentals for the development of a humane, intelligent, environmentally sensitive site plan. It is then more likely that beauty (your definition is acceptable) in various respects will evolve in the development of the plan.

appendix A
Stations Providing Local Climatological Data*

Alabama
Birmingham C.O., Birmingham AP, Huntsville, Mobile, Montgomery

Alaska
Anchorage, Annette, Barrow, Barter Is., Bethel, Bettles, Big Delta, Cold Bay, Fairbanks, Gulkana, Homer, Juneau, King Salmon, Kodiak, Kotzebue, McGrath, Nome, St. Paul Is., Talkeetna, Unalakleet, Valdez, Yakutat

Arizona
Flagstaff, Phoenix, Tucson, Winslow, Yuma

Arkansas
Fort Smith, Little Rock, North Little Rock

California
Bakersfield, Bishop, Blue Canyon, Eureka, Fresno, Long Beach, Los Angeles AP, Los Angeles C.O., Mount Shasta, Red Bluff, Sacramento, San Diego, San Francisco AP, San Francisco C.O., Santa Maria, Stockton

Colorado
Alamosa, Colorado Springs, Denver, Grand Junction, Pueblo

Connecticut
Bridgeport, Hartford

Delaware
Wilmington

District of Columbia
Washington Dulles AP, Washington National AP

Florida
Apalachicola, Daytona Beach, Fort Myers, Jacksonville, Key West, Miami, Orlando, Pensacola, Tallahassee, Tampa, West Palm Beach

---

*Through the National Climatic Data Center in Asheville, North Carolina

Georgia
Athens, Atlanta, Augusta, Columbus, Macon, Savannah

Hawaii
Hilo, Honolulu, Kahului, Lihue

Idaho
Boise, Lewiston, Pocatello

Illinois
Cairo, Chicago, Moline, Peoria, Rockford, Springfield

Indiana
Evansville, Fort Wayne, Indianapolis, South Bend

Iowa
Des Moines, Dubuque, Sioux City, Waterloo

Kansas
Concordia, Dodge City, Goodland, Topeka, Wichita

Kentucky
Jackson, Lexington, Louisville

Louisiana
Baton Rouge, Lake Charles, New Orleans, Shreveport

Maine
Caribou, Portland

Maryland
Baltimore

Massachusetts
Blue Hill, Boston, Worcester

Michigan
Alpena, Detroit, Flint, Grand Rapids, Houghton Lake, Lansing, Marquette, Muskegon, Sault Ste. Marie

Minnesota
Duluth, International Falls, Minneapolis–St. Paul, Rochester, Saint Cloud

Mississippi
Jackson, Meridian

Missouri
Columbia, Kansas City, Kansas City Downtown AP, St. Louis, Springfield

Montana
Billings, Glasgow, Great Falls, Havre, Helena, Kalispell, Miles City, Missoula

Nebraska
Grand Island, Lincoln, Norfolk, North Platte, Omaha Eppley AP, Omaha (North), Scottsbluff, Valentine

Nevada
Elko, Ely, Las Vegas, Reno, Winnemucca

New Hampshire
Concord, Mount Washington

New Jersey
Atlantic City AP, Atlantic City C.O., Newark

New Mexico
Albuquerque, Clayton, Roswell

New York
Albany, Binghamton, Buffalo, New York C. Park, New York Kennedy AP, New York LaGuardia AP, Rochester, Syracuse

North Carolina
Asheville, Cape Hatteras, Charlotte, Greensboro (High Point), Raleigh, Wilmington

North Dakota
Bismarck, Fargo, Williston

Ohio
Akron, Greater Cincinnati AP, Cleveland, Columbus, Dayton, Mansfield, Toledo, Youngstown

Oklahoma
Oklahoma City, Tulsa

Oregon
Astoria, Burns, Eugene, Medford, Pendleton, Portland, Salem, Sexton Summit

Pacific Islands
Guam, Johnston Island, Koror, Marshall Islands (Kwajalein, Majuro), American Samoa (Pago Pago), E. Caroline Islands (Ponape, Truk), W. Caroline Islands (Yap), Wake Is.

Pennsylvania
Allentown, Avoca, Erie, Harrisburg, Philadelphia, Pittsburgh, Williamsport

Puerto Rico
San Juan

Rhode Island
Block Island, Providence

South Carolina
Charleston AP, Columbia, Greenville–Spartanburg AP

South Dakota
Aberdeen, Huron, Rapid City, Sioux Falls

Tennessee
Bristol–Johnson City–Kingsport, Chattanooga, Knoxville, Memphis, Nashville, Oak Ridge

Texas
Abilene, Amarillo, Austin, Brownsville, Corpus Christi, Dallas–Fort Worth, Del Rio, El Paso, Galveston, Houston, Lubbock, Midland–Odessa, Port Arthur, San Angelo, San Antonio, Victoria, Waco, Wichita Falls

Utah
Milford, Salt Lake City

Vermont
Burlington

Virginia
Lynchburg, Norfolk, Richmond, Roanoke, Wallops Island

Washington
Olympia, Quillayute, Seattle C.O., Seattle Sea-Tac AP, Spokane, Stampede Pass, Walla Walla, Yakima

West Virginia
Beckley, Charleston, Elkins, Huntington

Wisconsin
Green Bay, La Crosse, Madison, Milwaukee

Wyoming
Casper, Cheyenne, Lander, Sheridan

appendix B

Sun Pegs
for Various Latitudes

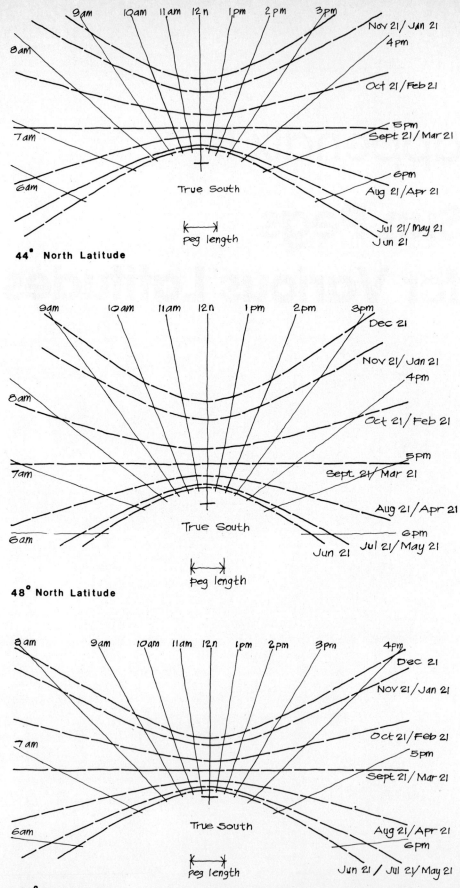

44° North Latitude

48° North Latitude

36° North Latitude

314

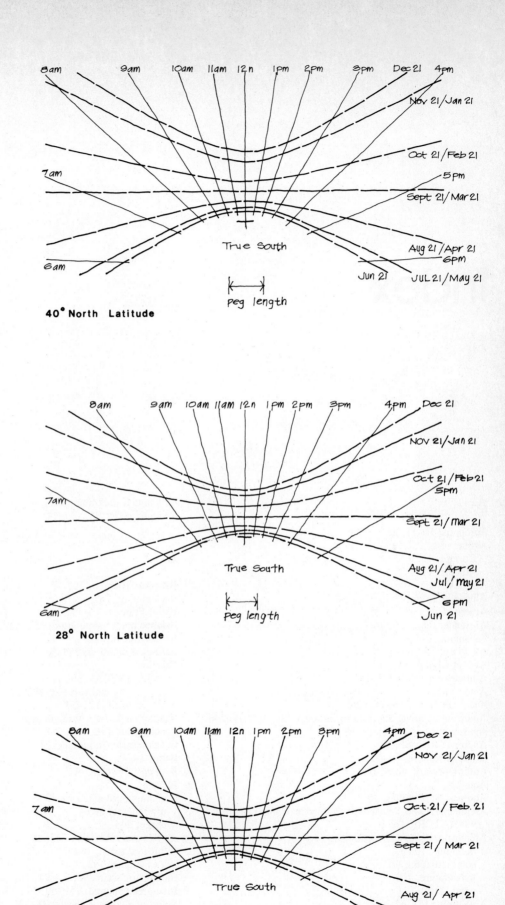

40° North Latitude

28° North Latitude

32° North Latitude

Index